enVision® Mathematics

Volume 2 Topics 9-15

Authors

Randall I. Charles
Professor Emeritus
Department of Mathematics
San Jose State University
San Jose, California

Jennifer Bay-Williams
Professor of Mathematics Education
College of Education and Human Development
University of Louisville
Louisville, Kentucky

Robert Q. Berry, III
Professor of Mathematics Education
Department of Curriculum, Instruction and Special Education
University of Virginia
Charlottesville, Virginia

Janet H. Caldwell
Professor Emerita
Department of Mathematics
Rowan University
Glassboro, New Jersey

Zachary Champagne
Assistant in Research
Florida Center for Research in Science, Technology, Engineering, and Mathematics (FCR-STEM)
Jacksonville, Florida

Juanita Copley
Professor Emerita, College of Education
University of Houston
Houston, Texas

Warren Crown
Professor Emeritus of Mathematics Education
Graduate School of Education
Rutgers University
New Brunswick, New Jersey

Francis (Skip) Fennell
Professor Emeritus of Education and Graduate and Professional Studies
McDaniel College
Westminster, Maryland

Karen Karp
Professor of Mathematics Education
School of Education
Johns Hopkins University
Baltimore, Maryland

Stuart J. Murphy
Visual Learning Specialist
Boston, Massachusetts

Jane F. Schielack
Professor Emerita
Department of Mathematics
Texas A&M University
College Station, Texas

Jennifer M. Suh
Associate Professor for Mathematics Education
George Mason University
Fairfax, Virginia

Jonathan A. Wray
Mathematics Supervisor
Howard County Public Schools
Ellicott City, Maryland

Mathematicians

Roger Howe
Professor of Mathematics
Yale University
New Haven, Connecticut

Gary Lippman
Professor of Mathematics and Computer Science
California State University, East Bay
Hayward, California

ELL Consultants

Janice R. Corona
Independent Education Consultant
Dallas, Texas

Jim Cummins
Professor
The University of Toronto
Toronto, Canada

Reviewers

Katina Arnold
Teacher
Liberty Public School District
Kansas City, Missouri

Christy Bennett
Elementary Math and Science Specialist
DeSoto County Schools
Hernando, Mississippi

Shauna Bostick
Elementary Math Specialist
Lee County School District
Tupelo, Mississippi

Samantha Brant
Teacher
Platte County School District
Platte City, Missouri

Jamie Clark
Elementary Math Coach
Allegany County Public Schools
Cumberland, Maryland

Shauna Gardner
Math and Science Instructional Coach
DeSoto County Schools
Hernando, Mississippi

Kathy Graham
Educational Consultant
Twin Falls, Idaho

Andrea Hamilton
K-5 Math Specialist
Lake Forest School District
Felton, Delaware

Susan Hankins
Instructional Coach
Tupelo Public School District
Tupelo, Mississippi

Barb Jamison
Teacher
Excelsior Springs School District
Excelsior Springs, Missouri

Pam Jones
Elementary Math Coach
Lake Region School District
Bridgton, Maine

Sherri Kane
Secondary Mathematics Curriculum Specialist
Lee's Summit R7 School District
Lee's Summit, Missouri

Jessica Leonard
ESOL Teacher
Volusia County Schools
DeLand, Florida

Jill K. Milton
Elementary Math Coordinator
Norwood Public Schools
Norwood, Massachusetts

Jamie Pickett
Teacher
Platte County School District
Kansas City, Missouri

Mandy Schall
Math Coach
Allegany County Public Schools
Cumberland, Maryland

Marjorie Stevens
Math Consultant
Utica Community Schools
Shelby Township, Michigan

Shyree Stevenson
ELL Teacher
Penns Grove-Carneys Point Regional School District
Penns Grove, New Jersey

Kayla Stone
Teacher
Excelsior Springs School District
Excelsior Springs, Missouri

Sara Sultan
PD Academic Trainer, Math
Tucson Unified School District
Tucson, Arizona

Angela Waltrup
Elementary Math Content Specialist
Washington County Public Schools
Hagerstown, Maryland

Savvas Learning Company LLC, 15 East Midland Avenue, Paramus, NJ 07652

ISBN-13: 978-0-13-495366-3
ISBN-10: 0-13-495366-5
11 2022

You'll be using these digital resources throughout the year!

Digital Resources

Go to SavvasRealize.com

Interactive Student Edition

Access online or offline.

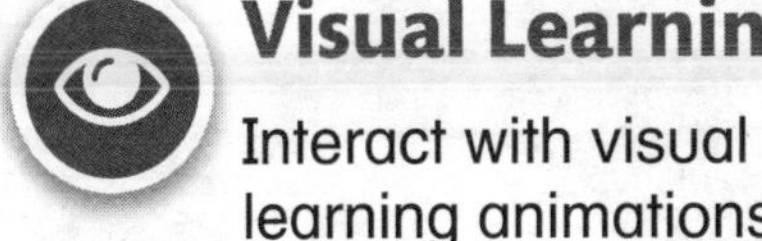

Visual Learning

Interact with visual learning animations.

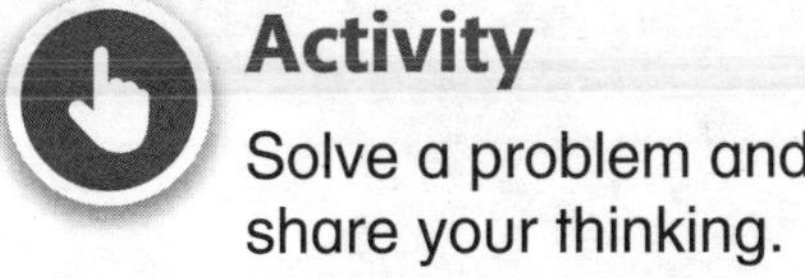

Activity

Solve a problem and share your thinking.

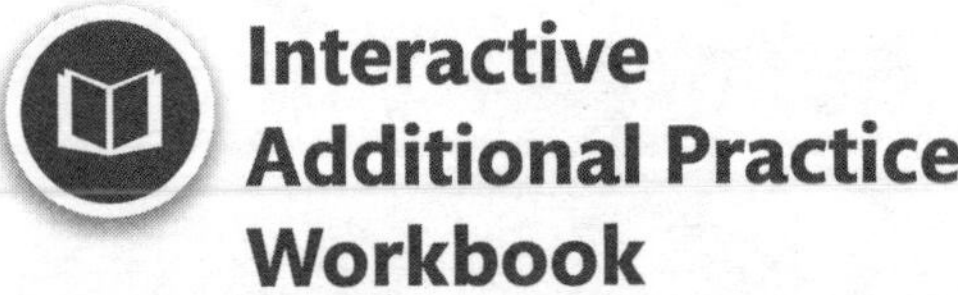

Interactive Additional Practice Workbook

Access online or offline.

Videos

Watch Math Practices Animations, Another Look Videos, and clips to support 3-Act Math.

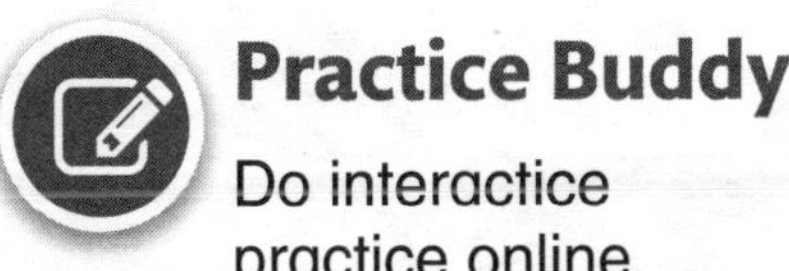

Practice Buddy

Do interactice practice online.

Math Tools

Explore math with digital tools.

Games

Play math games to help you learn.

Glossary

Read and listen in English and Spanish.

Assessment

Show what you've learned.

SAVVAS realize™ Everything you need for math anytime, anywhere

Hi, we're here to help you.
Let's have a great year!

Contents

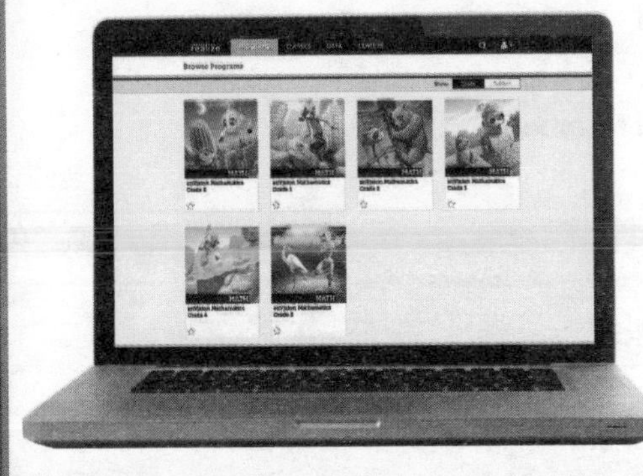

TOPICS

And remember your Interactive Student Edition is available at SavvasRealize.com!

TOPIC 1 in volume 1
Fluently Add and Subtract Within 20

TOPIC 2 in volume 1
Work with Equal Groups

TOPIC 3 in volume 1
Add Within 100 Using Strategies

TOPIC 4 in volume 1
Fluently Add Within 100

SavvasRealize.com

TOPIC 5 in volume 1

Subtract Within 100 Using Strategies

TOPIC 6 in volume 1

Fluently Subtract Within 100

TOPIC 7 in volume 1

More Solving Problems Involving Addition and Subtraction

TOPIC 8 in volume 1

Work with Time and Money

SavvasRealize.com

This shows how you can make 259 using place-value blocks.

TOPIC 9
Numbers to 1,000

This shows how you can use mental math and place-value blocks to find 243 + 100.
243 + 100 = ?
Add 1 hundred

TOPIC 10
Add Within 1,000 Using Models and Strategies

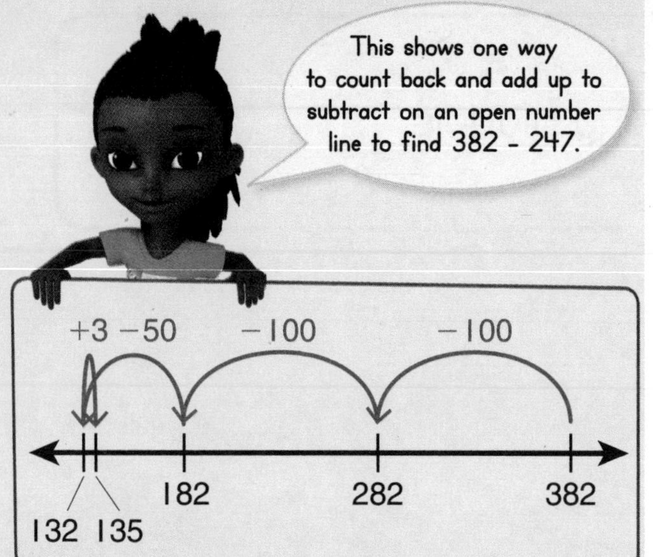
This shows one way to count back and add up to subtract on an open number line to find 382 - 247.
+3
−50
−100
−100
132
135
182
282
382

TOPIC 11
Subtract Within 1,000 Using Models and Strategies

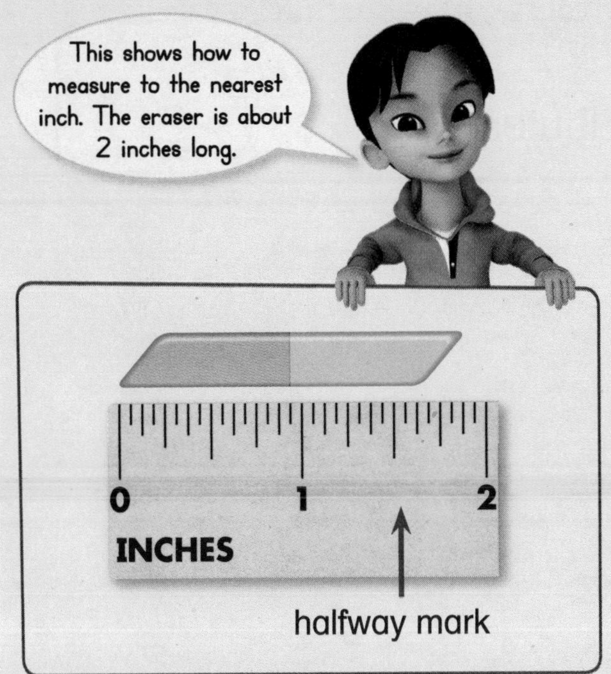

This shows how to measure to the nearest inch. The eraser is about 2 inches long.
0
1
2
INCHES
halfway mark

TOPIC 12
Measuring Length

This shows a
way you can draw
a cube.

TOPIC 13
Shapes and Their Attributes

This shows how you can represent whole numbers as lengths and subtract on a number line.

Amelia buys 17 feet of rope. She cuts off 8 feet of rope to make a jump rope.

How many feet of rope does she have left?

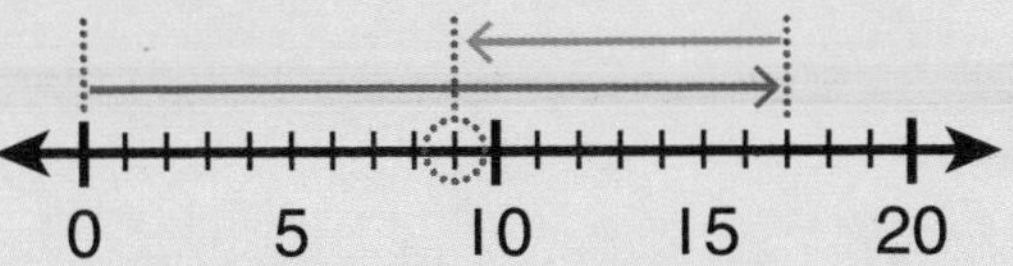

TOPIC 14
More Addition, Subtraction, and Length

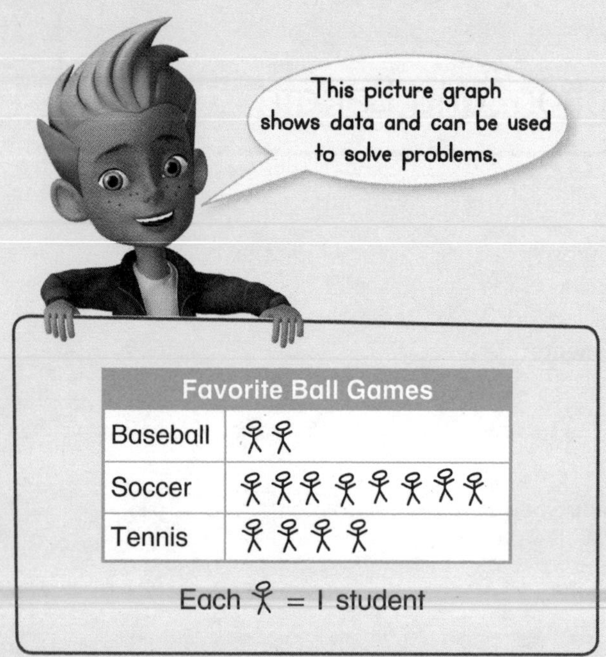
This picture graph shows data and can be used to solve problems.
Favorite Ball Games
Baseball
Soccer
Tennis
Each = 1 student

TOPIC 15
Graphs and Data

Math Practices and Problem Solving Handbook

The **Math Practices and Problem Solving Handbook** is available at SavvasRealize.com.

Math Practices

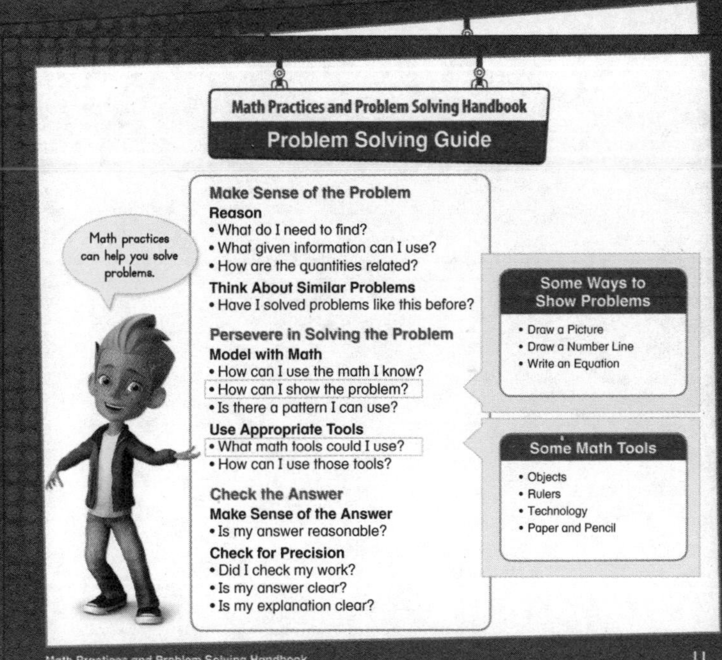

Problem Solving Guide
Problem Solving Recording Sheet

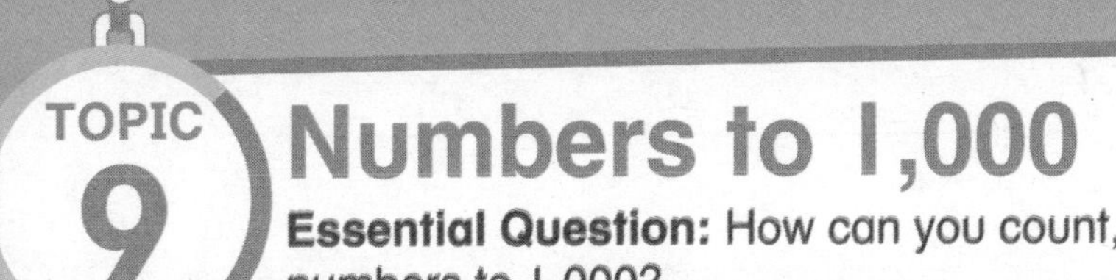

TOPIC 9 Numbers to 1,000

Essential Question: How can you count, read, and show numbers to 1,000?

Digital Resources

Interactive Student Edition · Activity · Visual Learning · Video · Practice · Assessment · Games · Tools · Glossary

Look at the model of a bird! How many pieces do you think it took to make it?

What else could you make with the same pieces?

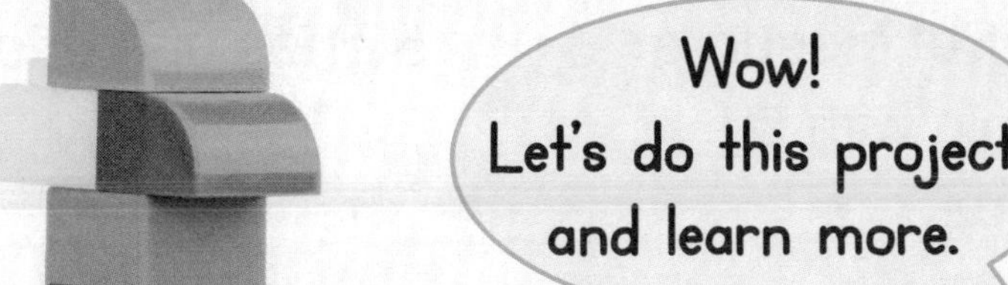

Wow!
Let's do this project and learn more.

enVision® STEM Project: Breaking Apart and Putting Together

Find Out Collect sets of building blocks. Take turns and work together. Use the blocks to build a model. Then take that model apart and use the same blocks to build a different model.

Journal: Make a Book Show your models in a book. In your book, also:

- Tell how many pieces you used to build your models.
- Show how to use place-value blocks to model different names for the same number.

Name ______________________________

Review What You Know

Vocabulary

1. Circle the coin with the **least value**. Put a square around the coin with the **greatest value**.

2. Circle the number that has 5 **ones** and 4 **tens**.

54

45

40

5

3. Tom is having breakfast. The minute hand on the clock shows **half past 7 o'clock**. Circle the time on the clock.

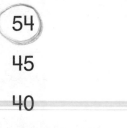

7:15 a.m.

7:30 a.m.

7:15 p.m.

7:30 p.m.

Counting Money

4. Circle coins that total 37¢.

Breaking Apart Numbers

5. Break apart each number into tens and ones.

23 = ______ + ______

47 = ______ + ______

96 = ______ + ______

Math Story

6. Howie has $13. A backpack costs $30. How much more money does Howie need to buy the backpack?

$______

Name ______________________________

PROJECT 9A

Which are the hottest planets in our solar system?

Project: Make a Planets Poster

PROJECT 9B

What is the height of the tallest waterfall in the world?

Project: Design a Waterfall Guide

PROJECT 9C

How much do large animals weigh?

Project: Create an Animal Riddle Booklet

3-ACT MATH PREVIEW

Math Modeling

Makes Cents

Video

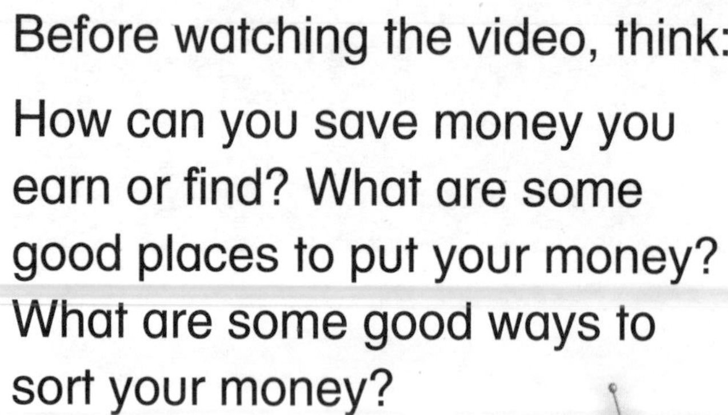

Before watching the video, think:
How can you save money you earn or find? What are some good places to put your money? What are some good ways to sort your money?

I can ...

model with math to solve a problem that involves skip counting by 5s, 10s, and 100s.

Name ______________________________

Lesson 9-1
Understand Hundreds

Solve & Share

What is another way to show 100? Draw a picture and explain.

I can ...
understand place value and count by hundreds to 1,000.

I can also use math tools correctly.

Way 1

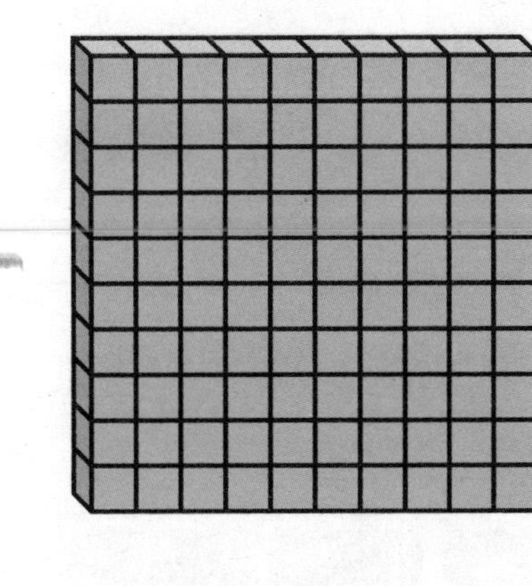

count by 1s

Way 2

count by 10s

Visual Learning A-Z Glossary

Visual Learning Bridge

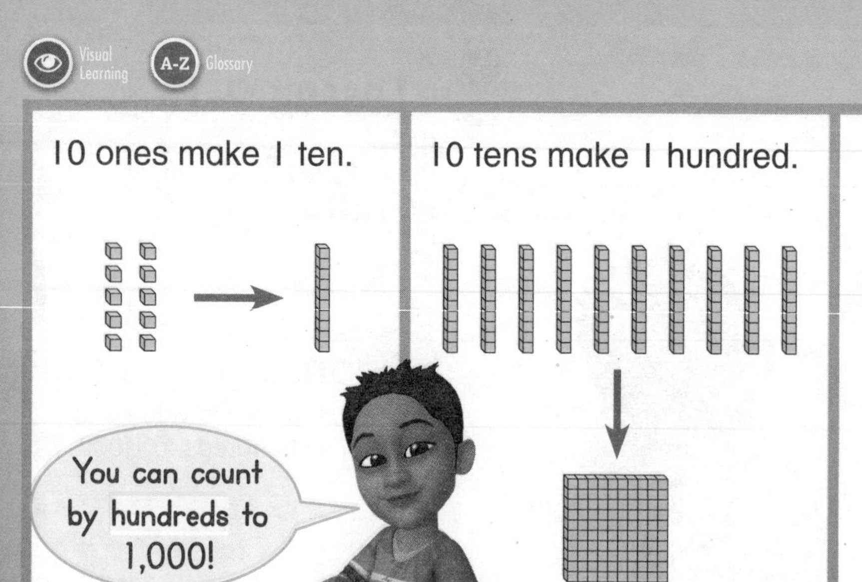

10 ones make 1 ten.
You can count by hundreds to 1,000!

10 tens make 1 hundred.

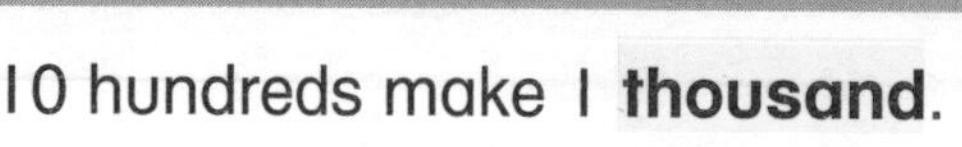

10 hundreds make 1 **thousand**.

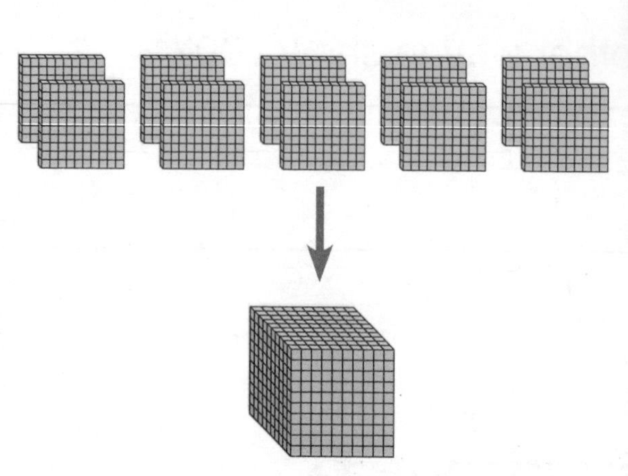

What is the number?

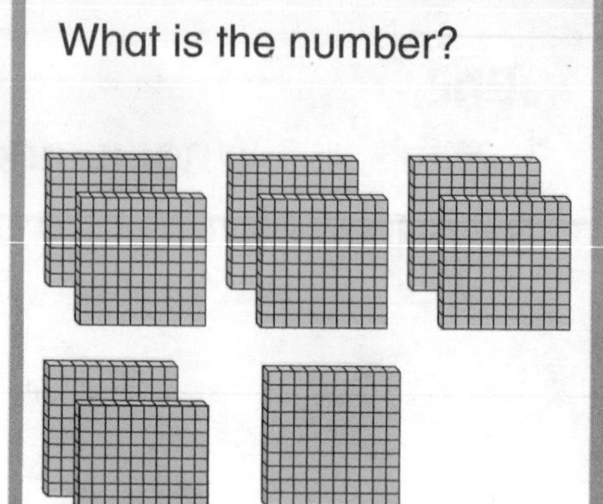

900 equals 9 hundreds, 0 tens, and 0 ones.

Convince Me! 10 ones make 1 ten. 10 tens make 1 hundred. 10 hundreds make 1 thousand. Do you see a pattern? Explain.

Guided Practice Complete each sentence. Use place-value blocks and your workmat to help.

1. 600 equals 6 hundreds, 0 tens, and 0 ones.

2. 800 equals 8 hundreds, 0 tens, and 0 ones.

Name ____________________

Independent Practice

Complete each sentence. Use models if needed.

3. 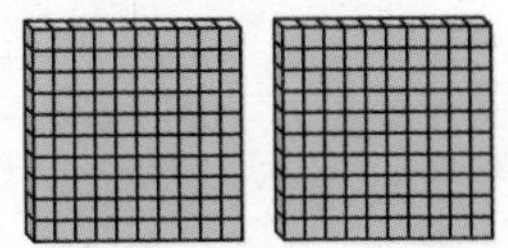

____ equals ____ hundreds, ____ tens, and ____ ones.

4. 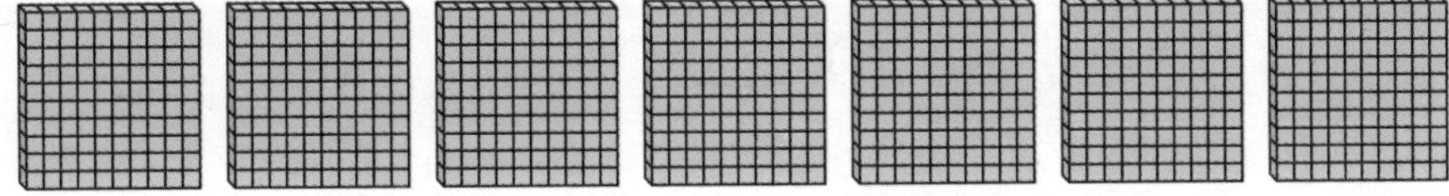

____ equals ____ hundreds, ____ tens, and ____ ones.

5. 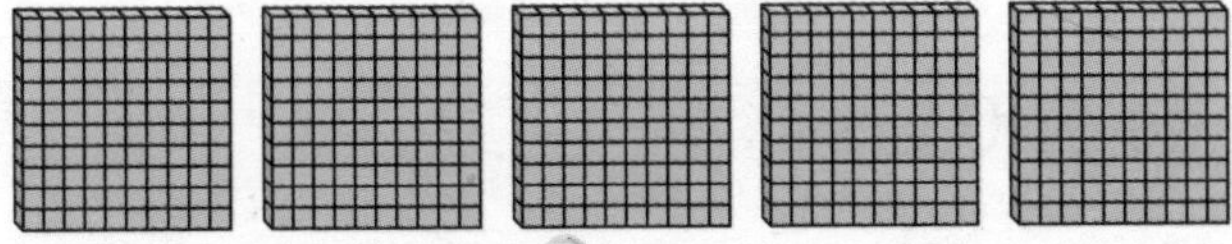

____ equals ____ hundreds, ____ tens, and ____ ones.

6. 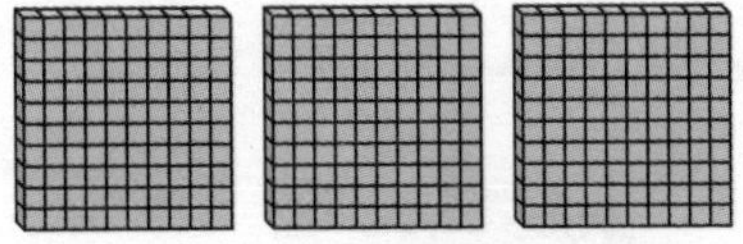

____ equals ____ hundreds, ____ tens, and ____ ones.

7. **Number Sense** Complete the pattern.

100	200	300		500		700	800	900	

Problem Solving Solve each problem. Use models if needed.

8. **Use Tools** Lucy picked a number. She says her number has 8 hundreds, 0 tens, and 0 ones.

What is Lucy's number?

9. **Vocabulary** Complete the sentences using the words below.

hundred **tens** **ones**

There are 100 ________ in one hundred.

There are 10 ________ in one ________.

Higher Order Thinking Farrah and Cory are playing beanbag toss. Circle the two other numbers they each must get to score 1,000 points.

10. Farrah has 300 points.

200 500 600 300

11. Cory has 500 points.

100 200 400 700

12. **Assessment Practice** Each box has 100 pencils. Count by hundreds to find the total. Which number tells how many pencils are in the boxes?

Ⓐ 170 Ⓒ 800

 Ⓑ 700 Ⓓ 900

Name ______________________

Lesson 9-2
Models and 3-Digit Numbers

I can ...
use place-value blocks and drawings to model and write 3-digit numbers.

I can also use math tools correctly.

Solve & Share

How can you use place-value blocks to show 125? Explain.

Draw your blocks to show what you did.

1 2 5

125

1+2+5=8

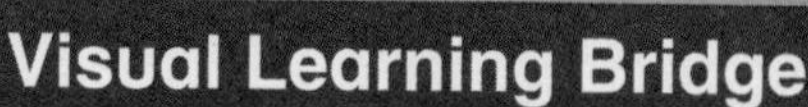

Visual Learning Bridge

What number do the models show?

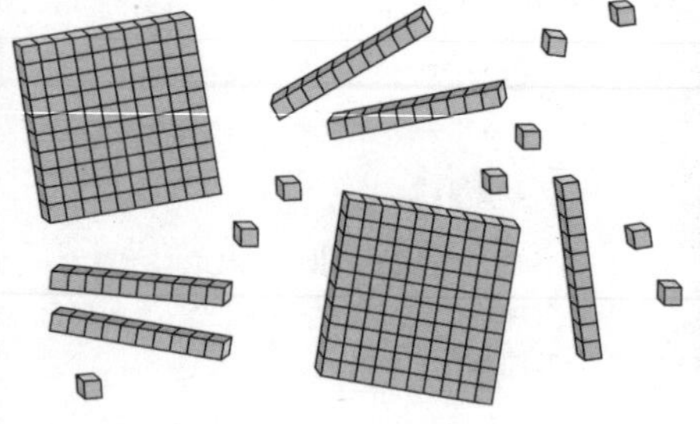

Remember, 10 ones make 1 ten.
10 tens make 1 hundred.

First, count the hundreds.

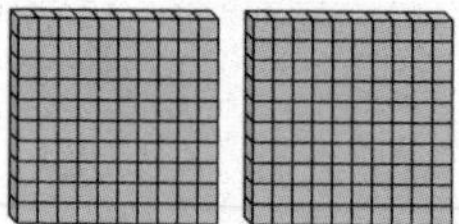

Use a **place-value chart** to show the value of each **digit**.

Hundreds	Tens	Ones
2		

Then count the tens.

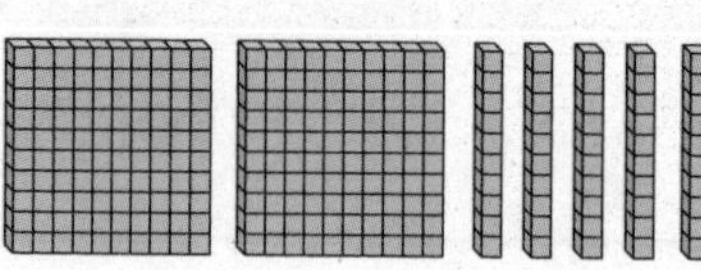

Hundreds	Tens	Ones
2	5	

Then count the ones.

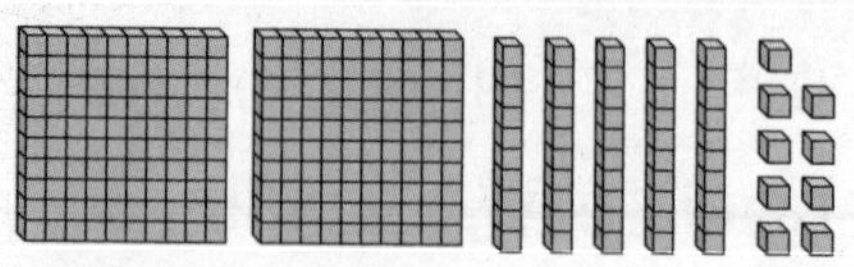

Hundreds	Tens	Ones
2	5	9

The models show 259.
259 has 3 digits.

Convince Me! How many hundreds are in 395? How many tens? How many ones?

☆ **Guided Practice** ☆ Write the numbers shown. Use place-value blocks and your workmat if needed.

1.

Hundreds	Tens	Ones
	7	0

70

2.

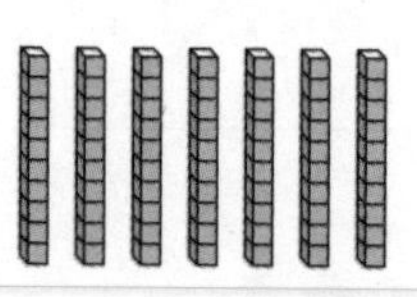

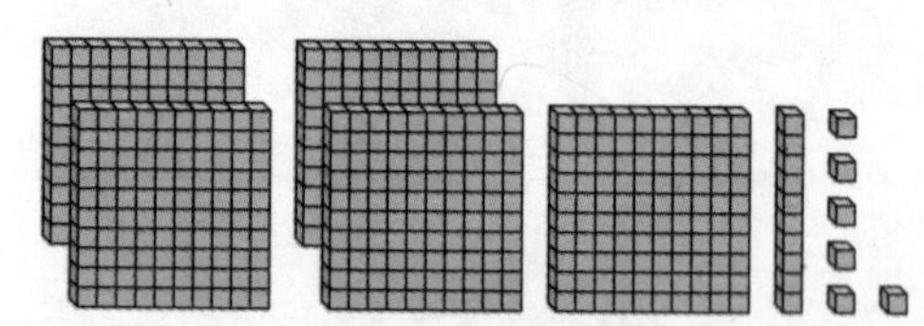

Hundreds	Tens	Ones
5	1	6

516

Name ______________________________

Independent Practice

Write the numbers shown. Use models and your workmat if needed.

3.

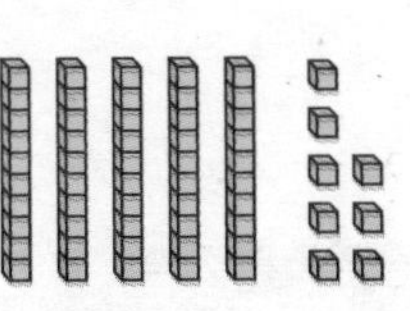

Hundreds	Tens	Ones
	5	8

58

4.

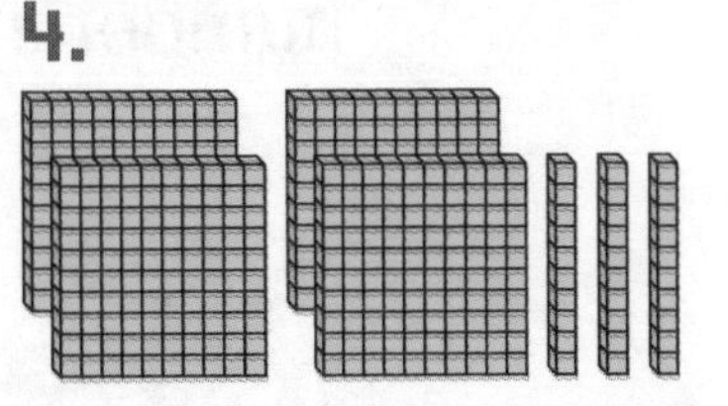

Hundreds	Tens	Ones
4	3	

43

5.

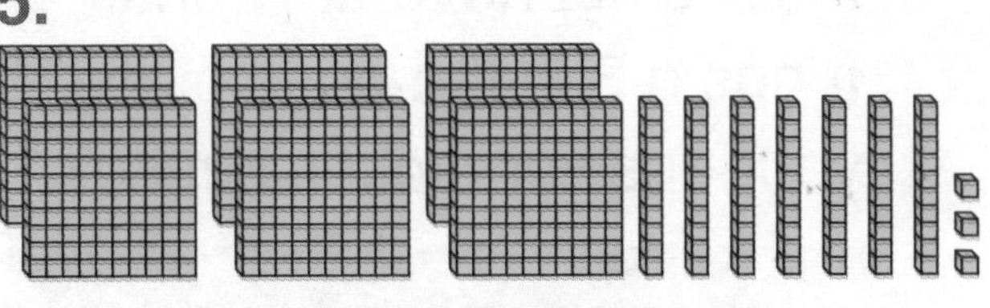

Hundreds	Tens	Ones
6	7	3

673

6.

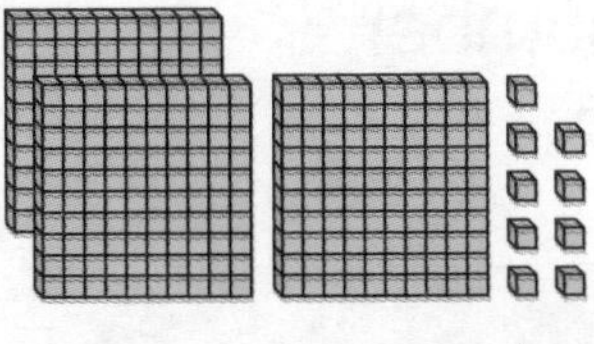

Hundreds	Tens	Ones
3		9

39

7.

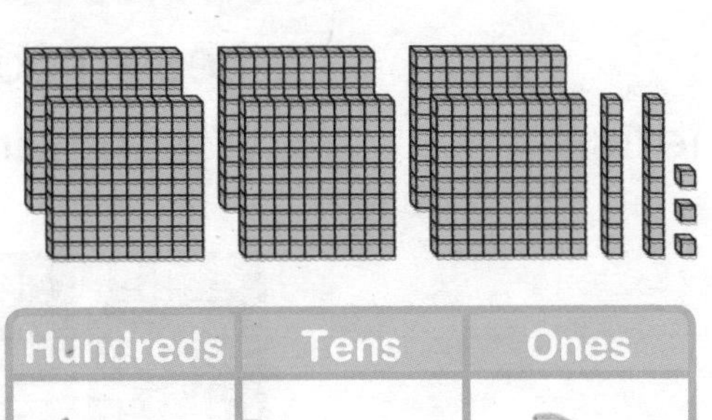

Hundreds	Tens	Ones
6	2	3

623

8.

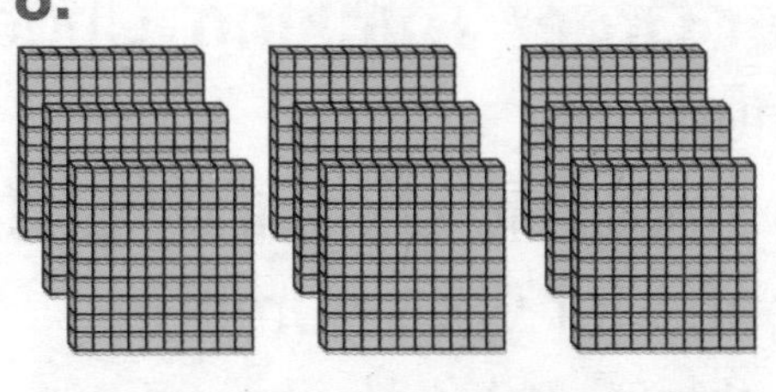

Hundreds	Tens	Ones
9		

9

9. Higher Order Thinking Find the number. It has 5 hundreds. The digit in the tens place is between 5 and 7. The number of ones is 2 less than 4. ______

Problem Solving Solve the problems below.

10. Make Sense Complete the chart. A number has an 8 in the hundreds place. It does not have any tens. It has a 3 in the ones place. Check that your answer makes sense.

Hundreds	Tens	Ones
8		3

What is the number? 83

11. Draw models to show 1 hundred, 4 tens, and 3 ones. Then write the number in the chart.

Hundreds	Tens	Ones
4	4	3

12. Higher Order Thinking Choose a three-digit number.
Draw models to show the hundreds, tens, and ones for your number.
Write the number below.

13. Assessment Practice Katie used these models to show a number. Which number is shown?

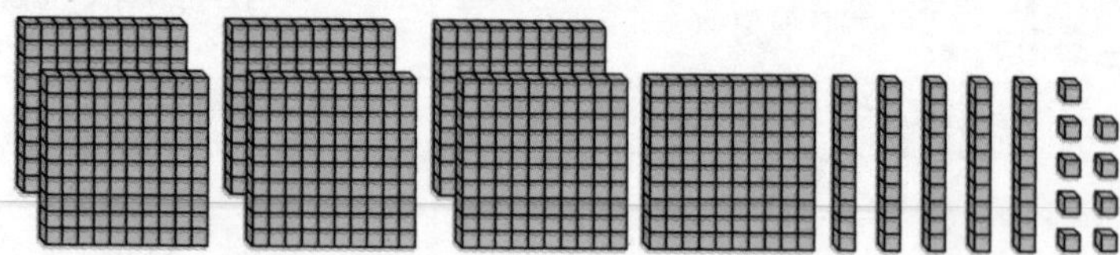

Ⓐ 759

Ⓑ 768

Ⓒ 858

Ⓓ 859

Name ________________________________

Activity

Lesson 9-3

Name Place Values

I can ...
tell the value of a digit by where it is placed in a number.

I can also model with math.

Solve & Share

Jake says the 3 in 738 has a value of 3. He shows this with 3 ones blocks. Do you agree with Jake? Explain. Use the chart to help.

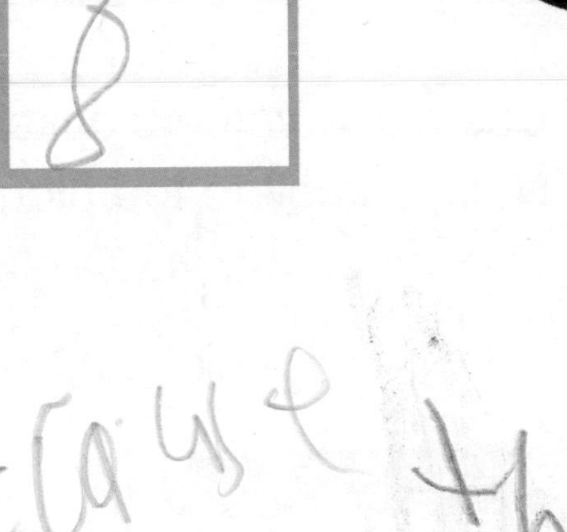

Hundreds	Tens	Ones
7	3	8

yes Becaus the 3 in thee middle

Visual Learning Bridge

What is the value of each digit in 354?

You can build the number with blocks.

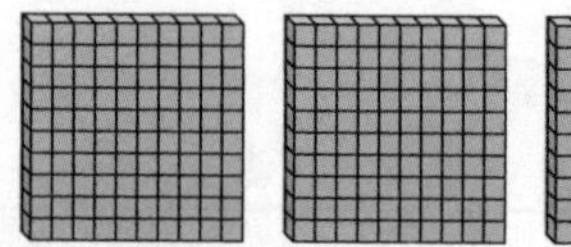

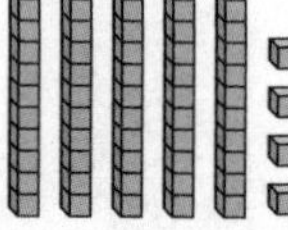

Remember, you can use a place-value chart to show the value of each digit.

Hundreds	Tens	Ones
3	5	4

The position of a digit tells its value.

354

The 3 has a value of 3 hundreds or 300.

The 5 has a value of 5 tens or 50.

The 4 has a value of 4 ones or 4.

Convince Me! How can you find the value of a digit using a place-value chart?

their is no prace value charts

Guided Practice Use place-value blocks to show the number. Next, complete the place-value chart. Then write the value of each digit.

1. 348

Hundreds	Tens	Ones
3	4	8

The 3 has a value of 3 hundreds or 300.

The 4 has a value of 4 tens or 40.

The 8 has a value of 8 ones or 8.

Name ____________________

Independent Practice

Circle the correct values for the underlined digit in each number.

2.	173	3	30	3 hundreds	3 ones	3 tens
3.	439	4 tens	4 hundreds	4	40	400
4.	661	6 hundreds	60	6 tens	600	6 ones
5.	518	500	5 tens	5 hundreds	5	50
6.	742	20	200	2	2 tens	2 ones

7. Use the number to answer each question.

902

What is the value of the 9?

____

What is the value of the 0?

____

What is the value of the 2?

____

8. Higher Order Thinking Write the number that has the following values.

- The tens digit has a value of 70.
- The ones digit has a value of 5 ones.
- The hundreds digit has a value of 8 hundreds.

Problem Solving

Use place value to solve each problem.

9. Complete the chart to find the number.

The number has 9 hundreds.
It has 5 tens.
It has 8 ones.

Hundreds	Tens	Ones
9	5	8

What is the number? 958

10. Model Courtney drew a picture of place-value blocks to show the number 793. Draw the blocks to show what Courtney's picture may have looked like.

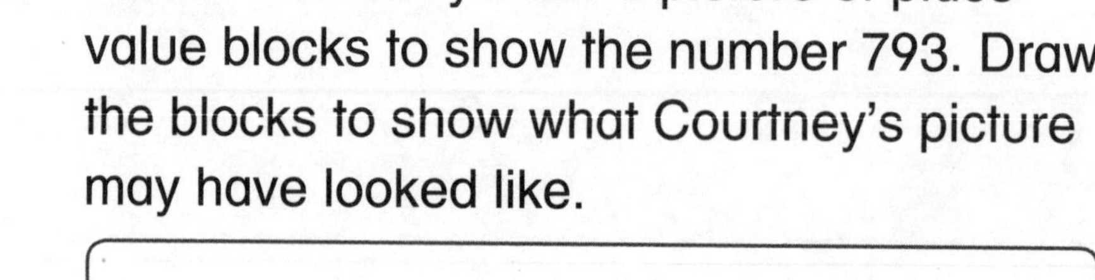

11. Higher Order Thinking A class needs to build the number 123 with place-value blocks but does **NOT** have any hundreds blocks. How can they build 123 using other place-value blocks?

12. Assessment Practice What is the value of the 6 in the number 862?

Ⓐ 6

Ⓑ 10

Ⓒ 60

Ⓓ 600

Name ______________________________

Lesson 9-4
Read and Write 3-Digit Numbers

I can ...
read and write 3-digit numbers in expanded form, standard form, and word form.

I can also model with math.

Solve & Share

What is another way to write the number 231? Explain.

Way 1

231

Way 2

Visual Learning Bridge

What number is shown by the models?

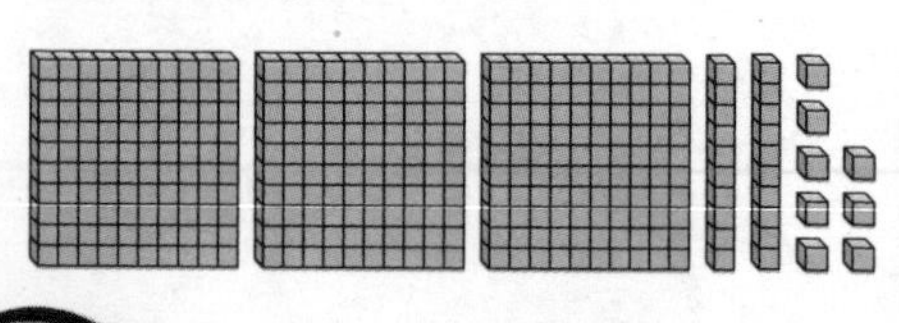

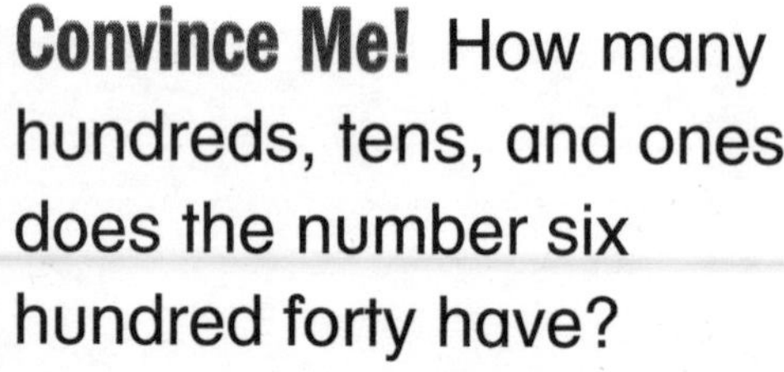

You can write the number in different ways.

Way 1
Write the number in **expanded form**.

300 + 20 + 8

Way 2
Write the number in **standard form**.

328

Write the hundreds first, then the tens, then the ones.

Way 3
Write the number in **word form**.

three hundred twenty-eight

All three ways show the same number!

328 = 300 + 20 + 8

Convince Me! How many hundreds, tens, and ones does the number six hundred forty have?

Guided Practice

Use the models to solve each problem.

1. Write the number in expanded form. Then write it in standard form.

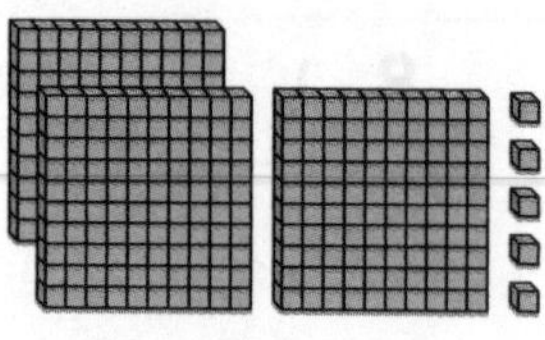

300 + 5

305

2. Write the number in expanded form. Then write it in word form.

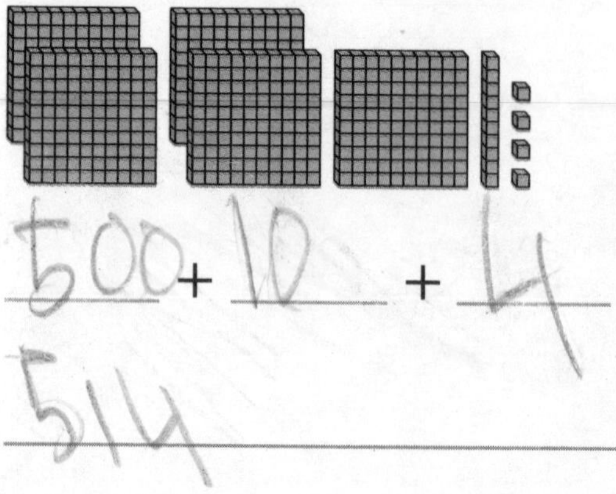

500 + 10 + 4

514

Name ______________________

Write the number in word form and standard form.

You can use place-value blocks to help!

3. 300 + 80 + 2

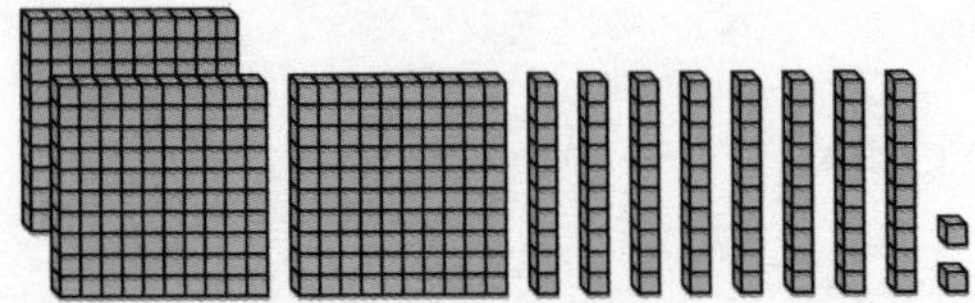

382

4. 200 + 6

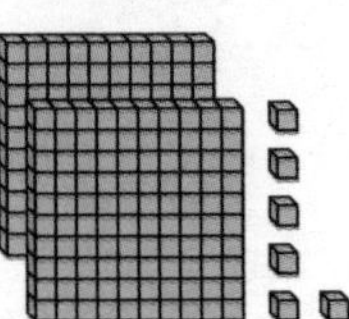

206

5. 600 + 90 + 5

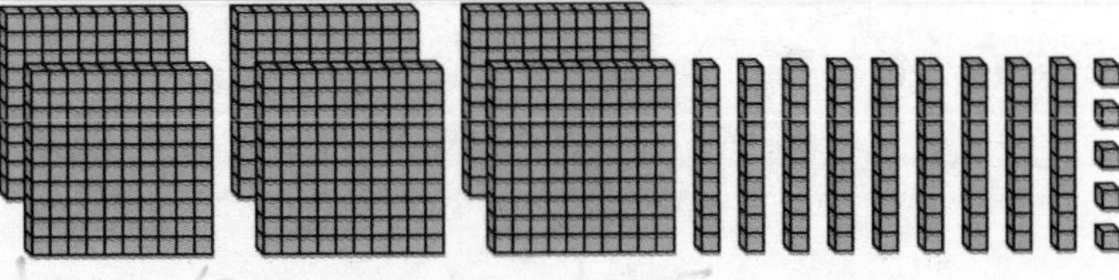

695

6. 500 + 30 + 3

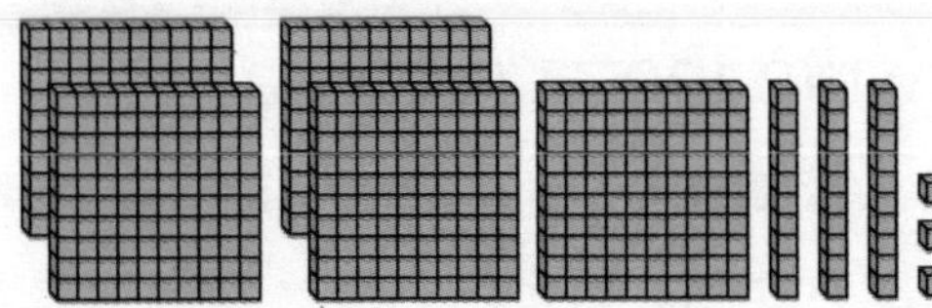

533

7. Write eight hundred seventy-four in expanded form and standard form.

800+7-4

874

8. Write 478 in expanded form and word form.

400+7+8

478

9. **Higher Order Thinking** Write the number in two different ways. It has 5 hundreds. The tens digit is 1 less than the hundreds digit. The ones digit is 2 more than the hundreds digit.

Standard form: 524 Expanded form: 500+2+1

Problem Solving

Use place-value models to help you solve the problems below.

10. **Vocabulary** There are 493 pages in a book.

Write the number 493 in **expanded form**.

_____ + _____ + _____

Write the number 493 in **word form**.

____

11. **Higher Order Thinking** Draw hundreds, tens, and ones to show a three-digit number. Next, write the number in expanded form. Then use the word form of the number in a sentence.

12. **Assessment Practice** The model shows a three-digit number. Which is the standard form of the number?

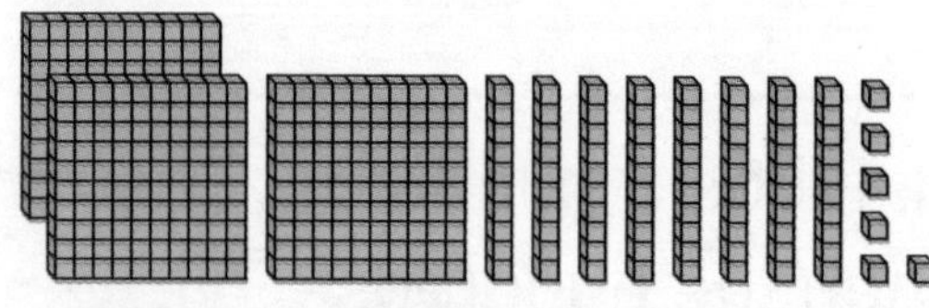

Ⓐ 300 + 80 + 6 Ⓑ 386 Ⓒ 300 + 90 + 7 Ⓓ 397

Name ______________________

Activity

Lesson 9-5

Different Ways to Name the Same Number

Solve & Share

Use place-value blocks. Show two ways to make 213. Then draw each way. Tell how your ways are alike and different.

I can ...

make and name a number in different ways to show the same value.

I can also reason about math.

Make your models here.

Draw your models here.

Way 1	**Way 2**
200 13	13 200

Visual Learning Bridge

You can show 123 in different ways. Here is one way.

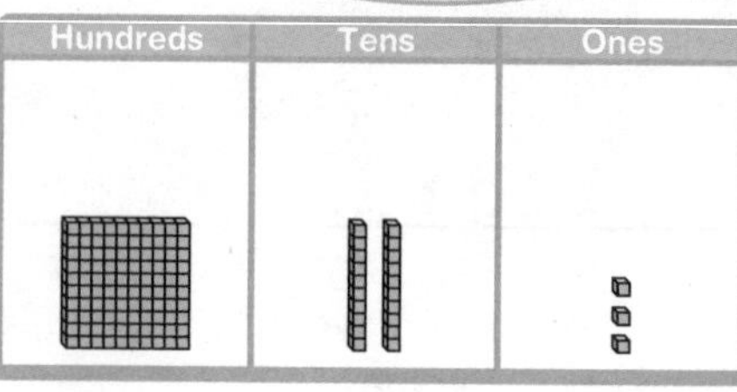

123 is 1 hundred, 2 tens, and 3 ones.
123 = 100 + 20 + 3

Or break apart the hundred to make 10 tens.

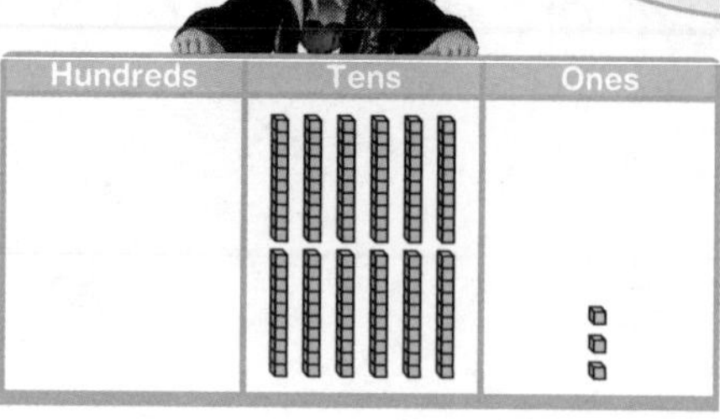

123 is 12 tens and 3 ones.
123 = 120 + 3

Or break apart a ten to make 10 ones.

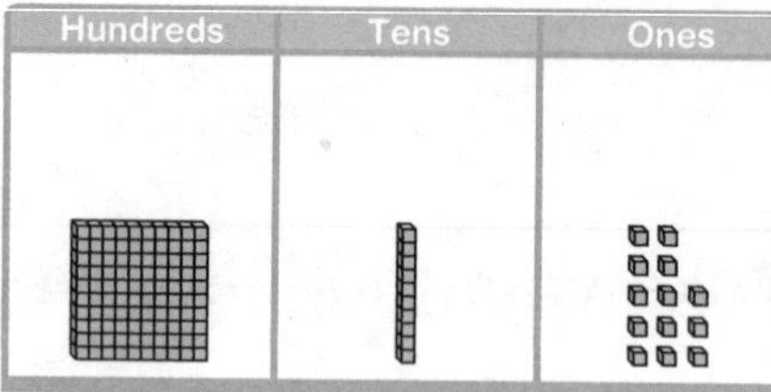

123 is 1 hundred, 1 ten, and 13 ones.
123 = 100 + 10 + 13

Convince Me! How can you show that 5 hundreds and 4 tens has the same value as 4 hundreds and 14 tens?

☆ **Guided Practice** ☆ Use place-value blocks to count the hundreds, tens, and ones. Show two other ways to make the number.

1.

Hundreds	Tens	Ones

132 = 100 + 30 + 2
132 = 10+30+2
132 = 100+30+2

Name ______________________

Independent Practice

Use place-value blocks to count the hundreds, tens, and ones. Then show two other ways to make the number.

2.

Hundreds	Tens	Ones

418 = ______

418 = ______

418 = ______

3.

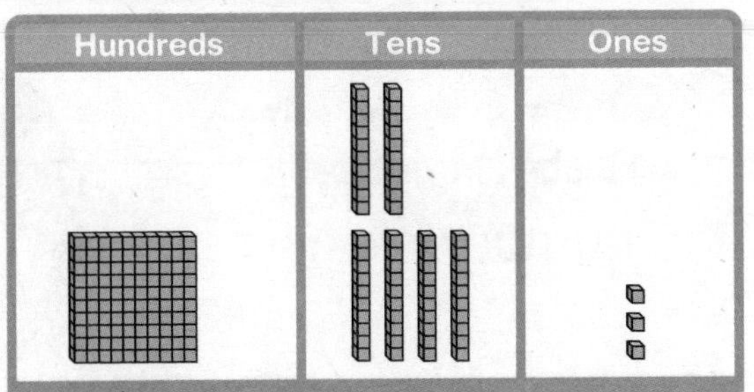

163 = ______

163 = ______

163 = ______

4.

Hundreds	Tens	Ones

225 = ______

225 = ______

225 = ______

Algebra Write the missing number.

5. 698 = 500 + ______ + 8

6. 939 = 900 + 20 + ______

Problem Solving Solve the problems below.

7. Carl made this model to show a number.

Hundreds	Tens	Ones

What number is shown? ______

Draw models to show another way Carl could make this number.

8. Explain Neha wants to make the same number in different ways. She says 300 + 130 + 9 equals the same number as 500 + 30 + 9. Do you agree with Neha? Explain.

____

____

____

Remember, you can show the same number in different ways.

9. Higher Order Thinking Make 572 as hundreds, tens, and ones. Write as many ways as you can.

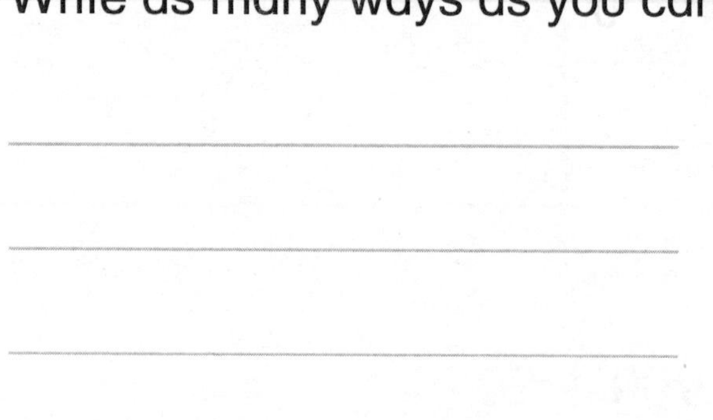

____

____

____

____

10. Assessment Practice Which is a way to show 687? Choose all that apply.

- ☐ 600 + 70 + 17
- ☐ 600 + 80 + 7
- ☐ 600 + 180 + 7
- ☐ 500 + 180 + 7

Name ______________________________

Activity

Lesson 9-6

Place-Value Patterns with Numbers

I can ...
use place-value patterns to mentally count by 1s and 10s from a given number.

I can also look for patterns.

Solve & Share

Write the missing numbers in the chart.
Be ready to explain how you found the missing numbers.

51	52	53	54	55	56	57	58	59	60
61	62	63	64	65	66	67	68	69	70
71	72	73	74	75	76	77	78	79	80
	82	83		85				89	
91			94		96	97	98		100
101	102	103	104	105	106	107	108	109	110
111	112	113	114	115	116	117	118	119	120
	122	123		125				129	
131			134				138		

 Visual Learning  Glossary

Visual Learning Bridge

You can use place-value patterns and mental math to count by 1s and 10s to 100.

37, 38, 39, 40, 41!

31	32	33	34	35	36	37
41	42	43	44	45	46	47
51	52	53	54	55	56	57

The ones digits go up by 1 from left to right.
The tens digits go up by 1 from top to bottom.

You can also use place-value patterns and mental math to count by 1s and 10s to 1,000.

537, 547, 557, 567!

531	532	533	534	535	536	537
541	542	543	544	545	546	547
551	552	553	554	555	556	557

The ones digits go up by 1 from left to right.
The tens digits go up by 1 from top to bottom.

Convince Me! Use mental math and place-value patterns to write each missing number.

538, 539, ______, 541, 542

481, 491, ______, 511, 521

Guided Practice Use place-value patterns and mental math to find the missing numbers.

1.

784	785	786	787	788	789	790
794	795	796	797	798	799	800
804	805	806	807	808	809	810

2.

412		414		416		418
422			425		427	
432	433		435	436	437	

Name ______________________________

Tools Assessment

Independent Practice

Use place-value patterns and mental math to find the missing numbers.

3.

884			887		889
	895			898	
904	905		907	908	

4.

	146	147			150
155				159	
	166	167		169	170

5. 456, 457, 458, ______, ______, 461, 462, ______, ______, ______

6. 620, 630, 640, ______, 660, ______, 680, 690, ______, 710, ______

7. 232, 242, ______, 262, ______, ______, 292, 302, ______, ______

8. 991, 992, ______, ______, 995, ______, 997, ______, 999, ______

Number Sense Describe each number pattern.

9. 130 → 230 → 330 → 430 → 530

____

____

10. 320 → 330 → 340 → 350 → 360

____

____

Problem Solving Solve each problem.

11. **Look for Patterns** Sally sees a pattern in these numbers. Describe the pattern.

995, 996, 997, 998, 999, 1,000

____

____

____

12. **Look for Patterns** Yoshi sees a pattern in these numbers. Describe the pattern.

341, 351, 361, 371, 381, 391

____

____

____

13. **Higher Order Thinking** Write your own three-digit numbers. Describe the number pattern for your numbers.

_____, _____, _____, _____, _____

____

____

____

14. **Assessment Practice** Use the numbers on the cards. Write the missing numbers in the number chart.

222 214 224 231

210	211	212	213		215
220	221		223		225
230		232	233	234	235

Name ______________________

Solve & Share

Use the number line to skip count by 5s, starting at 0. Write the two missing numbers. Describe any patterns you see.

Lesson 9-7

Skip Count by 5s, 10s, and 100s to 1,000

I can ... skip count by 5s, 10s, and 100s using a number line.

I can also reason about math.

0 5 10 15 20 ☐ ☐

____

____

____

This number line shows skip counting by 5s.

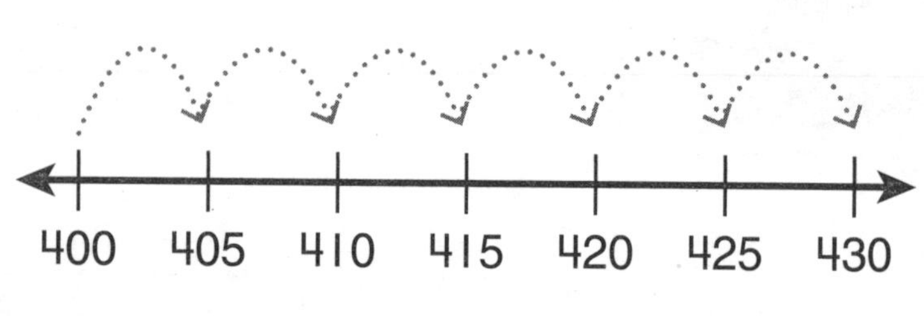

I see a pattern in the ones digits!

This number line shows skip counting by 100s.

400 500 600 700 800 900 1,000

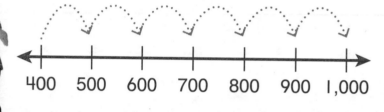

I see a pattern in the hundreds digits!

Convince Me! How could you use the number line in the first box above to skip count by 10s starting at 400?

Guided Practice Skip count on the number line. Write the missing numbers.

1.

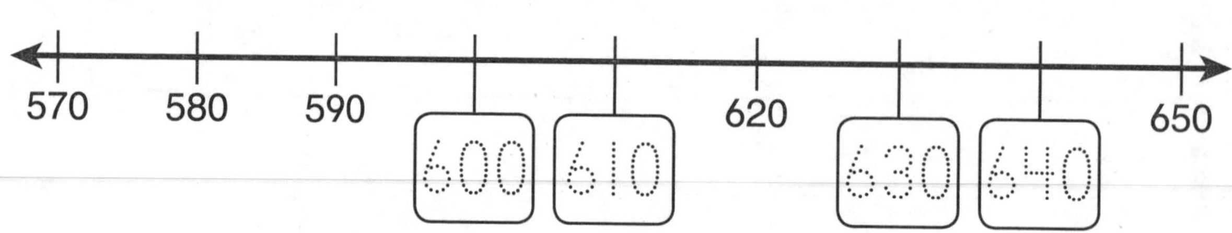

2.

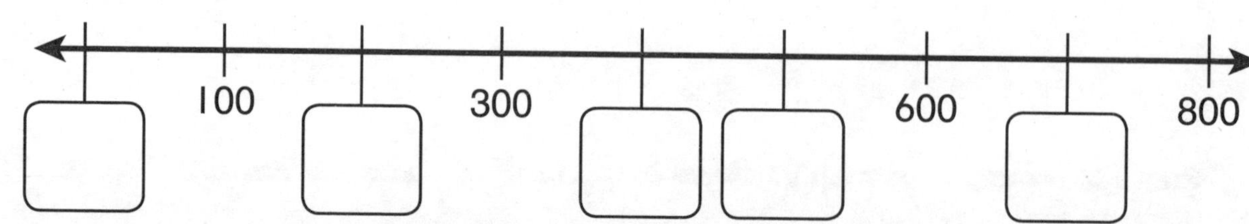

Name ______________________

Tools Assessment

Independent Practice

Skip count on the number line. Write the missing numbers.

3.

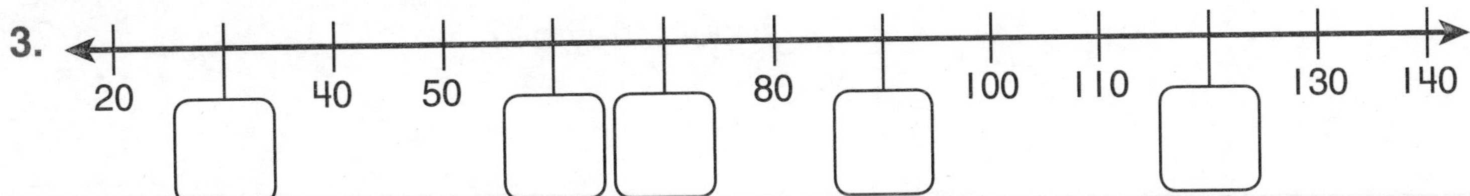

4.

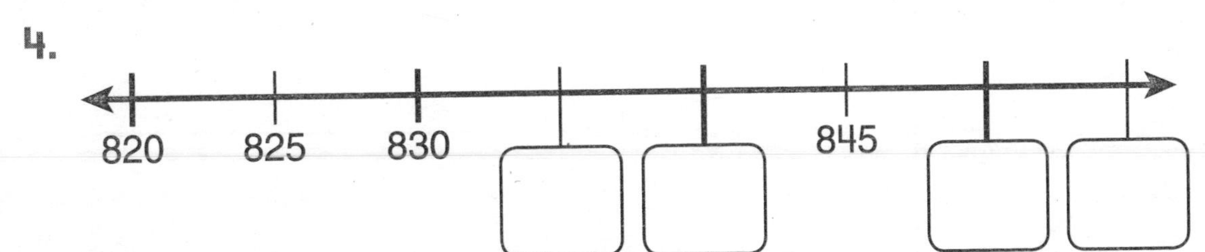

You can skip count by 5s, 10s, or 100s.

Look at the skip counting pattern. Write the missing numbers.

5. 100, 200, 300, 400, ______, ______

6. 950, 960, ______, 980, 990, ______

7. 480, 490, 500, ______, ______, 530

8. 745, 750, ______, ______, 765, ______

9. **Algebra** Write the missing numbers.

300 + ______ = 400

85 + ______ = 90

990 + ______ = 1,000

Problem Solving Solve the problems below.

10. **Reasoning** Greg is skip counting. He writes 430, 435, 440 on paper. Greg wants to write 3 more numbers after 440. What should they be?

_____, _____, _____

11. **Reasoning** Zoe is skip counting. She writes 500, 600, 700 on paper. Zoe wants to write 3 more numbers after 700. What should they be?

_____, _____, _____

12. **Higher Order Thinking** What number is used to skip count on this number line? How do you know? What numbers did the arrows land on at the jumps?

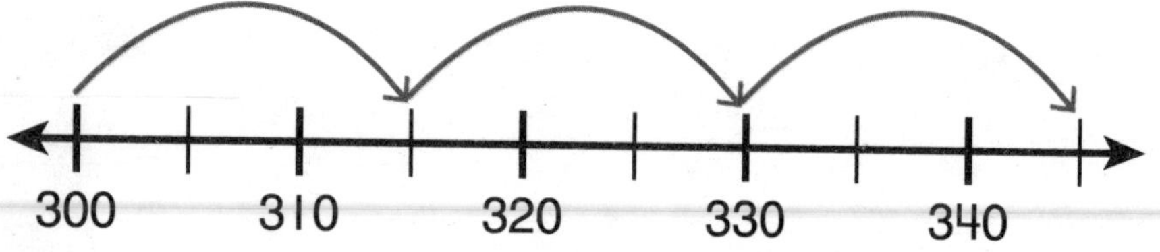

13. **Assessment Practice** Roy played 4 video games. He scored 110, 115, 120, and 125 points.

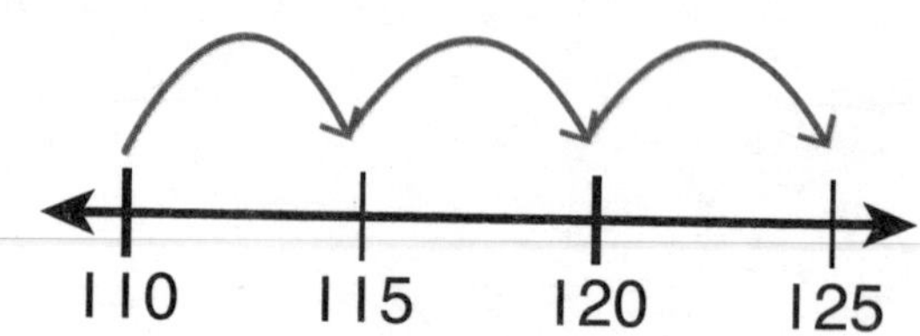

Skip counting by what number from 110 to 125 is shown on the number line?

Ⓐ 2 Ⓑ 5 Ⓒ 10 Ⓓ 100

Name ______________________________

Activity

Lesson 9-8

Compare Numbers Using Place Value

I can ...
compare numbers using place value.

I can also use repeated reasoning.

Solve & Share Joy and Zach flipped three number cards. Then they each made a number. Joy made 501 and Zach made 510.

Who made the greater number? How do you know? Use place-value blocks to help you solve.

Hundreds	Tens	Ones

_____ is greater than _____.

Visual Learning Bridge

Use place-value blocks to show each number. To compare the numbers, start with the digit that has the greatest place value.

Compare 325 and 225.

Hundreds	Tens	Ones
3	2	5
2	2	5

Compare the hundreds first.

300 is **greater than** 200.

So, 325 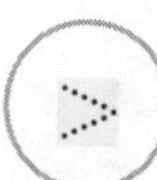 225.

Compare 736 and 756.

Hundreds	Tens	Ones
7	3	6
7	5	6

If the hundreds are equal, compare the tens.
30 is **less than** 50.

So, 736 < 756.

Compare 897 and 897.

Hundreds	Tens	Ones
8	9	7
8	9	7

The hundreds, the tens, and the ones are **equal**.
897 is equal to 897.

So, 897 = 897.

Convince Me! How would you compare 995 and 890? Explain.

Guided Practice

Use place-value blocks to show each number. Compare. Write greater than, less than, or equal to. Then write >, <, or =.

1. 264 is greater than 178.

264 > 178

Hundreds	Tens	Ones
2	6	4
1	7	8

2. 816 is ______ 819.

816 ◯ 819

Hundreds	Tens	Ones

Name ______________________

Tools Assessment

Independent Practice

Use place-value blocks to show each number. Compare.
Write greater than, less than, or equal to. Then write >, <, or =.

3. 572 is ______________ 577.

572 ◯ 577

4. 256 is ______________ 243.

256 ◯ 243

5. 837 is ______________ 837.

837 ◯ 837

6. 486 is ______________ 468.

486 ◯ 468

7. 208 is ______________ 208.

208 ◯ 208

8. 936 is ______________ 836.

936 ◯ 836

9. 821 is ______________ 821.

821 ◯ 821

10. 347 is ______________ 437.

347 ◯ 437

11. 286 is ______________ 189.

286 ◯ 189

12. Higher Order Thinking Find one number that will make all three comparisons true.

_____ < 111 _____ > 109 _____ = 110

Problem Solving Compare. Write >, <, or =. Then answer the question.

13. Reasoning Ming sells 319 tickets. Josie sells 315 tickets. Who sells more tickets?

319 ◯ 315

________ sells more tickets.

How can you use symbols to relate the numbers?

14. Reasoning Jared earned 189 pennies doing chores.
Tara earned 200 pennies doing chores.
Who earned more pennies?

189 ◯ 200

________ earned more pennies.

15. Higher Order Thinking Compare the numbers 298 and 289. Write the comparison two ways. Then explain your thinking.

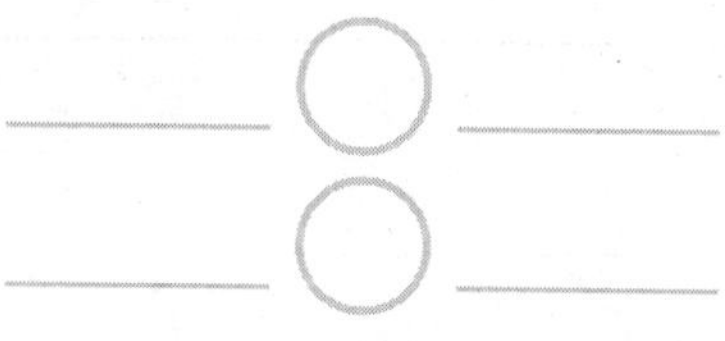

____

____

____

____

____

16. Assessment Practice Solve the riddle to find the number of coins in the second chest. Then compare the numbers.

The two numbers have the same digits.
The hundreds digits are the same.
The tens and ones digits are in different orders.

Ⓐ 556 < 665

Ⓑ 556 > 565

Ⓒ 556 = 565

Ⓓ 556 < 565

Name ___________________________

Lesson 9-9

Compare Numbers on the Number Line

I can ...
compare and write a three-digit number that is greater than or less than another three-digit number.

I can also reason about math.

Solve & Share This number line shows only one number. Name a number that is greater than 256. Then, name a number that is less than 256. Show your numbers on the number line and explain why you are correct.

256

_____ is greater than 256.

_____ is less than 256.

Visual Learning Bridge

You can write numbers that are greater than or less than another number, using a number line.

324 < 325

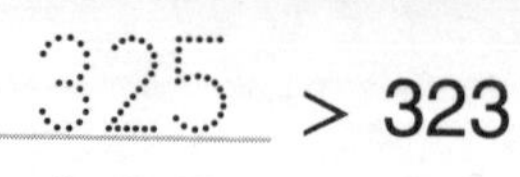

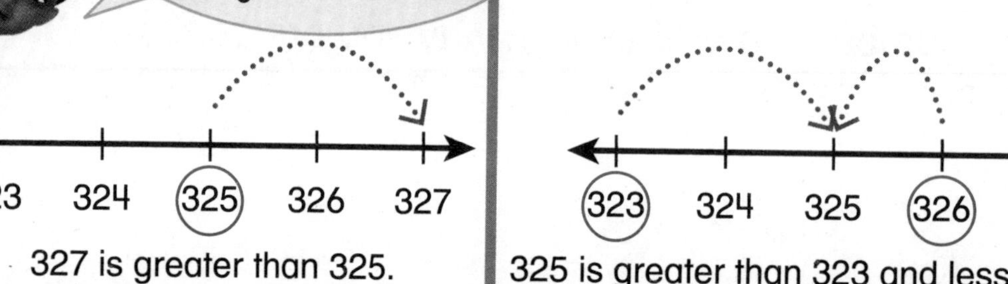

On a number line, the numbers to the left are less. 323 and 324 are both less than 325.
On a number line, the numbers to the right are greater. 326 and 327 are both greater than 325.

323 324 (325) 326 327

324 is less than 325.

327 > 325

323 324 (325) 326 327

327 is greater than 325.

325 > 323

325 < 326

(323) 324 325 (326) 327

325 is greater than 323 and less than 326.

Convince Me! Can you write a number that is less than 325, and that is not shown on the number line above? Explain.

Guided Practice Write a number to make each comparison correct. Draw a number line to help if needed.

1. 461 < 467

2. ____ < 470

3. 132 < ____

4. 263 < ____

5. 675 > ____

6. 684 = ____

Name ____________________

Tools Assessment

Independent Practice

Write a number to make each comparison correct. Draw a number line to help if needed.

7. 421 > ____

8. ____ < 884

9. 959 < ____

10. ____ < 619

11. 103 = ____

12. 566 > ____

13. 394 < ____

14. ____ < 417

15. ____ > 789

Write <, >, or = to make each comparison correct.

16. 107 ◯ 106

17. 630 ◯ 629

18. 832 ◯ 832

19. Higher Order Thinking Write a number to make each comparison correct. Place the numbers on the number lines.

____ < 780 < ____

____ > 457 > ____

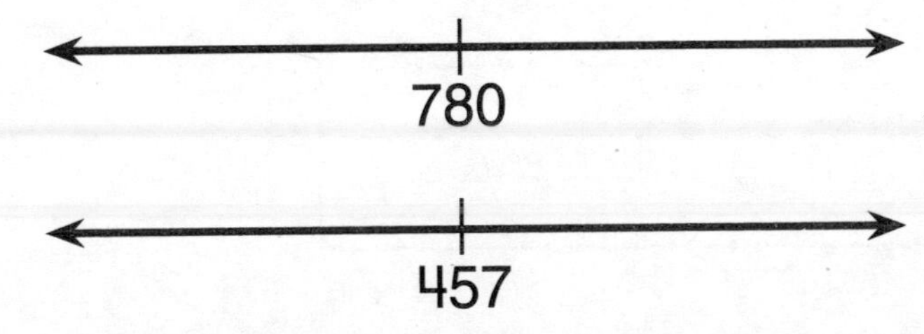

Problem Solving Solve the problems below.

20. Reasoning Kim is thinking of a number.
It is greater than 447.
It is less than 635.
What could the number be?

_____

21. Reasoning Don is thinking of a number.
It is less than 982.
It is greater than 950.
What could the number be?

_____

Think about how the numbers relate.

22. Higher Order Thinking Monty picked a number card. The number is greater than 282. It is less than 284. What is the number? _____

Explain how you know.

____

____

____

____

____

____

23. **Assessment Practice** Which number is neither greater than nor less than the number shown?

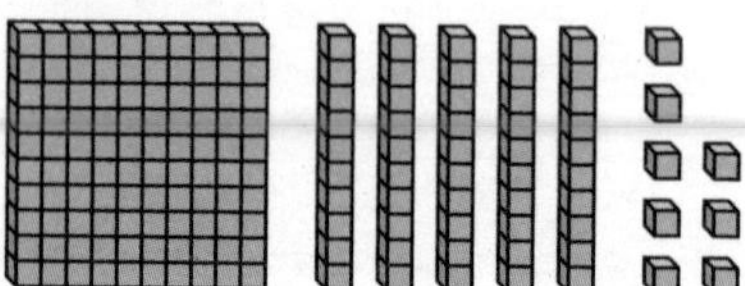

Ⓐ 157

Ⓑ 158

Ⓒ 159

Ⓓ 168

Name ______________________

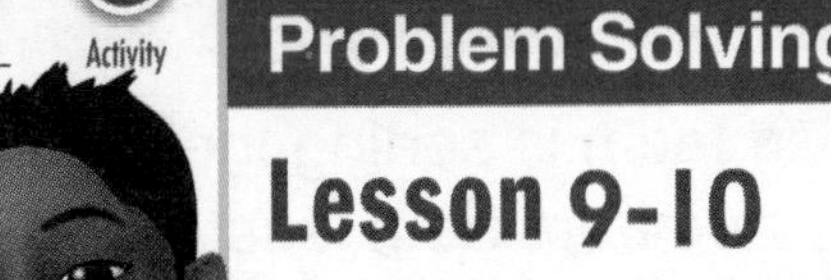

Lesson 9-10
Look For and Use Structure

Solve & Share

Sort the numbers 500, 800, 600, 400, and 700 from least to greatest.
Describe any number patterns that you see.
Are there any other numbers that fit the pattern?

I can ...
look for patterns to help me solve problems.

I can also describe number patterns.

Number patterns

Thinking Habits
Are there things in common that help me?
Is there a pattern? How does it help?

Visual Learning
A-Z Glossary

Visual Learning Bridge

The red team is sorting their jersey numbers from least to greatest. What is the next jersey number?

324
424
524
224

First sort the numbers. Then look for a number pattern.

How can I use patterns to help me solve the problem?

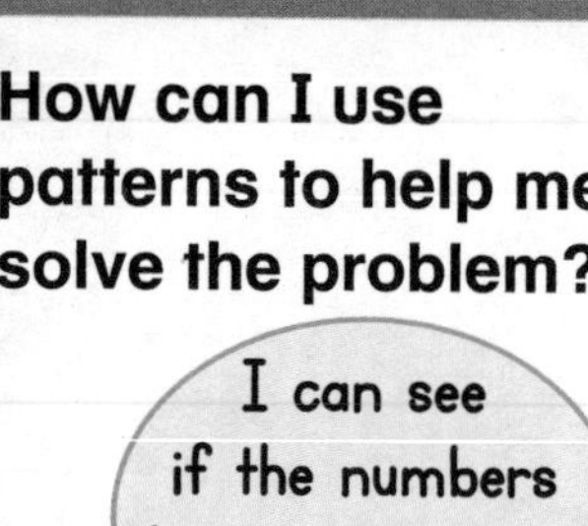
I can see if the numbers have anything in common.

224
324
424
524
?

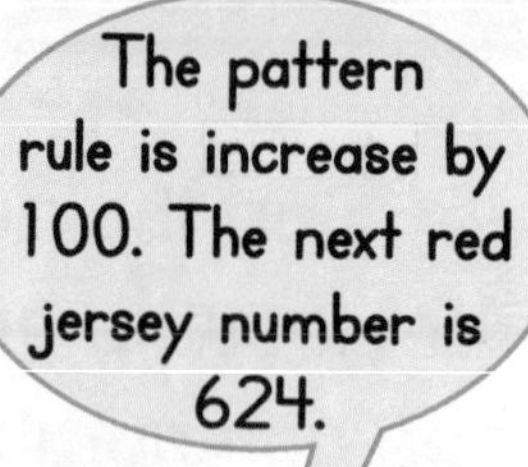
The tens and ones digits do not change. The hundreds increase by one hundred each time.
The pattern rule is increase by 100. The next red jersey number is 624.

The pattern will decrease if the team sorts the numbers from greatest to least.
224
324
424
524
624

Convince Me! How can you use the pattern to find the next three red jersey numbers?

Guided Practice Look for a pattern to solve each problem.

1. The yellow team is sorting their uniforms.

420
440
410
430
?

Sort the first four jersey numbers from least to greatest.

_____, _____, _____, _____

2. Look for a pattern in the sorted jersey numbers. What is the pattern rule?

____

3. What is the next greatest yellow jersey number? _____

Name ________________

Independent Practice

Break the problem into simpler parts to solve. Use a hundreds chart, a number line, or place value chart if you need to.

4. The blue team wants to sort their jersey numbers from greatest to least. After they sort the numbers, what number would come next?

List the jersey numbers from greatest to least.

_____, _____, _____, _____

Compare two numbers at a time to help you put the numbers in order.

Look for a pattern in the sorted jersey numbers. What is the pattern rule?

____

What jersey number is next in the pattern?

_____

5. A librarian sorted these books.
Find the missing book number. _____

Describe one pattern you notice.

____

____

____

Performance Task

Mail Delivery

Sam delivered mail to four houses numbered 115, 120, 110, and 105. He started at the house with the least number and continued to the house with the greatest number.

If the number pattern continues, what are the next three house numbers?

6. **Reasoning** Sort the numbers of the first four houses from least to greatest. Then write the sorted numbers on the houses in the top row above.

7. **Look for Patterns** What is the pattern rule for the four house numbers you sorted?

   What are the next three house numbers?

   Write the numbers of the houses in the bottom row of houses above.

8. **Explain** Why do you sort the numbers before looking for a pattern? Explain.

Name ______________________________

Fluency Practice Activity

Color a path from **Start** to **Finish**. Follow the sums and differences that are even numbers. You can only move up, down, right, or left.

I can ... add and subtract within 100.

I can also be precise in my work.

Start

66 – 28	15 + 12	64 – 27	57 + 36	99 – 66	53 – 14	23 + 46	75 – 22	52 + 13
15 + 35	59 – 28	57 + 22	87 – 74	56 – 12	78 – 52	61 + 15	42 – 29	29 + 16
53 + 43	44 + 39	90 – 18	47 – 23	61 + 39	61 – 36	24 + 38	15 + 58	73 – 52
85 – 39	56 + 17	43 – 11	25 + 26	81 – 28	61 + 14	53 – 37	33 + 38	45 – 18
33 + 57	78 – 52	56 + 12	87 – 32	16 + 45	93 – 24	63 + 15	26 + 44	27 – 19

Finish

TOPIC 9

Vocabulary Review

Glossary

Word List

- compare
- decrease
- digits
- equals (=)
- expanded form
- greater than (>)
- hundred
- increase
- less than (<)
- ones
- place-value chart
- standard form
- tens
- thousand
- word form

Understand Vocabulary

Write *standard form*, *expanded form*, or *word form*.

1. 400 + 30 + 7 ______

2. four hundred thirty-seven ______

3. 437 ______

Label each picture. Use terms from the Word List.

4. 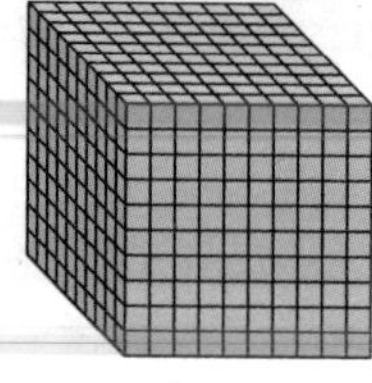 ______

5. 

______

6. 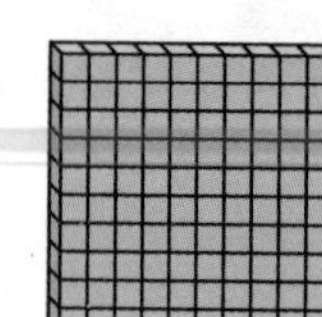 ______

Compare. Complete each sentence.

7. 901 is ______ 910.

8. 429 ______ 400 + 20 + 9.

Use Vocabulary in Writing

9. What is the next number in the pattern?

911, 921, 931, 941, ______

Explain how you solved the problem. Use terms from the Word List.

Name ___________________________

TOPIC 9

Reteaching

Set A

10 tens make 1 hundred.
You can count by hundreds.

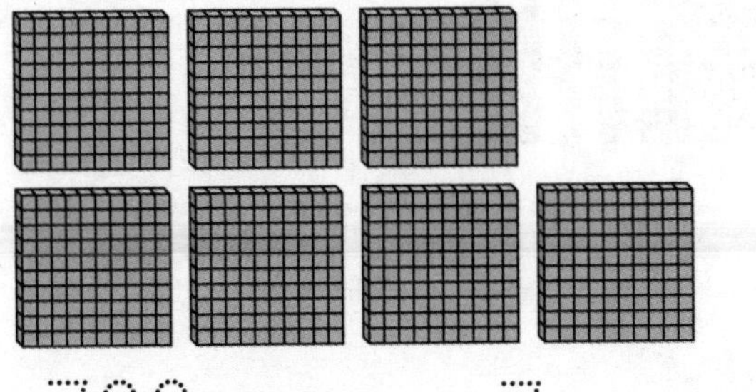

700 equals 7 hundreds,
0 tens, and 0 ones.

Complete the sentence. Use models if needed.

1. 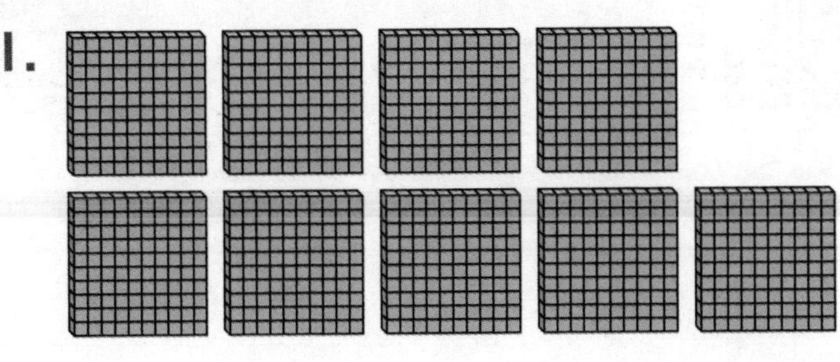

_____ equals _____ hundreds,
_____ tens, and _____ ones.

Set B

You can use place value to help you write numbers.

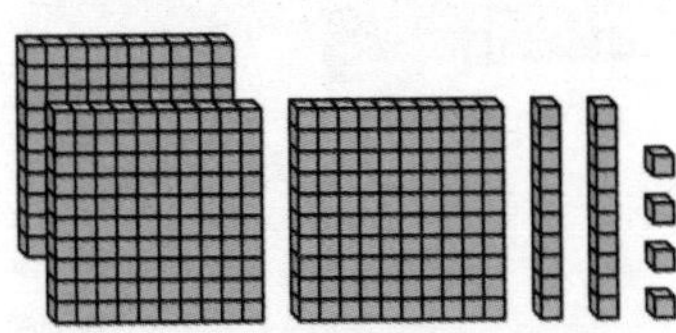

Hundreds	Tens	Ones
3	2	4

324

There are 3 hundreds, 2 tens, and 4 ones in 324.

Write the numbers. Use models and your workmat if needed.

2. 

Hundreds	Tens	Ones

_____

3. 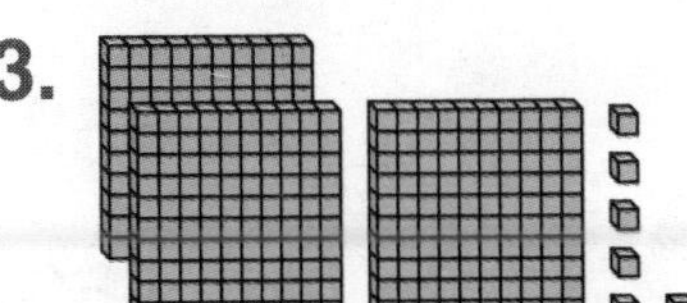

Hundreds	Tens	Ones

_____

Set C

You can write a number using the standard form, expanded form, and word form.

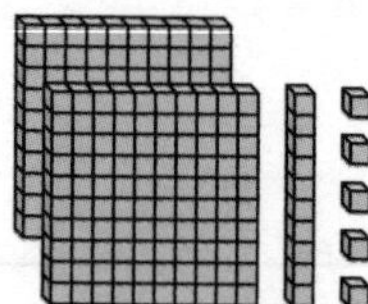

215

200 + 10 + 5

two hundred fifteen

Write the number in standard form, expanded form, and word form.

4. 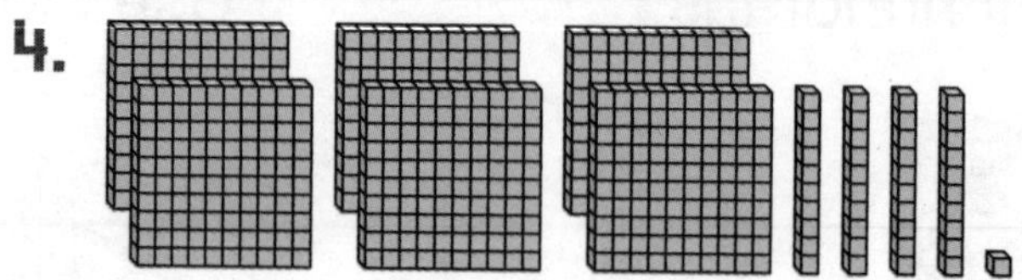

______

______ + ______ + ______

____

Set D

You can show different ways to make numbers.

Hundreds	Tens	Ones

238 = 200 + 30 + 8

238 = 200 + 20 + 18

238 = 230 + 8

Look at the models in the chart.
Show three different ways to make the number.

5. 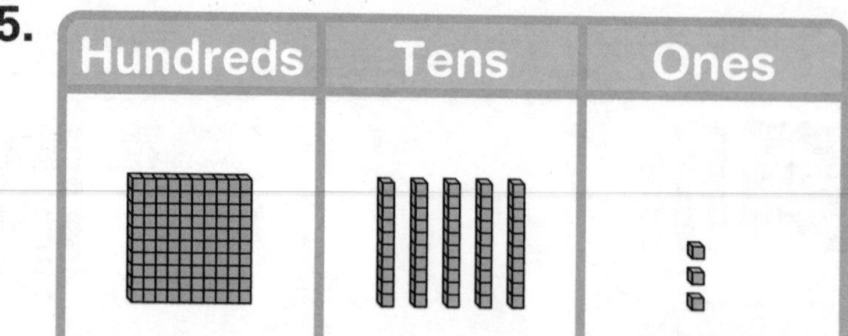

153 = ______ + ______ + ______

153 = ______ + ______ + ______

153 = ______ + ______

Name ______________________________

Set E

You can look for patterns with numbers on a hundreds chart.

342	343	344	345	346	347
352	353	354	355	356	357
362	363	364	365	366	367

From left to right, the ones digit goes up by 1.

From top to bottom, the tens digit goes up by 1.

Use place-value patterns to find the missing numbers.

6.

574		576	577	578	
584		586		588	589
	595	596	597		

7.

	222		224	225	
	232		234	235	236
241	242		244		246

Set F

You can skip count by 5s, 10s, and 100s on a number line.

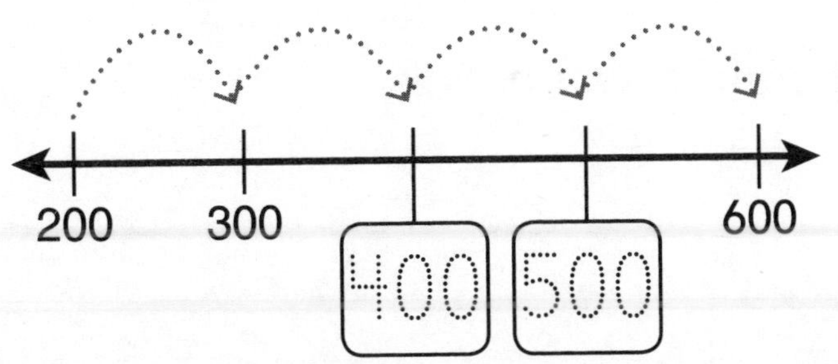

Skip count on the number line. Write the missing numbers.

8.

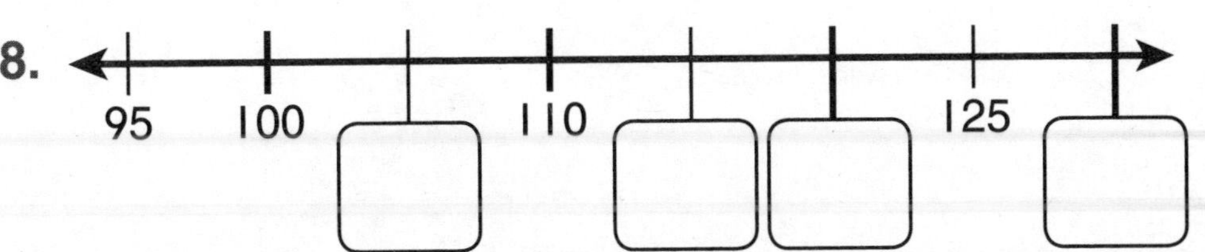

Set G

You can use place value to compare numbers.

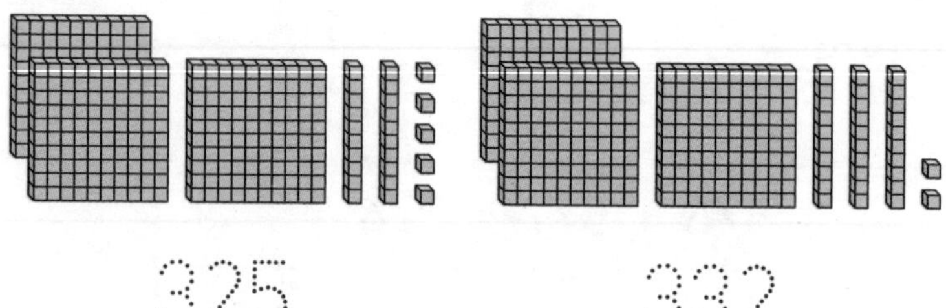

325 332

The hundreds are equal, so compare the tens. 20 is less than 30.

So, 325 < 332.

Compare each pair of numbers. Write >, <, or =.

9. 785 ◯ 793
10. 199 ◯ 198
11. 452 ◯ 452
12. 805 ◯ 810
13. 902 ◯ 897
14. 451 ◯ 516
15. 636 ◯ 629
16. 754 ◯ 754

Set H

Thinking Habits

Look For and Use Structure

Are there things in common that help me?

Is there a pattern? How does it help?

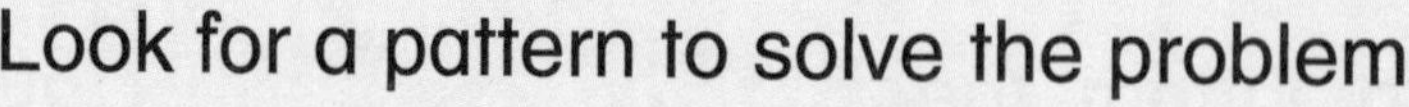

Look for a pattern to solve the problem.

17. These tags are in a drawer.

Describe a pattern you notice.

____

____

What is the missing number? ______

Name ________________________________

1. Each box has 100 crayons.
Count by hundreds to find the total.
How many crayons are in all of the boxes? Explain.

____

____

____

____

____

2. Danny made this model.
Write the number in three different forms.

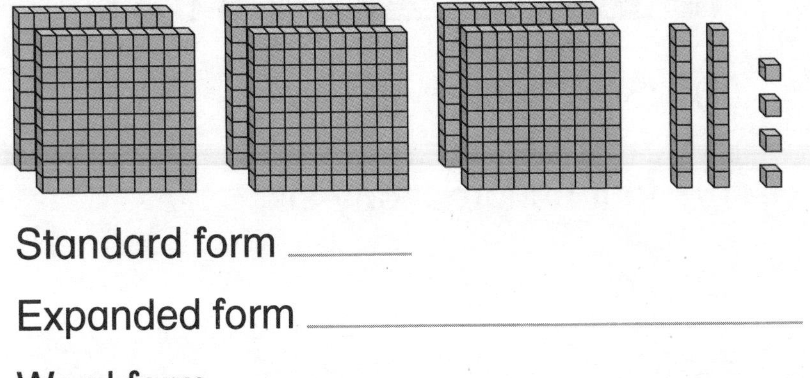

Standard form ______

Expanded form ______________________

Word form ______________________

____

3. Write the number the model shows.
Use the chart.

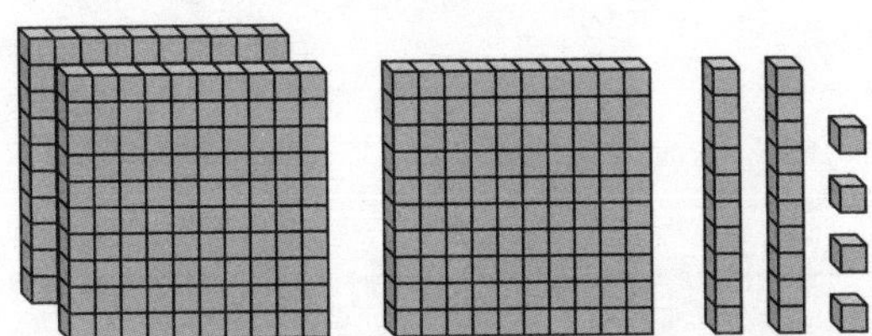

Hundreds	Tens	Ones

4. What is the value of the 8 in the number 789? What is the expanded form of 789?

____

____

____

5. Which is the word form of the number shown by the blocks?

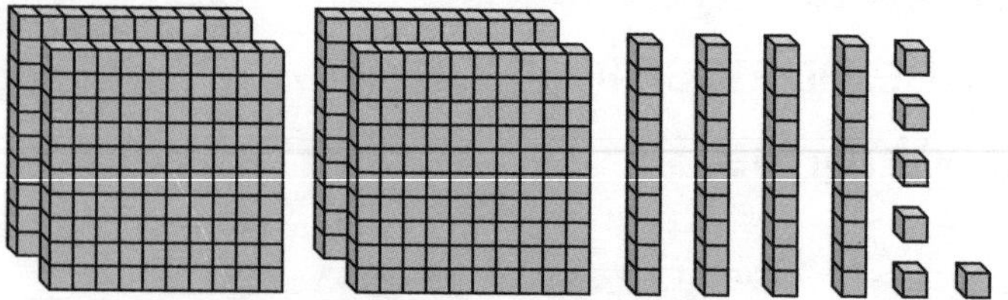

Ⓐ four hundred fifty-six

Ⓑ four hundred forty-six

Ⓒ 400 + 40 + 6

Ⓓ 446

6. Which is the standard form of the number shown by the blocks?

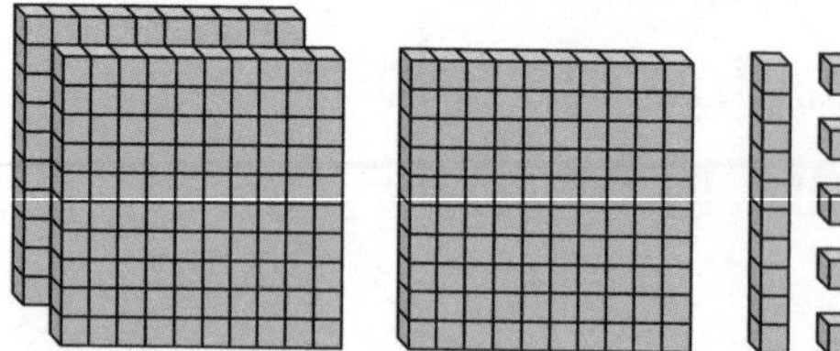

Ⓐ 315

Ⓑ three hundred fifteen

Ⓒ 300 + 10 + 5

Ⓓ 351

7. Draw a line from each number form to its example.

word form	standard form	expanded form
100 + 20 + 1	one hundred twenty-one	121

8. Kate made this model. What number does it show? Write the number and complete the sentence.

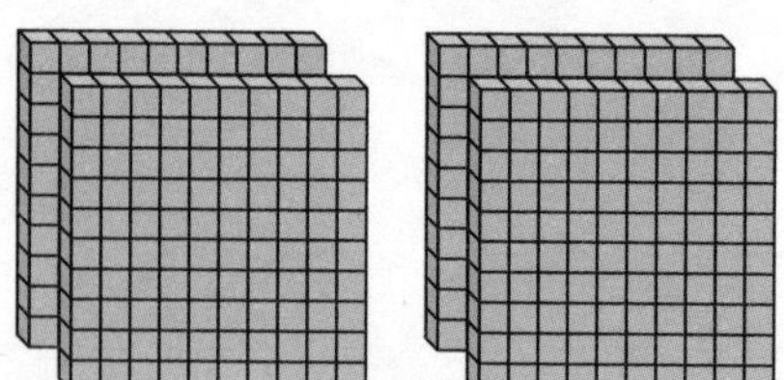

_____ equals _____ hundreds, _____ tens, and _____ ones.

Name ______________________________

9. Lee and Maria collect pennies.
Lee has 248 pennies.
Maria has 253 pennies.
Who has more pennies?

____

Write <, =, or > to compare the number of pennies.

248 ◯ 253

10. Jeff is thinking of a number.
The number has 2 hundreds.
It has more ones than tens.
It has 7 tens.

Which could be the number?
Choose all that apply.

- ☐ 276
- ☐ 279
- ☐ 267
- ☐ 278
- ☐ 289

11. Compare. Write <, =, or >.

429 ◯ 294 849 ◯ 984

12. Write a number that will make each comparison correct.

$327 <$ ____ $716 >$ ____

13. There are 326 boys at a school. Which is the expanded form for the number of boys?

Ⓐ 200 + 30 + 6 Ⓑ 300 + 20 + 6 Ⓒ 300 + 60 + 2 Ⓓ 300 + 60 + 7

14. Which is a way to show 576? Choose all that apply.

- ☐ 500 + 60 + 16
- ☐ 500 + 70 + 6
- ☐ 500 + 6
- ☐ 400 + 170 + 6
- ☐ 500 + 60 + 7

15. Use the numbers on the cards. Write the missing numbers in the number chart.

333 340 321 331

320		322	323	324
330		332		334
	341	342	343	344

16. Candy counts 405, 410, 415, 420, 425, 430. By what number does Candy skip count?

Ⓐ 2

Ⓑ 5

Ⓒ 10

Ⓓ 100

17. Skip count on the number line. Write the missing numbers.

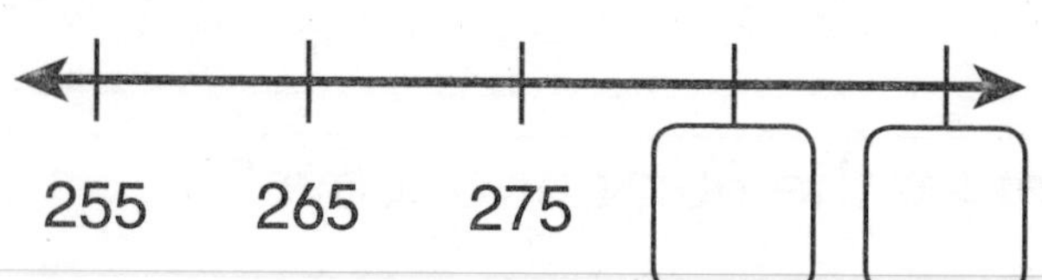

18. Choose all the comparisons that are correct.

- ☐ $576 < 675$
- ☐ $899 < 799$
- ☐ $435 > 354$
- ☐ $698 < 896$
- ☐ $856 > 859$

Name ______________________________

Reading Record
These students love to read!
These books show the number of pages each student has read so far this year.

1. Write the number of pages Tim read in expanded form.

____ + ____ + ____

Write the number in word form.

____

2. Complete the place-value chart to show the number of pages Ruth read.

Hundreds	Tens	Ones

Show two other ways to write the number.

____ + ____ + ____

____ + ____ + ____

3. Show two ways to compare the number of pages that Luisa read with the number of pages that Ruth read. Use > and <.

____ ◯ ____

____ ◯ ____

4. This number line shows the total number of minutes Diane read each week for 3 weeks.

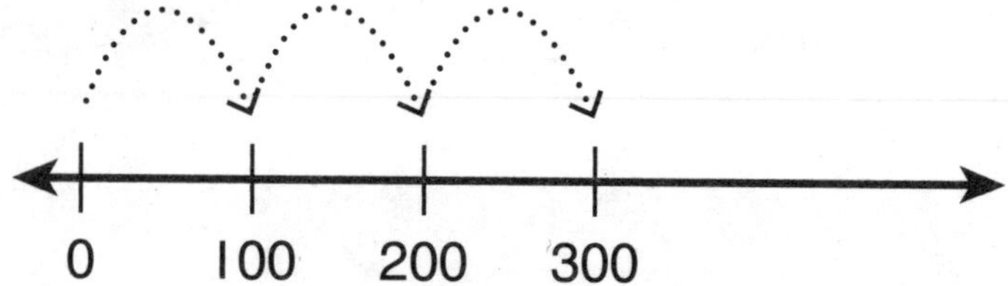

How many minutes did she read after the first week? ______ minutes

After the second week? ______ minutes

After the third week? ______ minutes

How many minutes did she read each week? Explain how you know.

5. Diane reads the same number of minutes each week. How many minutes does she read after 4 weeks? After 5 weeks? Skip count on the number line above to find the answers.

After 4 weeks: ______ minutes

After 5 weeks: ______ minutes

6. The table shows how many pages Jim read in three different months. If he follows the pattern, how many pages will Jim read in April and May?

Number of Pages Read	
January	210
February	220
March	230
April	?
May	?

Part A

What pattern do you see in the table?

Part B

How many pages will Jim read in April and May?

TOPIC 10

Add Within 1,000 Using Models and Strategies

Essential Question: What are strategies for adding numbers to 1,000?

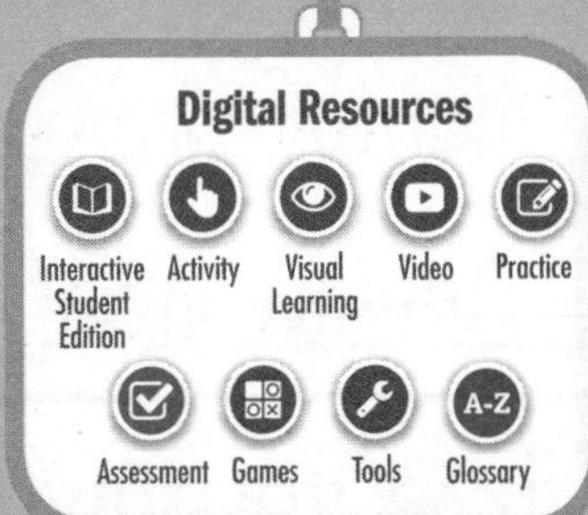

Look at all the tall buildings!

It takes a lot of planning to build a tall building. Would you like to try?

Wow! Let's do this project and learn more.

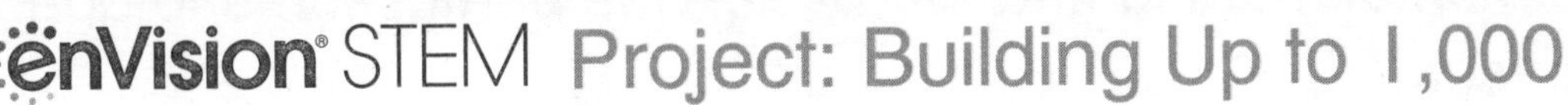

Find Out Use drinking straws and pieces of tape. The total number of straws and pieces of tape cannot be more than 1,000. First, decide how many of each to use. Then share. Build the tallest buildings you can.

Journal: Make a Book Describe your building in a book. In your book, also:

- Tell how many drinking straws and pieces of tape you used.
- Tell how you would make a better building if you did it again.

Name ______________________________

Vocabulary

1. Circle all of the **hundreds digits** in the numbers below.

   5 0 2

   5 8

   1,0 0 0

2. Write the **expanded form** of the number.

   846

   ____

3. Write the **word form** of the number.

   265

   ____

   ____

Open Number Lines

4. Use the open number line to find the sum.

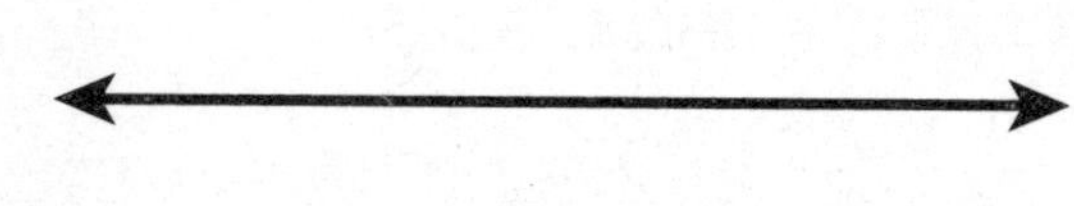

$54 + 13 =$ ______

Mental Math

5. Use mental math to find each sum.

   $40 + 37 =$ ______

   $6 + 77 + 4 =$ ______

Partial Sums

6. Use partial sums to add.

$$\begin{array}{r} 46 \\ +\,53 \\ \hline \end{array} \qquad \begin{array}{r} 29 \\ +\,61 \\ \hline \end{array}$$

Name ______________________

Pick a Project

PROJECT 10A

What are the run times of two of your favorite movies?

Project: Write Movie Reviews

PROJECT 10B

How many shots do basketball teams block?

Project: Make a Basketball Poster

PROJECT 10C

How many miles are between a State Capital and other cities?

Project: Draw a State Map

PROJECT 10D

How far can people hike in the Sierra Nevada Mountains?

Project: Create a Hiking Guide

Name ______________________

Lesson 10-1
Add 10 and 100

I can ...
add 10 and 100 mentally using what I know about place value.

I can also look for patterns.

Solve & Share

Forest Park Nursery sells trees.
Sal buys a maple tree for \$125.
A spruce tree costs \$10 more than a maple tree.
An elm tree costs \$100 more than a maple tree.
What is the cost of a spruce tree? An elm tree?

Use dollar bills, place-value blocks, or mental math to solve.
Be ready to explain how you solved the problem.

Visual Learning Bridge

You can use mental math to add 10 or 100 to three-digit numbers.

Find 243 + 10.
Find 243 + 100.

243
How can I add 10 or 100 mentally?

243 + 10 = ?

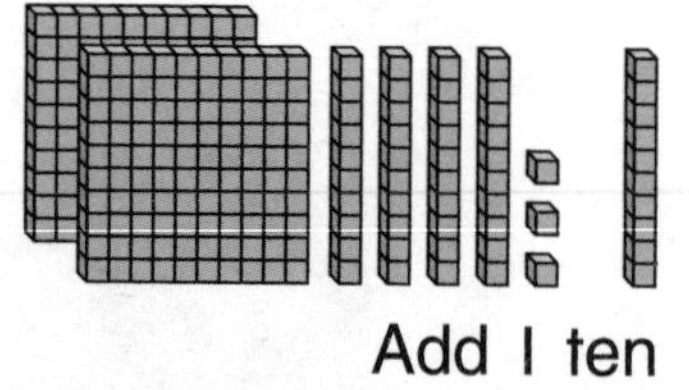

Add 1 ten
4 tens plus 1 ten equals 5 tens.
So, 243 + 10 = 253.

243 + 100 = ?

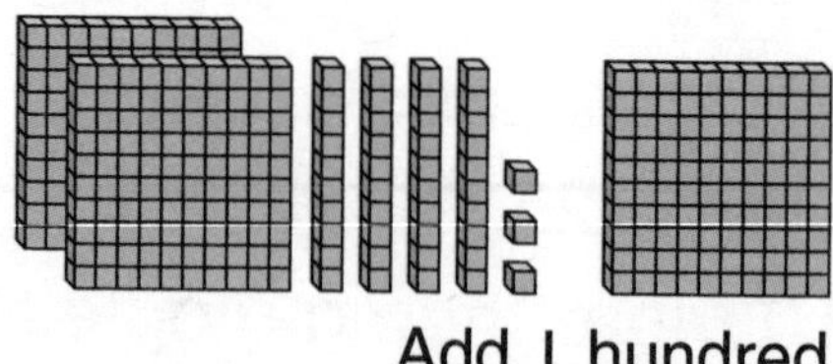

Add 1 hundred
2 hundreds plus 1 hundred equals 3 hundreds.
So, 243 + 100 = 343.

Sometimes adding 10 changes the tens and hundreds digits.

Find 290 + 10.

I know 290 = 29 tens. 29 tens plus 1 ten equals 30 tens or 300. So, 290 + 10 = 300.

Convince Me! Use mental math to find 567 + 10 and 567 + 100. Explain your reasoning.

Guided Practice

Add. Use place-value blocks or mental math.

1.

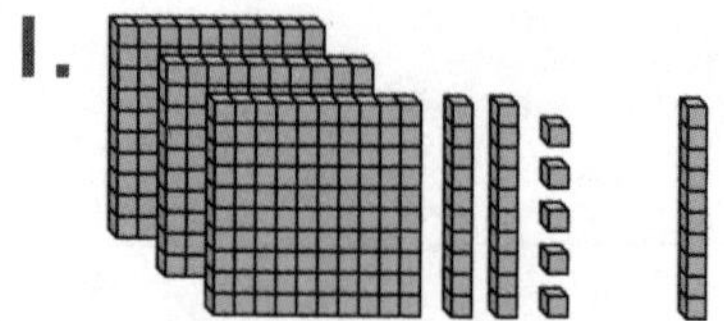

325 + 10 = 335

2.

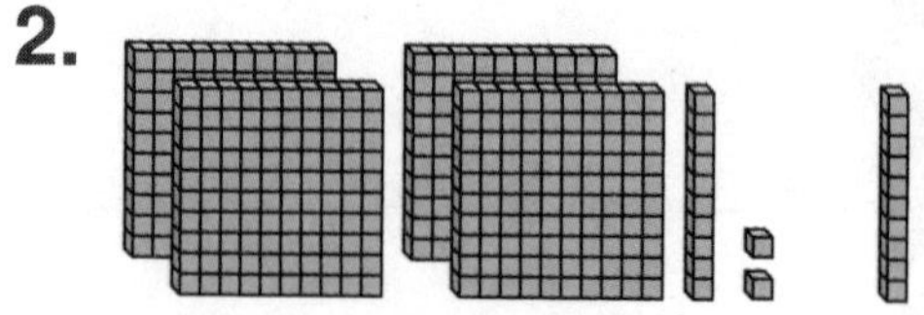

____ + ____ = ____

3.

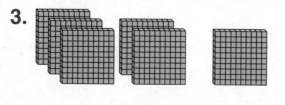

____ + ____ = ____

4.

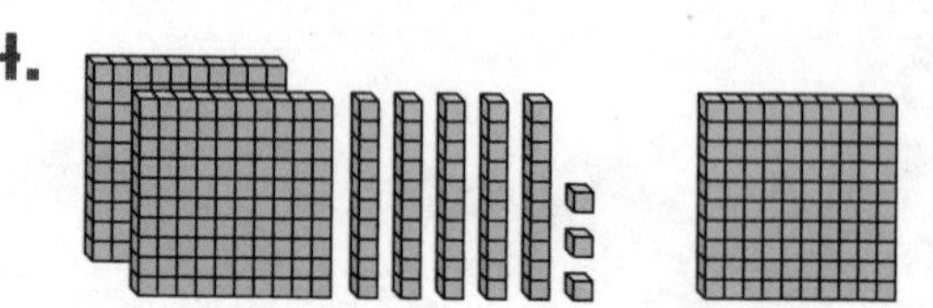

____ + ____ = ____

Name ______

Tools Assessment

Independent Practice

Add. Use place-value blocks or mental math.

5. 164 + 100 = ______

6. \$837 + \$10 = ______

7. 329 + 100 = ______

8. 610 + 10 = ______

9. 295 + 10 = ______

10. \$497 + \$100 = ______

11. 790 + 10 = ______

12. 693 + 100 = ______

13. 900 + 100 = ______

14. 460 + 10 = ______

15. 185 + 10 = ______

16. 723 + 100 = ______

Algebra Find the missing numbers. Use mental math to solve.

17. 572 + ☐ = 672

18. 285 + ☐ = 385

19. 709 = 699 + ☐

20. 422 = 322 + ☐

21. 615 + ☐ = 625

22. 600 = ☐ + 590

Problem Solving Solve each problem. Show your work.

23. **enVision® STEM** The Science Club asked 178 people about recycling. The club wants to ask a total of 188 people about recycling.

How many more people will the Science Club need to ask?

______ more people

24. **Use Structure** Jordan has four $100 bills, three $20 bills, one $10 bill, and seven $1 bills. What will Jordan's total be if Jayla gives him one more $10 bill? What will his total be if she gives him one more $100 bill?

______

______

Is there a shortcut that makes sense?

25. **Higher Order Thinking** Think of a 3-digit number. Write a story about adding 100 to your number. Then write an equation to show your solution.

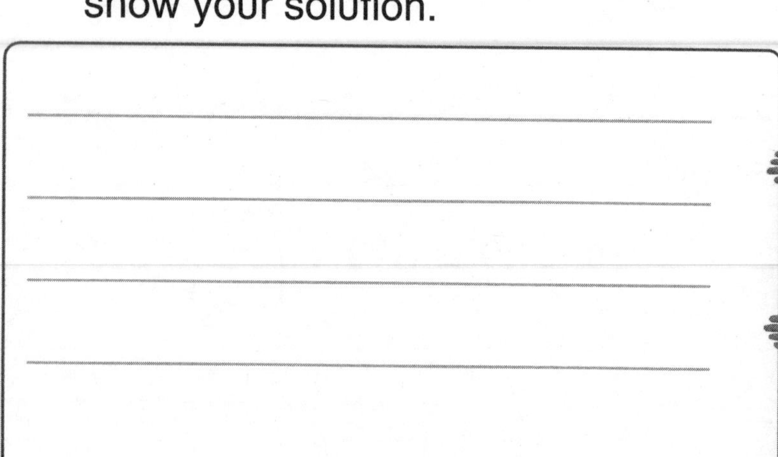

______ + ______ = ______

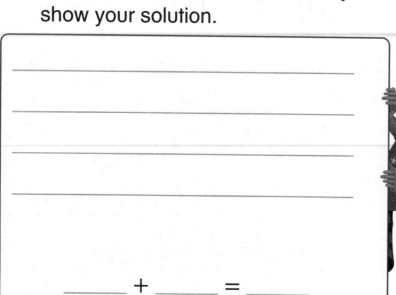

26. **Assessment Practice** Which equations are true? Choose all that apply.

- ☐ $251 + $10 = $351
- ☐ 528 + 100 = 628
- ☐ 528 + 10 = 538
- ☐ $251 + $100 = $351

Name ______

Lesson 10-2

Add on an Open Number Line

I can ...
use an open number line to add 3-digit numbers.

I can also use math tools correctly.

Solve & Share

Use the open number line to find 598 + 123. Explain your work.

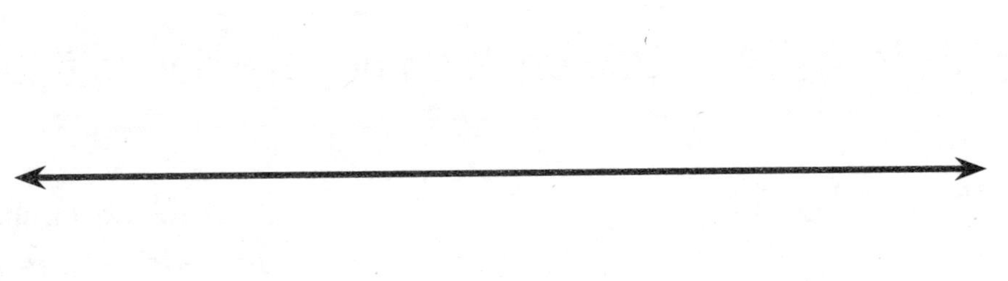

____ + ____ = ____

Find 481 + 122. Use an open number line.

One Way

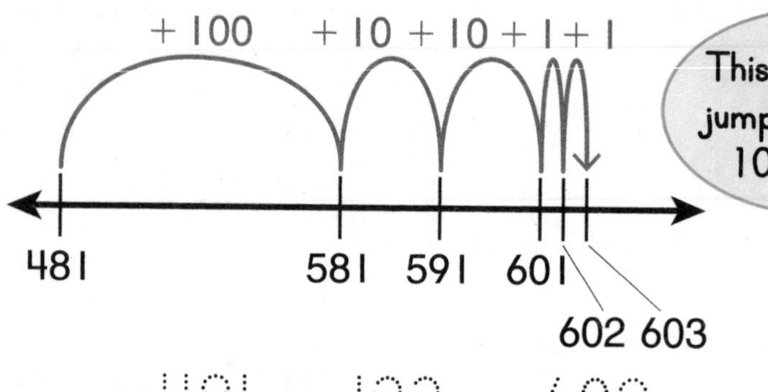

This way shows jumps by 100s, 10s, and 1s.

Another Way

This way shows how you can make bigger jumps.

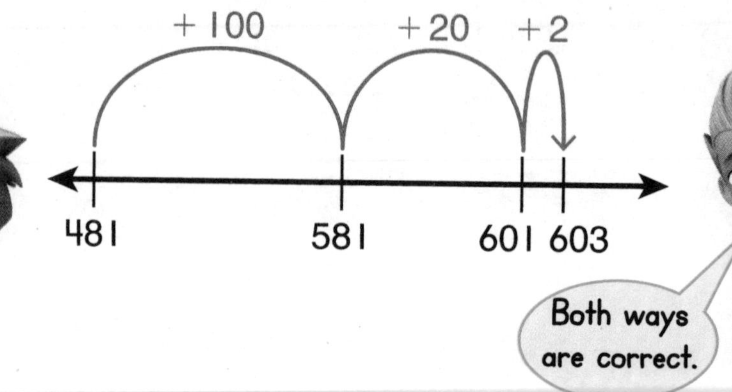

Both ways are correct.

Convince Me! Explain how you can use an open number line to find 599 + 205.

Guided Practice Use an open number line to find each sum.

1. 375 + 118 = ______

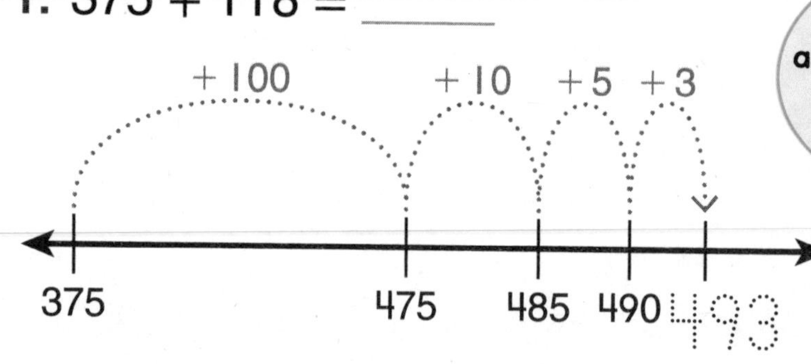

Breaking apart an addend does not change the value being added.

2. 670 + 232 = ______

Name ______________________________

Independent Practice

Use an open number line to find each sum.

3. 269 + 156 = ______

4. 637 + 242 = ______

5. 886 + 114 = ______

6. 208 + 598 = ______

7. **Higher Order Thinking** Lisa finds 550 + 298 using the open number line below. Is her work correct? Explain.

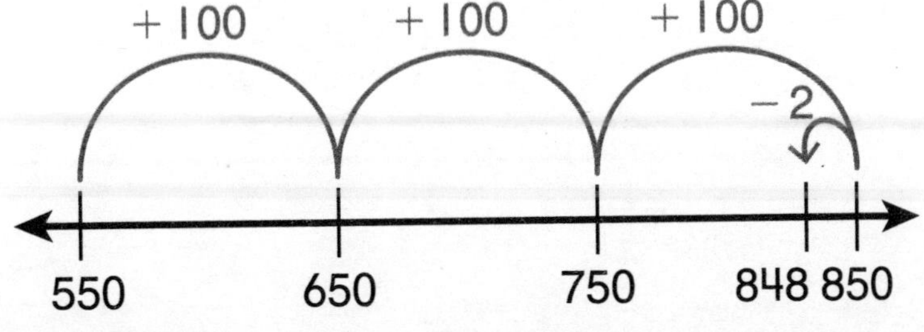

Problem Solving ☆ Use an open number line to find each sum.

8. **Reasoning** José has 181 cards. He collects 132 more cards. How many cards does he have now?

_____ cards

9. **Vocabulary** Complete the sentence using two of these terms.

add **tens** **open number line** **rule**

An _______________

can be used to _______________.

10. **Higher Order Thinking** Use open number lines to find 446 + 215 in two different ways.

446 + 215 = _____

11. **Assessment Practice** Mary uses an open number line to find 286 + 137. All of the jumps she draws are greater than 1. Draw what Mary could have done. Write the sum.

286 + 137 = _____

Name ______

Lesson 10-3

Add Using Models

Solve & Share

Use place-value blocks to find 243 + 354. Tell which place value you added first and why. Then draw a picture to show your work.

I can ...
use models to add 3-digit numbers and then explain my work.

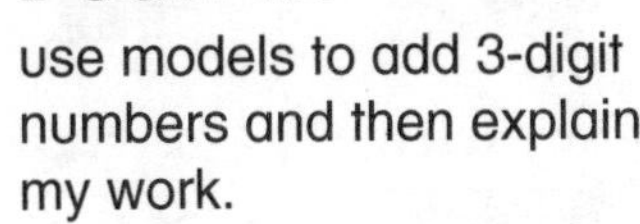

I can also use math tools correctly.

243 + 354 = ______

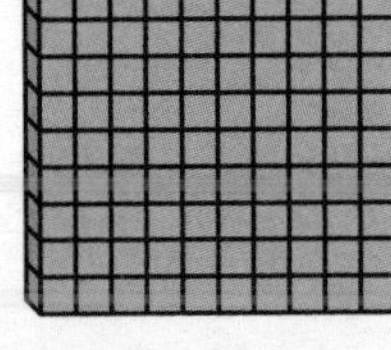

 Visual Learning  Glossary

Visual Learning Bridge

Find 238 + 126.

Hundreds	Tens	Ones
2 hundreds	3 tens	8 ones
1 hundred	2 tens	6 ones

You can show each addend with place-value blocks.

Join the hundreds, the tens, and the ones. Regroup if you can.

Hundreds	Tens	Ones
3 hundreds	5 tens	14 ones or 1 ten and 4 ones
3 hundreds 300	6 tens 60	4 ones 4

You can regroup 10 ones as 1 ten.

So, 238 + 126 = 364.

Convince Me! Are the tens regrouped in the example above? How do you know?

Guided Practice

Use place-value blocks to find each sum. Regroup if needed.

1. 223 + 106 = ____

Hundreds	Tens	Ones

2. 149 + 362 = ____

Hundreds	Tens	Ones

Name ____________________

Independent Practice Use and draw blocks to find each sum. Regroup if needed.

3. 151 + 324 = ______

Hundreds	Tens	Ones

4. 250 + 298 = ______

Hundreds	Tens	Ones

5. 258 + 109 = ______

Hundreds	Tens	Ones

6. 187 + 246 = ______

Hundreds	Tens	Ones

7. 236 + 318 = ______

Hundreds	Tens	Ones

8. 432 + 365 = ______

Hundreds	Tens	Ones

9. **Number Sense** Jamal says that the sum of 183 + 198 is less than 300. Is Jamal's answer reasonable? Why or why not?

____

____

____

Both addends are close to 200.

Problem Solving Solve the problems below. Show your work.

10. Reasoning 156 children in a school are girls. 148 children in that school are boys. How many children go to that school?

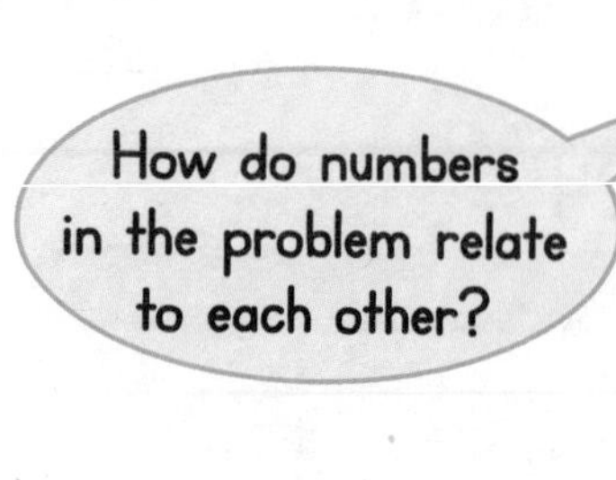

How do numbers in the problem relate to each other?

______ children

11. Higher Order Thinking Write an addition problem about stickers. Use 3-digit numbers. Then solve the problem.

____

____

____

____

12. Assessment Practice Which is the sum of 129 + 268?

Hundreds	Tens	Ones

Ⓐ 292

Ⓑ 294

Ⓒ 389

Ⓓ 397

Name ______________________

Activity

Lesson 10-4

Continue to Add Using Models and Place Value

I can ...
use models and place value to add 3-digit numbers.

I can also model with math.

Solve & Share

Oak School has 256 students. Pine School has 371 students. How many students do the schools have in all? Use place-value blocks to help. Draw your blocks below and solve.

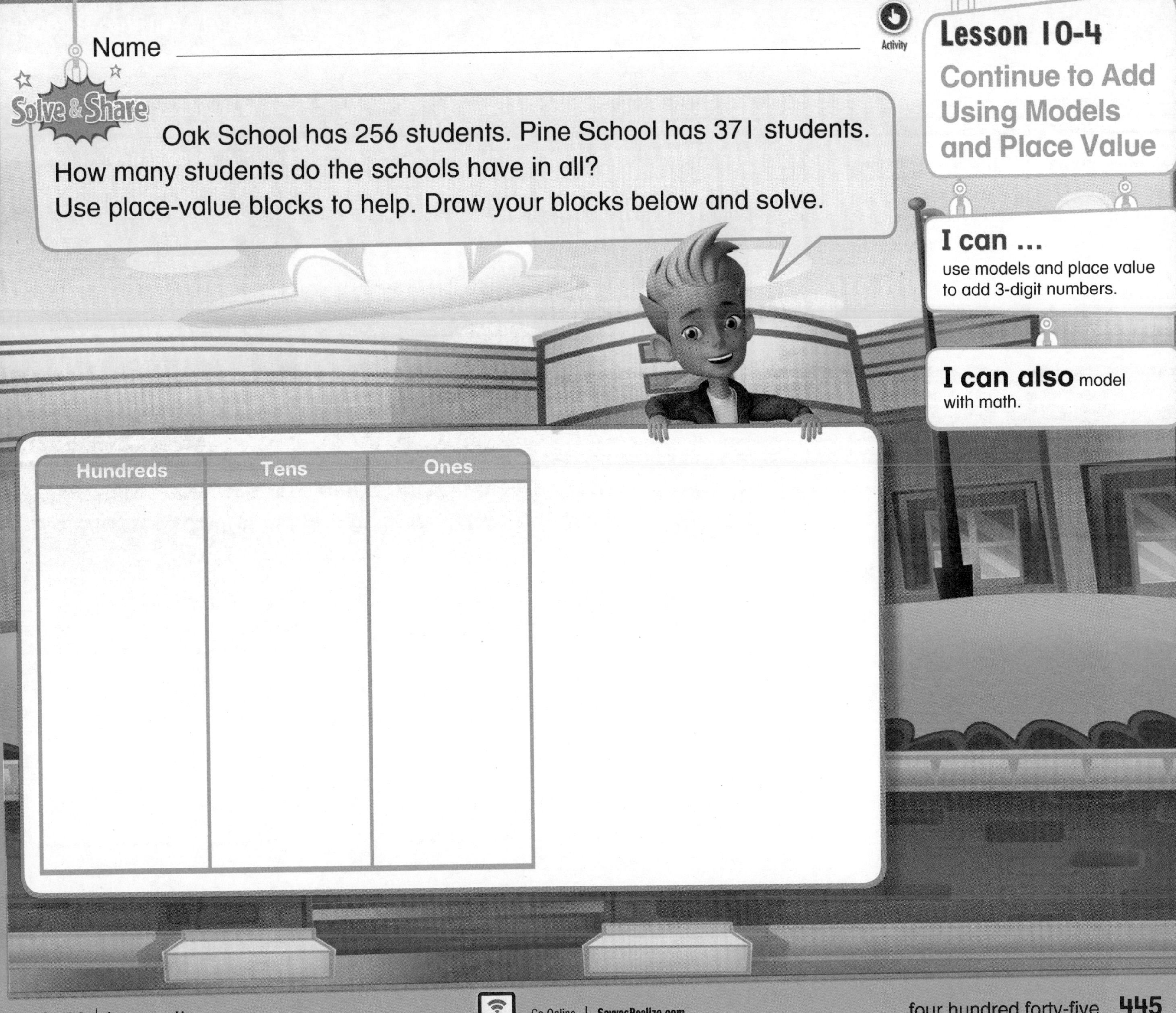

Hundreds	Tens	Ones

Visual Learning Bridge

Find 372 + 145.
Draw place-value blocks.

Hundreds	Tens	Ones
3 hundreds	7 tens	2 ones
1 hundred	4 tens	5 ones

Join the the hundreds, the tens, and the ones.

Hundreds	Tens	Ones
4 hundreds	11 tens	7 ones
400	110	7

The partial sums are 400, 110, and 7.

Add the partial sums to get the final sum.

$$\begin{array}{r} 400 \\ 110 \\ +\ \ 7 \\ \hline 517 \end{array}$$

So, 372 + 145 = 517.

Convince Me! Look at the example above. Why don't the 11 tens need to be regrouped to get the final sum?

Guided Practice Draw blocks to find the partial sums. Record the partial sums to find the sum.

1. 236 + 252 = ____

Hundreds	Tens	Ones

$$\begin{array}{r} 400 \\ 80 \\ +\ \ 8 \\ \hline 488 \end{array}$$

2. 328 + 124 = ____

Hundreds	Tens	Ones

Name ______________________________

Independent Practice

Draw blocks to find the partial sums.
Record the partial sums to find the sum.

3. 372 + 281 = ______

Hundreds	Tens	Ones

4. 429 + 163 = ______

Hundreds	Tens	Ones

5. 174 + 245 = ______

Hundreds	Tens	Ones

6. Higher Order Thinking Ben said that the sum of 157 and 137 is 284. Nikki said that Ben made a mistake. Who is correct? Explain.

____

____

____

Add 157 and 137.
Do you get the same
sum as Ben?

Problem Solving

Solve each problem below. You can use models to help.

You can draw blocks to model the problem. Use partial sums to solve.

7. Model On Friday, 354 people went to the fair. On Saturday, 551 people went to the fair.

How many people went to the fair in all?

Hundreds	Tens	Ones

_____ people

8. Higher Order Thinking Write an addition problem in which the partial sum for tens is greater than 10 tens. Draw blocks and show partial sums to solve.

_____ + _____ = _____

Hundreds	Tens	Ones

9. Assessment Practice Find 448 + 323. Draw place-value blocks and show partial sums to solve.

448 + 323 = _____

Hundreds	Tens	Ones

Name ______________________

On Monday, 248 people visit the museum.
On Tuesday, 325 people visit the museum.
How many people visit the museum on Monday and Tuesday?
Solve any way you choose. Be prepared to explain your thinking.

______ people

Lesson 10-5

Add Using Place Value and Partial Sums

I can ...
add 3-digit numbers using place value and partial sums.

I can also look for patterns.

Visual Learning Bridge

Find 257 + 384.
You can draw blocks to show the addends.

Hundreds	Tens	Ones
2 hundreds	5 tens	7 ones
3 hundreds	8 tens	4 ones

Add the partial sums to find the sum.

	Hundreds	Tens	Ones
	2	5	7
+	3	8	4
Hundreds:	5	0	0
Tens:	1	3	0
Ones:		1	1
Sum =	6	4	1

Here is how you can write the addition.

$$\begin{array}{r} 257 \\ +\,384 \\ \hline 500 \\ 130 \\ +\,11 \\ \hline 641 \end{array}$$

So, 257 + 384 = 641.

Convince Me! Can the problem above be solved by adding the ones first, then the tens, and then the hundreds? Explain.

Guided Practice

Add. Use partial sums. Show your work. Use place-value blocks if needed.

1. 425 + 148 = ____

	Hundreds	Tens	Ones
	4	2	5
+	1	4	8
Hundreds:	5	0	0
Tens:		6	0
Ones:		1	3
Sum =			

2. 394 + 276 = ____

$$\begin{array}{r} 394 \\ +\,276 \\ \hline \end{array}$$

Keep place values in line when you write each partial sum.

Name ______________________

Tools Assessment

Independent Practice

Add. Use partial sums. Show your work.

3.
```
  347
+ 242
```

4.
```
  183
+ 249
```

5.
```
  278
+ 406
```

6.
```
  367
+ 493
```

7.
```
  518
+ 347
```

8. **Higher Order Thinking** Mark found the sum of 127 and 345. Explain his mistake. What is the correct sum?

Mark's Work:

```
             127
           + 345
Hundreds:    400
Tens:          6
Ones:       + 12
             418
```

____

____

____

9. **Reasoning** Rhea has a $100 bill, four $20 bills, one $10 bill, and three $5 bills. Is this amount greater or less than $210? Explain.

____

____

____

____

Problem Solving

Solve each problem. Show your work.

10. **Look for Patterns** 349 people are on a boat. 255 people are on another boat. How many people are on both boats?

You can use place value and partial sums to add.

_____ people

11. 163 students are in first grade. 217 students are in second grade. How many students are in both grades?

_____ students

12. **Higher Order Thinking** Choose a number between 100 and 400. Add 384 to your number. What is the sum? Show your work.

Explain the steps you took to find the sum.

_____

_____

_____

13. **Assessment Practice** Which is the same amount as 238 + 164? Choose all that apply.

☐ 200 + 190 + 12 ☐ 300 + 90 + 12 ☐ 402 ☐ 400 + 10 + 2

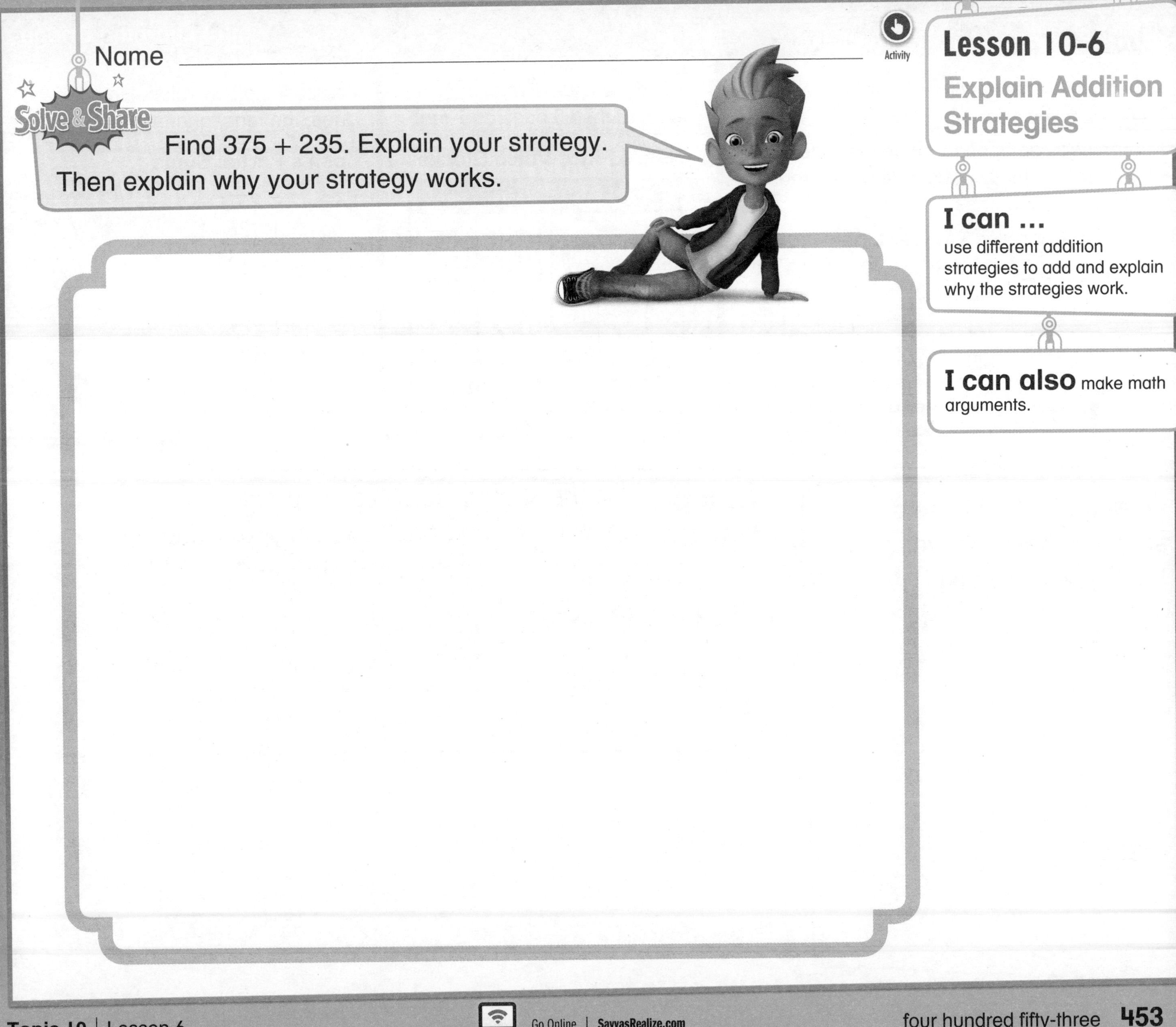

Name
Activity
Solve & Share
Find 375 + 235. Explain your strategy.
Then explain why your strategy works.

Lesson 10-6

Explain Addition Strategies

I can ...
use different addition strategies to add and explain why the strategies work.

I can also make math arguments.

Lauren, Nate, and Josh use different ways to find 257 + 126.

Lauren uses an open number line. She starts at 257 and mentally adds up the hundreds, the tens, and the ones.

Lauren's Number Line

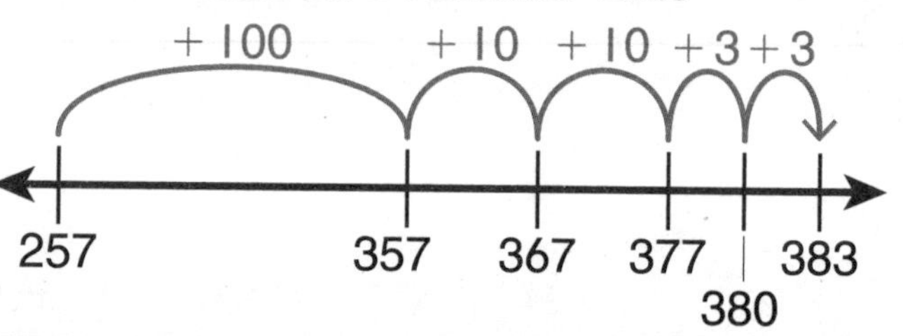

Nate draws place-value blocks. He regroups 10 ones as 1 ten.

Nate's Place-Value Blocks

Hundreds	Tens	Ones

257 + 126 = 383

Josh uses place value. He adds the ones, the tens, and then hundreds.

Josh's Partial Sums

$$\begin{array}{r} 257 \\ +\ 126 \\ \hline 13 \\ 70 \\ +\ 300 \\ \hline 383 \end{array}$$

Why does each strategy work?

Convince Me! Choose a strategy shown above. Explain why it works.

Guided Practice Use the strategy to solve the problem. Show your work. Then explain your work.

1. 624 + 248 = 872

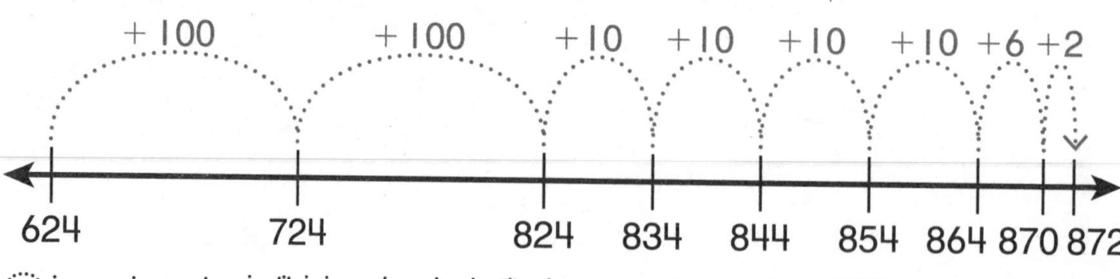

Start at 624. Add 2 hundreds. Then add 4 tens. Count on 6 to get to 870, then add 2 more to reach 872. The jumps add up to 248.

Name ______________________

Tools Assessment

Independent Practice Choose any strategy to solve each addition problem. Show your work. Then explain why the strategy works.

2. 212 + 487 = ______

____

____

3. 874 + 109 = ______

____

____

4. 419 + 532 = ______

____

____

How many different ways can you use?

5. 650 + 270 = ______

____

____

Problem Solving

Solve each problem any way you choose. Show your work.

6. **Reasoning** Lee School needs 407 folders for its students. Jefferson School needs 321 folders for its students. How many folders do both schools need?

_____ folders

7. **Reasoning** There are 229 people at the football game. 108 more people arrive at the game. How many people are at the football game now?

_____ people

8. **Higher Order Thinking** Tommy found 125 + 598. Since 598 is close to 600, he added 125 + 600 = 725. Then he subtracted 2 to get 723.

Why did Tommy subtract 2? Explain.

9. **Assessment Practice** There are 192 ants on an ant farm. 397 more ants join the ant farm. How many ants are on the ant farm now? Use the number line to solve. Explain.

Name ______________________________

Problem Solving

Lesson 10-7
Repeated Reasoning

I can ... solve problems and explain patterns I see.

I can also add three-digit numbers.

Solve & Share Solve these problems any way you choose. Explain patterns you see.

63 + 28 = ?

263 + 128 = ?

63 + 28 = ?	263 + 128 = ?

Thinking Habits

What can I use from one problem to help with another problem?

Are there things that repeat?

Visual Learning Bridge

How is adding 3-digit numbers like adding 2-digit numbers?

24 + 36 = ?

324 + 136 = ?

I can use what I know and look for things that repeat. I can check my work as I add each place.

Use two open number lines.

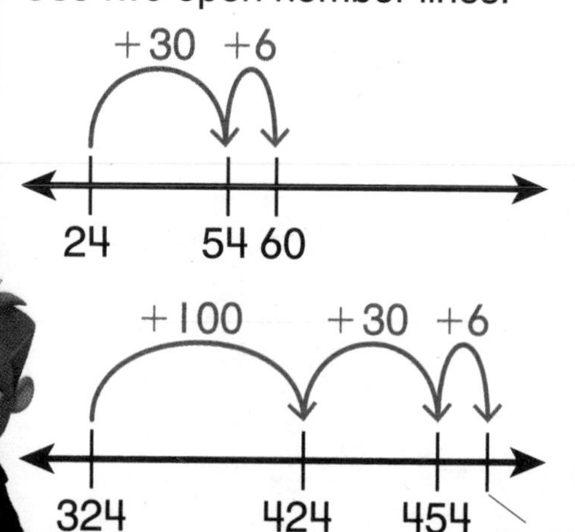
+30
+6
24
54
60
+100
+30
+6
324
424
454
460

Use partial sums.

```
   24        324
 + 36      + 136
   10         10
 + 50         50
   60      + 400
             460
```

24 + 36 = 60

324 + 136 = 460

I used repeated reasoning. I added the same ones to ones and tens to tens in both problems. I repeated this with two different strategies.

Convince Me! If you start with 36 and add on 24, in the example above, will you get the same sum? Explain.

Guided Practice Use repeated reasoning to solve the two problems. Circle the digits that are the same in the sums. Explain why the sums are different.

1. 57 + 29 = ____ 157 + 229 = ____

```
   57
 + 29
   16
 + 70
```

Name ______________________________

Tools Assessment

Independent Practice Solve each problem.

2. Write a problem where you need to regroup to make a ten or a hundred. Each addend must be three digits. Draw place-value blocks to solve your problem. Then explain why you needed to regroup.

_____ + _____ = _____

Hundreds	Tens	Ones

____

____

____

____

____

3. Write a problem where you do not need to regroup to make a ten or a hundred. Each addend must be three digits. Draw place-value blocks to solve your problem. Then explain why you did not need to regroup.

_____ + _____ = _____

Hundreds	Tens	Ones

____

____

____

____

____

Problem Solving

Performance Task

Tickets Sold
The table shows how many tickets were sold at a theater.

How many tickets were sold on Thursday and Saturday in all?

TICKETS

25145843

Tickets Sold	
Thursday	128
Friday	245
Saturday	367

25145843

4. **Make Sense** Which numbers and operation can you use to solve the problem?

____

____

____

5. **Model** Write an equation that shows the problem you need to solve.

___ ◯ ___ = ___

6. **Generalize** Use what you know about adding 3-digit numbers to solve the problem. Explain what you did.

____

____

____

____

Name ______________________________

Fluency Practice Activity

Find a partner. Get paper and a pencil. Each partner chooses a different color: light blue or dark blue.

Partner 1 and Partner 2 each point to a black number at the same time. Both partners subtract Partner 2's number from Partner 1's number.

If the answer is on your color, you get a tally mark. Work until one partner gets seven tally marks.

I can ...
subtract within 100.

I can also make math arguments.

Partner 1
59
78
92
82
64

53	19	43	62	37	30
48	65	81	32	51	76
14	71	58	66	48	25
44	37	55	47	33	67

Partner 2
45
27
16
11
34

Tally Marks for Partner 1	Tally Marks for Partner 2

Word List

- addend
- break apart
- digits
- hundreds
- mental math
- open number line
- partial sum
- sum

Understand Vocabulary

Choose a term from the Word List to complete each sentence.

1. When adding 193 + 564, the sum of 90 + 60 is called a

   ______________________.

2. In 709 + 187, 709 is an ______________________.

3. You can use an ______________________ to count on.

---

4. In 841, there are

   ______ hundreds.

5. Give the value of each digit in 610.

   ____

6. Use mental math to find 198 + 362.

   ____

Use Vocabulary in Writing

7. Use words to tell how to find 249 + 201. Use terms from the Word List.

Name ______________________________

Set A

You can use mental math to add 10 or 100 to 362.

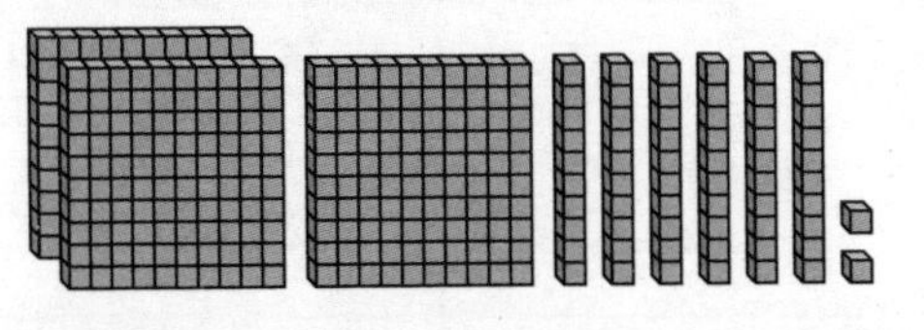

362 + 10 = 372

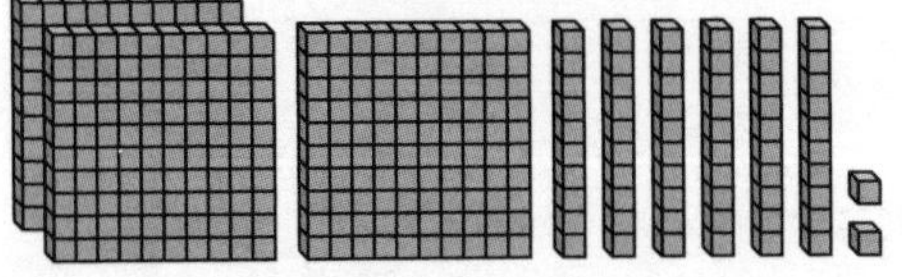

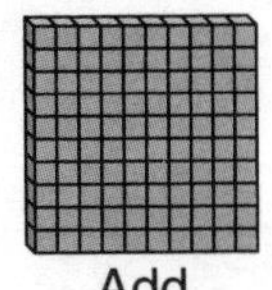

362 + 100 = 462

Add using place-value blocks or mental math.

1. 600 + 10 = ______

2. 345 + 100 = ______

3. 543 + 100 = ______

4. 800 + 100 = ______

5. 799 + 10 = ______

6. 119 + 10 = ______

Set B

You can use an open number line to add. Find 327 + 126.

First, place 327 on the line and then count on by 100s, 10s, and 1s.

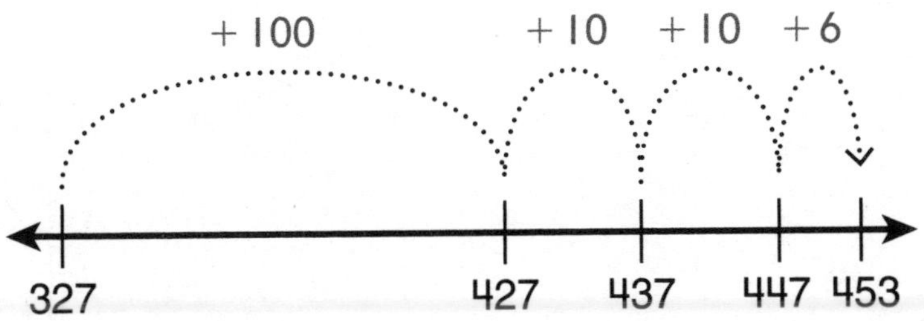

So, 327 + 126 = 453.

Use an open number line to find each sum.

7. 594 + 132 = ______

8. 157 + 245 = ______

Set C

You can use or draw place-value blocks and use partial sums to add. Find 276 + 137.

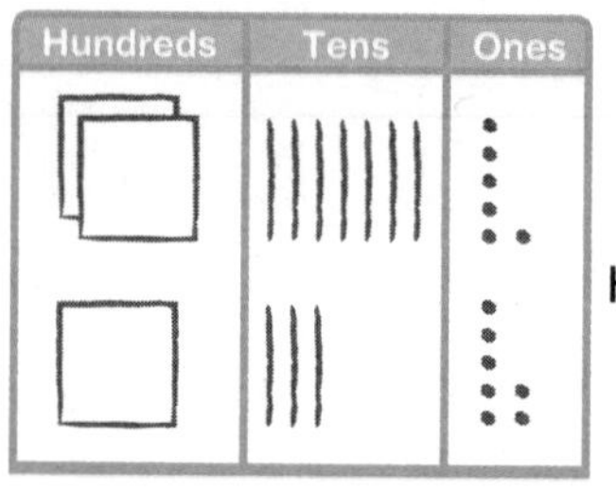

	Hundreds	Tens	Ones
	2	7	6
+	1	3	7
Hundreds:	3	0	0
Tens:	1	0	0
Ones:		1	3
Sum =	4	1	3

Add. Use partial sums. Show your work. Use drawings of blocks if needed.

9. 408 + 326 = ______

	Hundreds	Tens	Ones
	4	0	8
+	3	2	6
Hundreds:			
Tens:			
Ones:			
Sum =			

Set D

Thinking Habits

Repeated Reasoning

What can I use from one problem to help with another problem?

Are there things that repeat?

Solve each problem. Use partial sums and repeated reasoning. Use drawings of blocks if needed.

10.

$$\begin{array}{r} 68 \\ +\ 14 \\ \hline \end{array} \qquad \begin{array}{r} 168 \\ +\ 214 \\ \hline \end{array}$$

Circle the digits that are alike in each sum.

Name ______________________________

TOPIC 10

Assessment Practice

1. Emily has 100 sun stickers. She has 382 star stickers and 10 moon stickers. How many sun and star stickers does Emily have?

Ⓐ 492 Ⓒ 393

Ⓑ 482 Ⓓ 392

2. Tyrone collects baseball cards. He gives 138 cards to his friend. Now he has 428 cards. How many cards did Tyrone have before he gave some away?

_____ cards

3. Use the open number line to solve the problem. Write the missing numbers in the boxes.

421 + 250 = ?

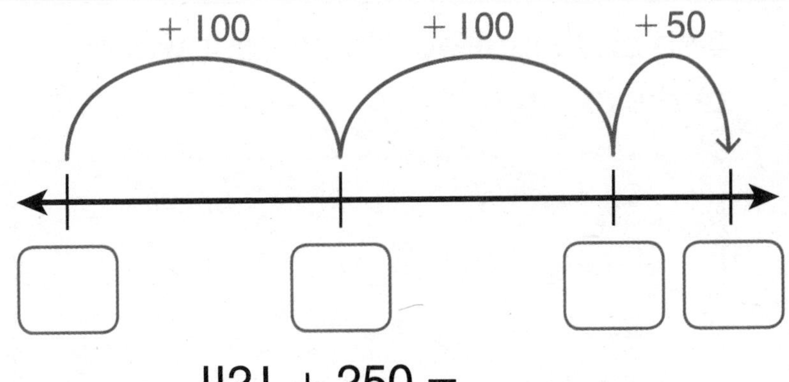

421 + 250 = _____

4. Which is the same amount as 528 + 167? Choose all that apply.

☐ 500 + 80 + 15 ☐ 500 + 180 + 15 ☐ 600 + 90 + 5 ☐ 600 + 80 + 15

5. Choose all the equations in which the sum is 488.

☐ 478 + 10 = ? ☐ 388 + 100 = ? ☐ 248 + 240 = ? ☐ 200 + 265 = ?

6. Rich has 335 pennies.
Beth has 58 more pennies than Rich.
How many pennies do they have in all?

Ⓐ 277
Ⓑ 393
Ⓒ 628
Ⓓ 728

Hundreds	Tens	Ones

7. Use place value and partial sums to find 472 + 256. Show your work.

	Hundreds	Tens	Ones
	4	7	2
+	2	5	6
Hundreds:			
Tens:			
Ones:			
Sum:			

472 + 256 = _____

8. Molly reads 184 pages. Pat reads 294 pages. What is the total number of pages they read in all?

Use any strategy. Show your work and explain.

_____ pages

9. On Saturday, 449 people visit the zoo.
On Sunday, 423 people visit the zoo.
How many people visit the zoo in all?

Use the open number line to solve.
Explain your work.

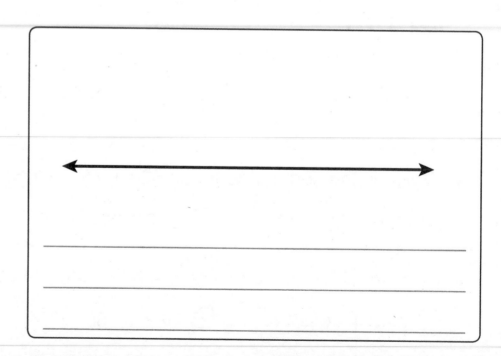

Name ____________________

Recycling Race

Westbrook School is having a recycling contest. The table shows the number of cans each grade collected in February.

Cans Collected in February	
First Grade	264
Second Grade	302
Third Grade	392
Fourth Grade	425

1. How many cans did the first-grade students and the second-grade students collect in all?
   Use the open number line to solve.

   ______ cans

2. Bruce used partial sums to find how many cans the third-grade students and fourth-grade students collected in all.

$$\begin{array}{rr} & 392 \\ & +\ 425 \\ \hline \text{Hundreds:} & 700 \\ \text{Tens:} & 11 \\ \text{Ones:} & +\ \ 7 \\ \hline & 718 \end{array}$$

Do you agree with his answer?
Circle **yes** or **no**.

Explain your answer.

3. Which two grades collected a total of 689 cans? Choose any strategy to solve the problem. Show your work. Explain which strategy you used.

The ________ grade and the ________ grade collected a total of 689 cans.

Here are some addition strategies you have learned.

Addition Strategies

- Open Number Line
- Compensation
- Mental Math
- Break Apart Numbers
- Partial Sums
- Place-Value Blocks
- Regrouping

4. The second-grade collected 432 cans in March. They collected 198 cans in April. Tom and Bill find how many cans the class collected in March and April.

Tom's Way	Bill's Way
432	432
+ 198	+ 198
10	10
120	12
+ 500	+ 500
630	522

Who added correctly? Explain.

Who answered incorrectly? What did he do?

TOPIC 11

Subtract Within 1,000 Using Models and Strategies

Essential Question: What are strategies for subtracting numbers to 1,000?

Digital Resources

Interactive Student Edition · Activity · Visual Learning · Video · Practice · Assessment · Games · Tools · Glossary

Bees help move pollen from one flower to another!

Moving the pollen helps plants grow fruit and vegetables.

Wow!
Let's do this project and learn more.

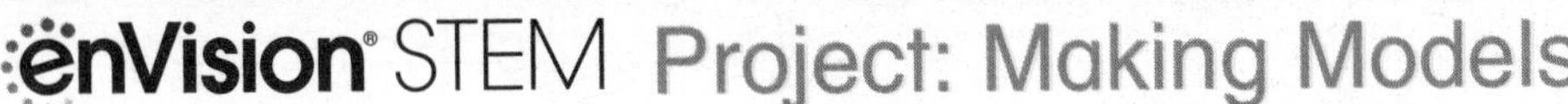

Find Out Use a paintbrush as a model of a bee's leg. Dip the brush in a bowl of sugar. Then dip the brush in a bowl of pepper. Take turns. What happens to the sugar? What happens to the pepper?

Journal: Make a Book Show what you learn in a book. In your book, also:

- Tell how bees help move pollen between plants.
- Show how to use a model to help subtract three-digit numbers.

Name ______________________________

Review What You Know

Vocabulary

1. Circle each number that is **less than** 607.

598

608

706

2. Circle each number that is **greater than** 299.

352

300

298

3. Circle the group of numbers that **decrease** by 100 from left to right.

650, 550, 450, 350

320, 420, 520, 620

570, 560, 550, 540

Subtraction Facts

4. Write each difference.

14 − 7 = ______

11 − 4 = ______

16 − 9 = ______

Think of addition facts to help.

Partial Differences

5. Use partial differences to find 54 − 29.

Math Story

6. Ben has 64 comic books. He gives 36 comic books to friends. How many comic books does Ben have left?

______ comic books

Name ___________________________________

Pick a Project

PROJECT 11A

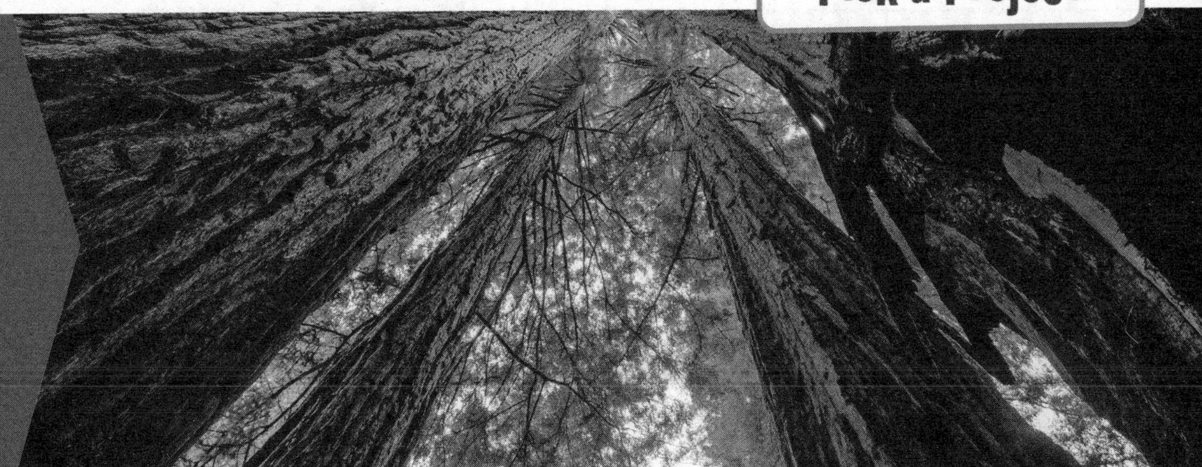

How tall is the world's tallest redwood tree?

Project: Create a Redwood Trees Booklet

PROJECT 11B

Where does a lot of snow fall?

Project: Build a Snow Sculpture

PROJECT 11C

How high are Florida's mountains?

Project: Make a Poster About Florida Mountains

3-ACT MATH PREVIEW

Math Modeling

The Chemistry Set

Before watching the video, talk to a classmate:

When was the last time you mixed something together? What happened to the items you mixed? How did they change?

I can ...

model with math to solve a problem that involves using strategies to add and subtract.

Name ________________________________

Activity

Lesson 11-1

Subtract 10 and 100

I can ...
subtract 10 or 100 mentally using what I know about place value.

I can also look for patterns.

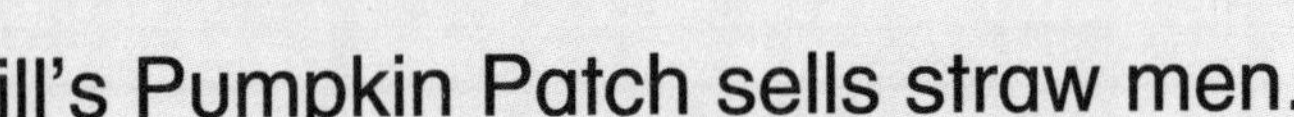

Solve & Share Jill's Pumpkin Patch sells straw men.
A large straw man costs $134.
A medium straw man costs $10 less than a large straw man.
A small straw man costs $100 less than a large straw man.
What is the cost of a medium straw man? A small straw man?

Use dollar bills, place-value blocks, or mental math to solve.
Be ready to explain how you solved the problem.

You can use mental math to subtract 10 or 100 from three-digit numbers.

Find 328 – 10.
Find 328 – 100.

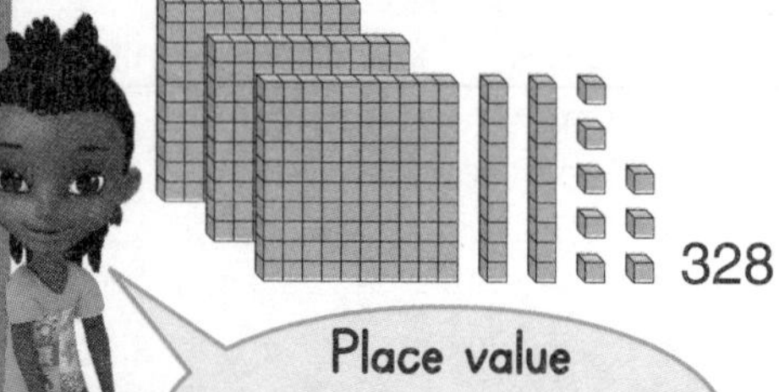

328
Place value can help me subtract mentally.

328 – 10 = ____

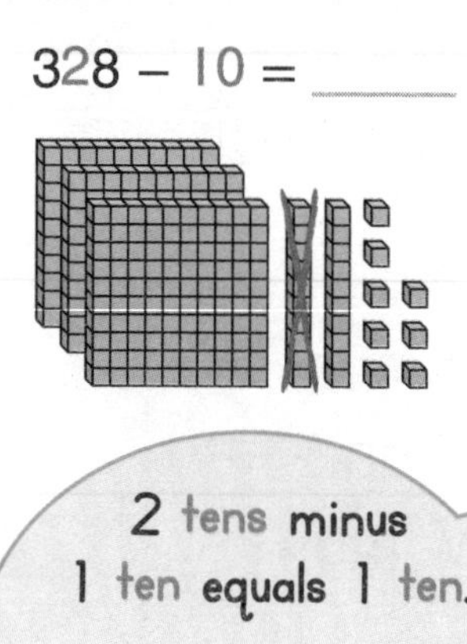

2 tens minus 1 ten equals 1 ten.
So, 328 – 10 = 318.

328 – 100 = ____

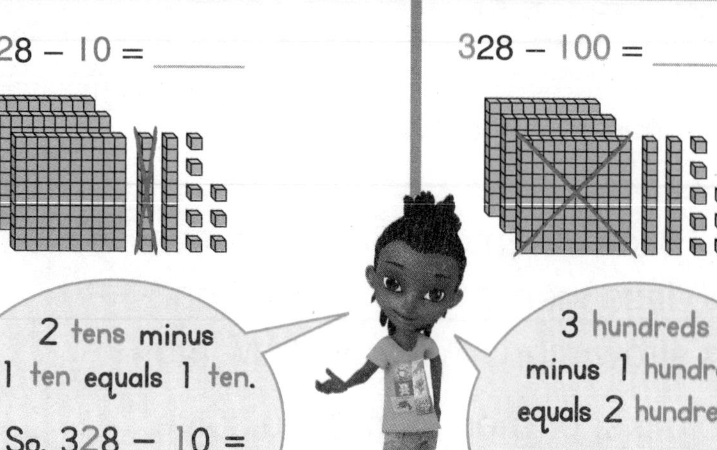

3 hundreds minus 1 hundred equals 2 hundreds.
So, 328 – 100 = 228.

Sometimes subtracting 10 changes the tens and hundreds digits.
Find 500 – 10.

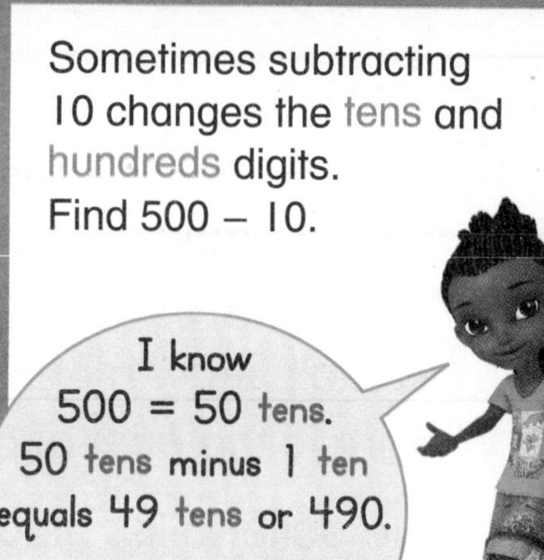

I know 500 = 50 tens.
50 tens minus 1 ten equals 49 tens or 490.
So, 500 – 10 = 490.

Convince Me! Use mental math to find 457 – 10 and 457 – 100. Explain your reasoning.

Guided Practice Subtract. Use place-value blocks or mental math. Then write an equation to show the subtraction.

1. 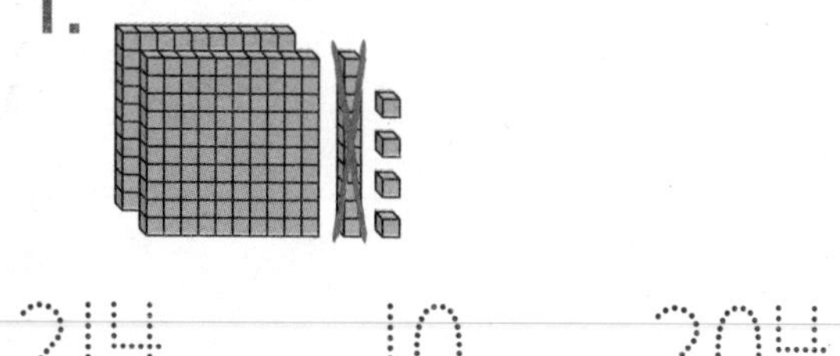

214 – 10 = 204

2. 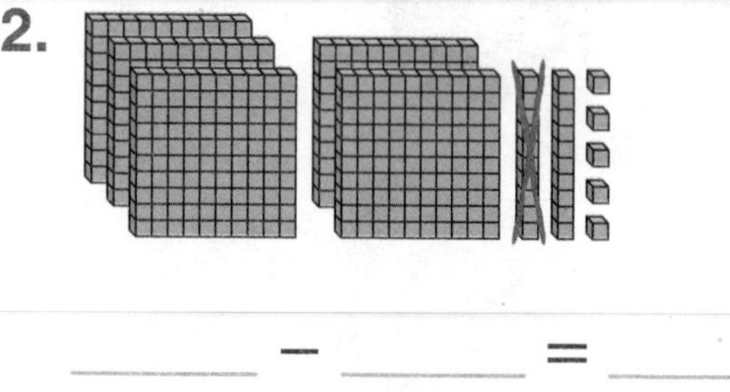

____ – ____ = ____

3. 

____ – ____ = ____

4. 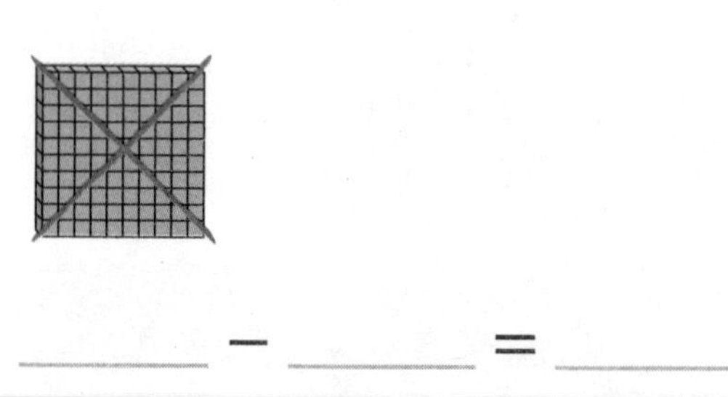

____ – ____ = ____

Name ________________________

Independent Practice

Subtract. Use place-value blocks or mental math.

5. 250 − 10 = ______

6. 604 − 10 = ______

7. \$102 − \$100 = ______

8. 719 − 10 = ______

9. \$400 − \$100 = ______

10. 308 − 10 = ______

11. 520 − 100 = ______

12. 975 − 10 = ______

13. 143 − 100 = ______

14. \$825 − \$10 = ______

15. 409 − 10 = ______

16. \$200 − \$100 = ______

Algebra Find the missing numbers. Use mental math to solve.

17. 362 − ☐ = 352

18. 801 − ☐ = 701

19. 449 = 549 − ☐

20. 657 − ☐ = 647

21. 215 − ☐ = 205

22. 700 − ☐ = 690

Problem Solving Solve each problem. Show your work.

23. **enVision® STEM** Marni is studying facts about bees. She finds that one type of bee can pollinate 955 plants each day. A different type of bee pollinates 100 fewer plants. How many plants does it pollinate?

_____ plants

24. **Model** Alex has five $100 bills, three $10 bills, and four $1 bills. He buys a pair of shoes for $100. How much money does he have left?

_____

25. **Higher Order Thinking** Think of a 3-digit number. Write a story about subtracting 100 from your number. Then complete the equation to show your subtraction.

_____ – _____ = _____

26. **Assessment Practice** Which equations are true? Choose all that apply.

- ☐ 303 – 10 = 293
- ☐ 493 – 100 = 393
- ☐ 563 – 10 = 453
- ☐ 309 – 100 = 299

Name ______

Activity

Lesson 11-2

Subtract on an Open Number Line

I can ...
use an open number line to add up to subtract 3-digit numbers.

I can also model with math.

There are 224 girls and some boys in a parade. There are 471 children in the parade. How many boys are in the parade?

Use the open number line to solve the problem. Show your work.

Find 382 – 247. Use an open number line.

Add up from 247, the number you are subtracting. Stop at 382.

One Way You can add up to find the difference.

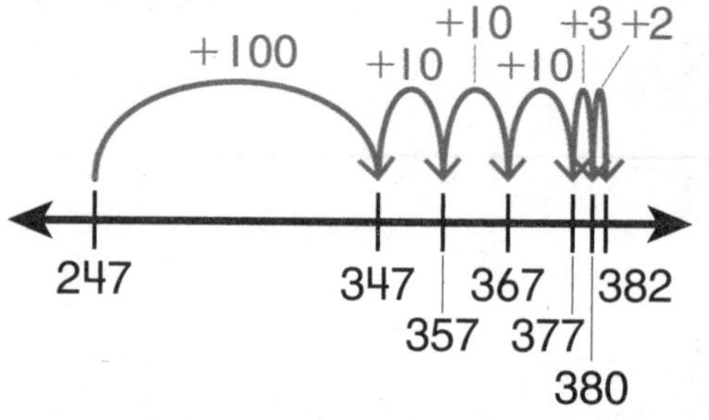

100 + 10 + 10 + 10 + 3 + 2 = 135

Another Way You can count back to find the difference.

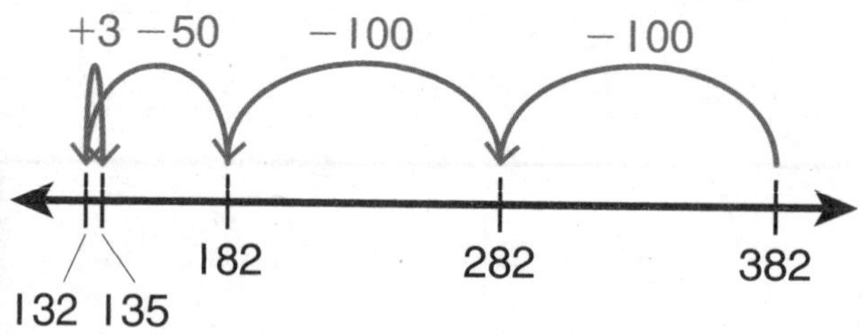

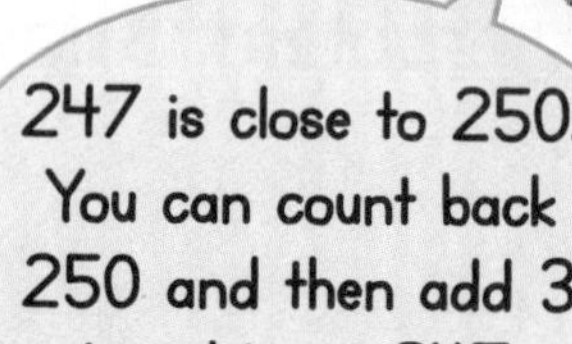

So, 382 – 247 = 135.

You can check your work by adding.

247 + 135 = 382.

So, 135 is correct.

247 is close to 250. You can count back 250 and then add 3 to subtract 247.

Convince Me! What is another way you could add up to find 382 – 247? Explain.

Guided Practice

Use the open number line to subtract.

1. 573 – 459 = ____

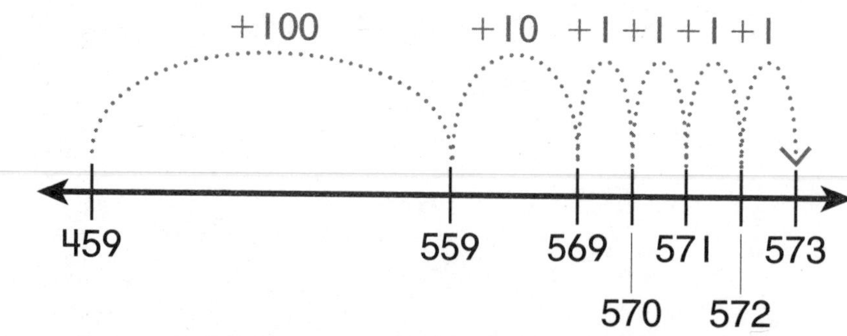

2. 672 – 547 = ____

Name ______

Tools Assessment

Independent Practice

Use the open number line to subtract.

3. 530 – 318 = ____

4. 735 – 429 = ____

5. 802 – 688 = ____

6. **Vocabulary** Complete the sentences using each word below once.

ones **add** **number**

You can add up to subtract on an open number line.

Start at the ________ you are subtracting.

________ up hundreds, tens, and ________.

Stop at the number you subtract from.

Problem Solving Solve each problem. Check your work.

7. **Reasoning** Yun has 780 blocks. Marsha has 545 fewer blocks than Yun. How many blocks does Marsha have?

Add up or count back to find the difference.

_____ blocks

8. **Higher Order Thinking** Use open number lines to find 463 – 258 in two different ways.

463 – 258 = _____

9. **Assessment Practice** Write a math story for 653 – 529. Then solve your story.

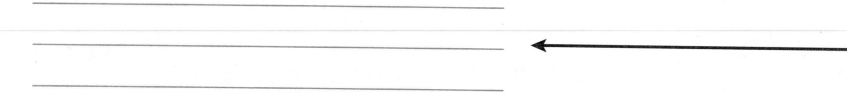

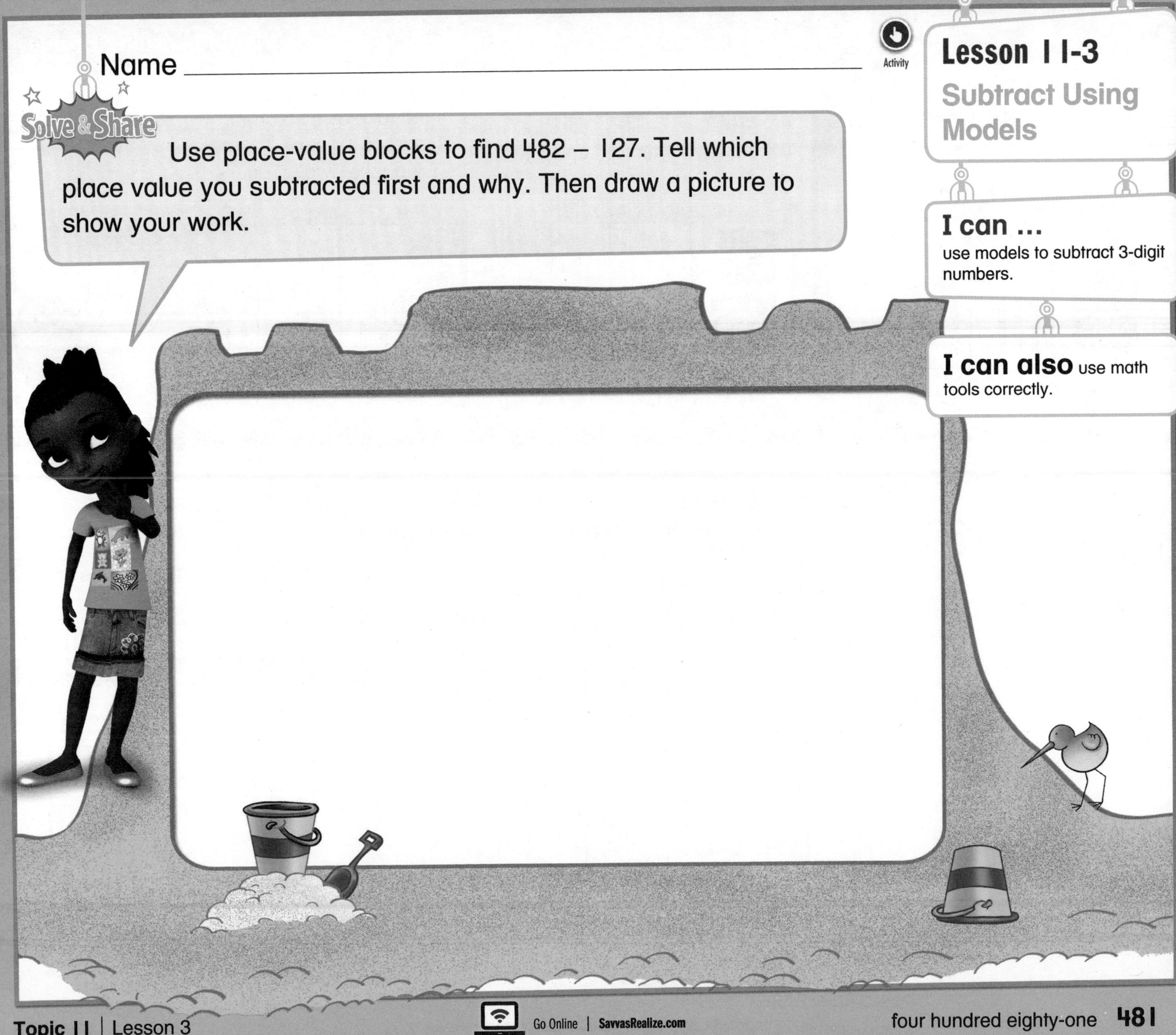
Name
Activity
Lesson 11-3
Subtract Using Models
I can ...
use models to subtract 3-digit numbers.
I can also use math tools correctly.
Solve & Share
Use place-value blocks to find 482 – 127. Tell which place value you subtracted first and why. Then draw a picture to show your work.

Visual Learning | A-Z Glossary

Visual Learning Bridge

Find 335 − 117.
Show 335 using hundreds, tens, and ones.

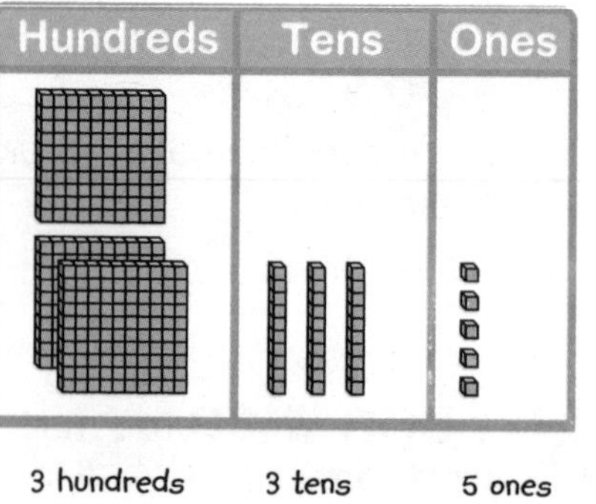

3 hundreds | 3 tens | 5 ones

You can start by taking away hundreds and tens.

Take away 1 hundred and 1 ten.

Hundreds	Tens	Ones
2 hundreds	2 tens	5 ones

Take away 7 ones.
First take away 5 ones.
Regroup 1 ten as 10 ones.
Then take away 2 ones.

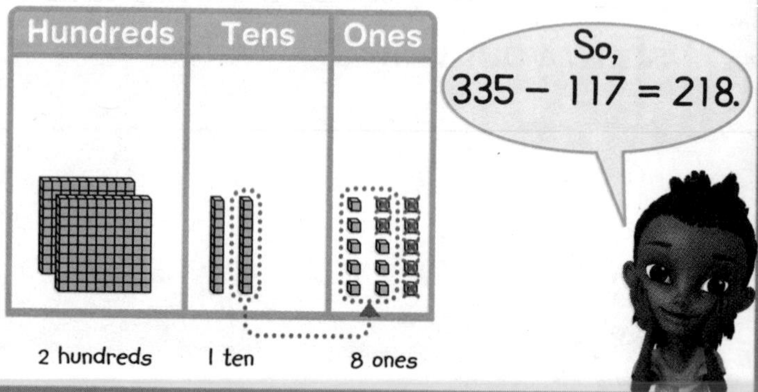

2 hundreds | 1 ten | 8 ones

Convince Me! Explain why regrouping works in the problem above.

Guided Practice Use and draw blocks to find each difference. Show your work.

1. 326 − 143 = 183

Hundreds	Tens	Ones

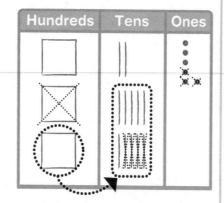

2. 363 − 127 = ______

Hundreds	Tens	Ones

3. 546 − 271 = ______

Hundreds	Tens	Ones

Name ______________________

Tools Assessment

Independent Practice

Use and draw blocks to find each difference. Show your work.

4. 314 − 152 = ______

Hundreds	Tens	Ones

5. 653 − 419 = ______

Hundreds	Tens	Ones

6. 438 − 162 = ______

Hundreds	Tens	Ones

7. 662 − 480 = ______

Hundreds	Tens	Ones

8. 999 − 834 = ______

9. 599 − 209 = ______

10. 954 − 738 = ______

11. Number Sense Tyler says that the difference of 676 − 367 is greater than 200. Is what Tyler says reasonable? Why or why not?

____

____

____

____

Sometimes it can help to use numbers that are close but easier to subtract.

Problem Solving

Solve each problem below.
Show your work.

12. Tia collected cans to raise money for school. She collected 569 cans on Monday. Tia collected some more cans on Tuesday. Now she has 789 cans. How many cans did Tia collect on Tuesday?

_____ cans

13. Make Sense Josh has these bills. How much money does he have?

_____

14. Higher Order Thinking Write a subtraction problem about recycling. Use 3-digit numbers. Then solve the problem.

____

____

____

____

15. Assessment Practice Use the place-value-blocks to find 864 − 319. Which is the difference?

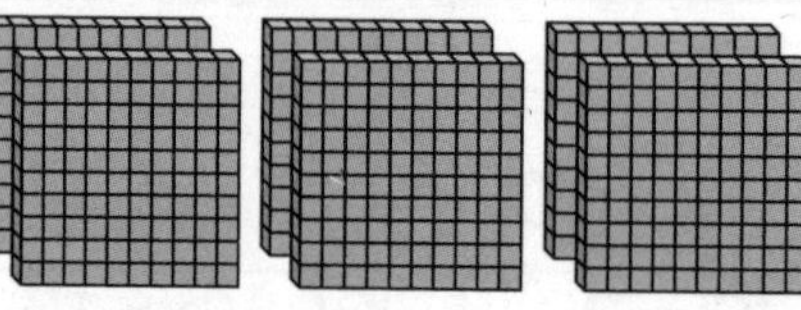
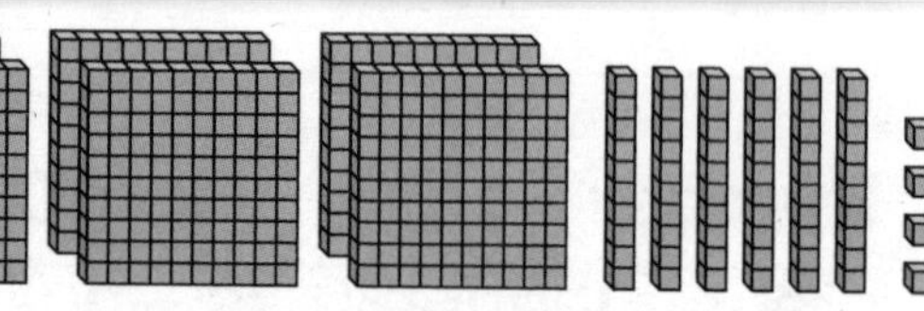
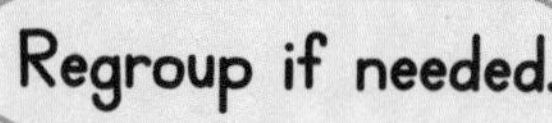

Ⓐ 454

Ⓑ 535

Ⓒ 545

Ⓓ 555

Name ______________________

Activity

Lesson 11-4

Subtract Using Models and Place Value

I can ...
use models and place value to subtract.

I can also model with math.

Solve & Share

Larissa has $353. She buys a pair of basketball shoes for $117. How much money does she have left over?

Use or draw place-value blocks to solve. Be ready to explain what you did and why it works.

Visual Learning Bridge

Find 328 − 133.

I can record partial differences.

One Way

Subtract 1 hundred from 3 hundreds.

$$\begin{array}{r} 328 \\ -\ 100 \\ \hline 228 \end{array}$$

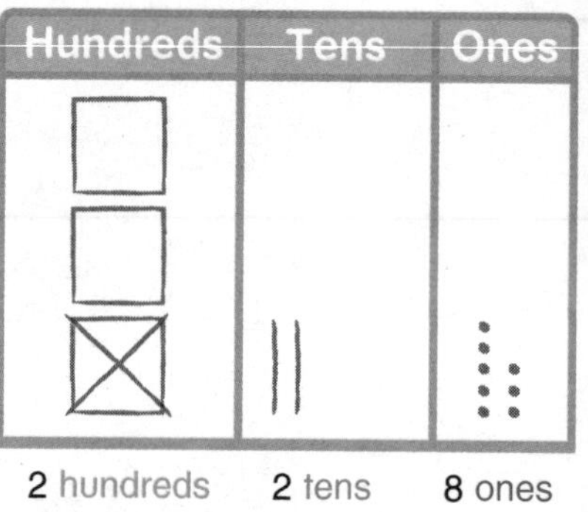

Subtract 3 tens.
First, subtract 2 tens.
Regroup 1 hundred as 10 tens.
Then subtract 1 ten.

$$\begin{array}{r} 328 \\ -\ 100 \\ \hline 228 \\ -\ 20 \\ \hline 208 \\ -\ 10 \\ \hline 198 \end{array}$$

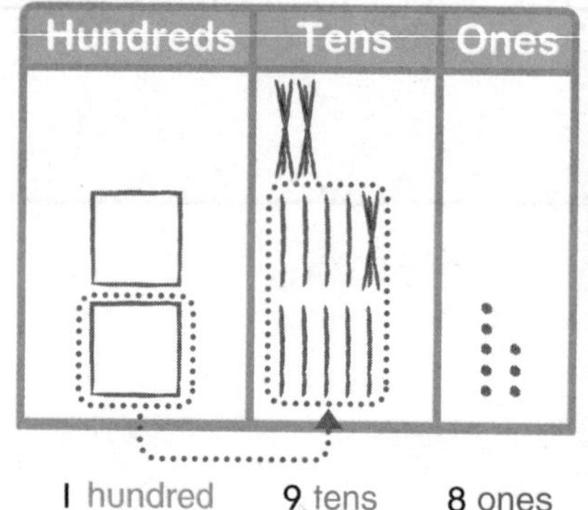

Subtract 3 ones from 8 ones.

$$\begin{array}{r} 328 \\ -\ 100 \\ \hline 228 \\ -\ 20 \\ \hline 208 \\ -\ 10 \\ \hline 198 \\ -\ 3 \\ \hline 195 \end{array}$$

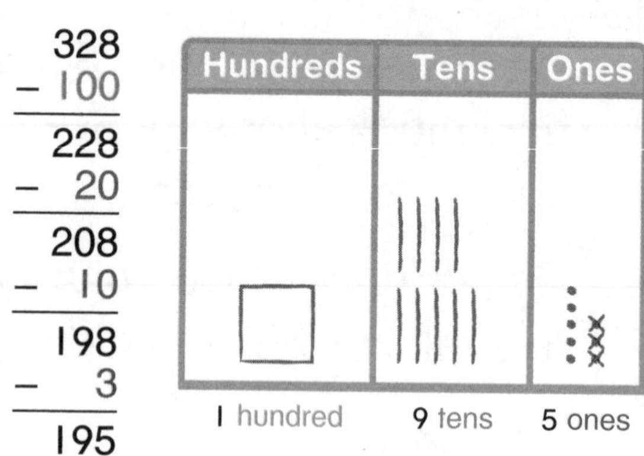

So, 328 − 133 = 195.

Convince Me! Find 254 − 174. Jason says he can subtract 100, and then 4, and then 70 to find the difference. Do you agree? Explain.

Guided Practice

Draw blocks to find the partial differences. Record the partial differences to find the difference.

1. 485 − 136 = 349

$$\begin{array}{r} 485 \\ -\ 5 \\ \hline 480 \\ -\ 1 \\ \hline 479 \\ -\ 30 \\ \hline 449 \\ -\ 100 \\ \hline 349 \end{array}$$

Subtract 5 ones.
Subtract 1 one.
Subtract 3 tens.
Subtract 1 hundred.

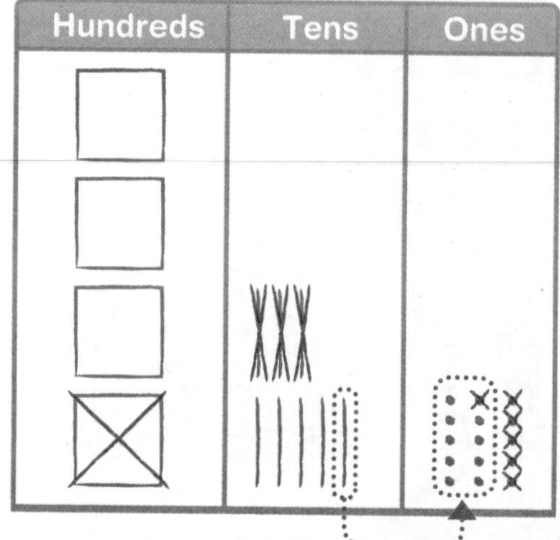

Name ______________________

Independent Practice

Draw blocks to find the partial differences. Record the partial differences to find the difference.

2. 598 – 319 = _____

Hundreds	Tens	Ones

3. 794 – 452 = _____

Hundreds	Tens	Ones

4. 871 – 355 = _____

Hundreds	Tens	Ones

Solve. Draw blocks to help.

5. Higher Order Thinking There were 642 people at the beach. There were 271 adults at the beach. The rest were children. How many children were at the beach?

Hundreds	Tens	Ones

_____ children

Problem Solving

Solve each problem. You can use models to help. Show your work.

6. Model Jeff has 517 baseball cards. He has 263 football cards. How many more baseball cards than football cards does he have?

Can you use drawings of place-value blocks to show partial differences?

Hundreds	Tens	Ones

______ more baseball cards

7. Reasoning Felipe has 453 stamps in his collection. Emily has 762 stamps in her collection. How many more stamps does Emily have?

Hundreds	Tens	Ones

______ more stamps

8. Assessment Practice Which numbers complete this partial difference problem for 423 – 219? Choose all that apply.

```
  423
-  10
  413
- 200
    ?
-   3
  210
-   6
    ?
```

☐ 213 ☐ 204

☐ 210 ☐ 200

Name ______________________

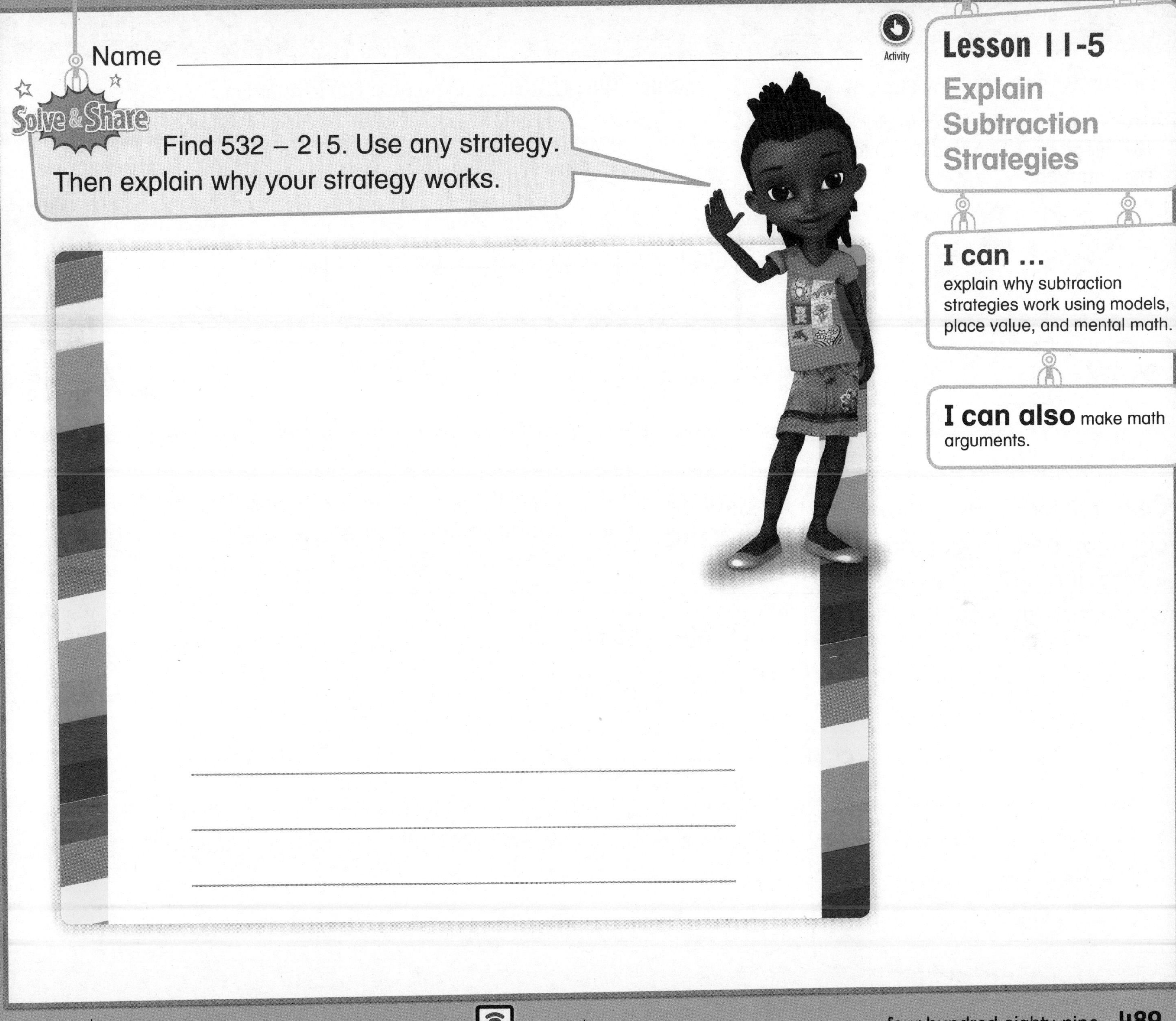

Find 532 − 215. Use any strategy. Then explain why your strategy works.

Lesson 11-5

Explain Subtraction Strategies

I can ...
explain why subtraction strategies work using models, place value, and mental math.

I can also make math arguments.

Find 437 – 245. Use any strategy.

One Way Draw place-value blocks to show 437. Regroup 1 hundred as 10 tens. Then subtract.

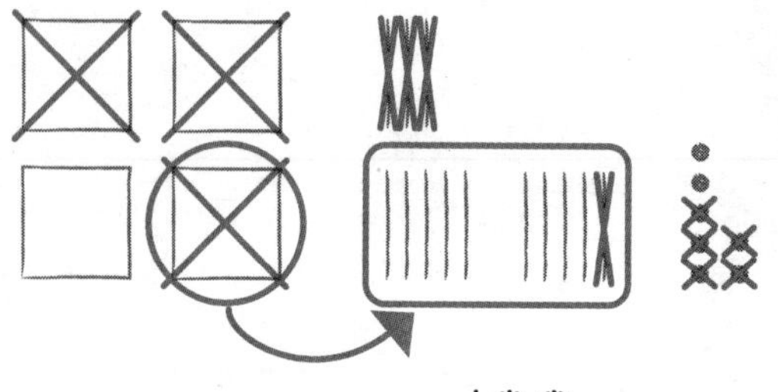

So, 437 – 245 = 192.

Another Way Use an open number line to subtract.

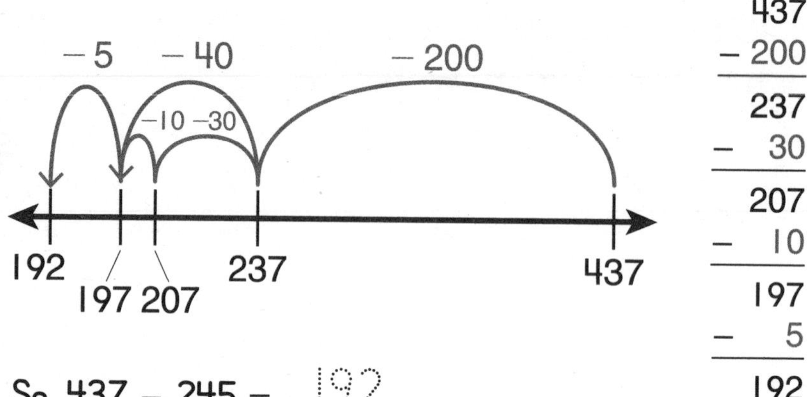

So, 437 – 245 = 192.

Convince Me! Show how to count up on the open number line to find 437 – 245. Explain why your way works.

Guided Practice Subtract any way you choose. Show your work. Then explain why the strategy works.

1. 345 – 116 = 229

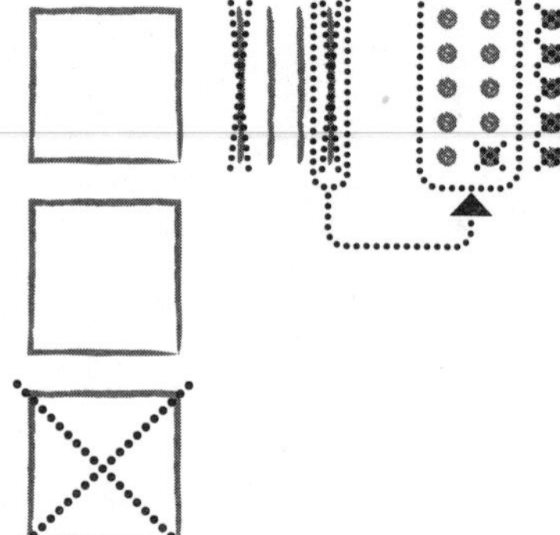

Name ____________________

Tools Assessment

Independent Practice Choose any strategy to solve each subtraction problem. Show your work. Then explain why the strategy works.

2. 312 − 179 = ____

3. 464 − 155 = ____

4. 612 − 478 = ____

5. Number Sense Use place value to find 748 − 319. Complete the equations.

319 = 300 + ____ + 9

Hundreds: 748 − ____ = ____

Tens: ____ − 10 = ____

Ones: ____ − ____ = ____

Problem Solving Solve each problem. Show your work.

6. **Explain** Ava wants to use mental math to find 352 − 149. Show how she could find the difference. Is this a good strategy for Ava to use? Explain why or why not.

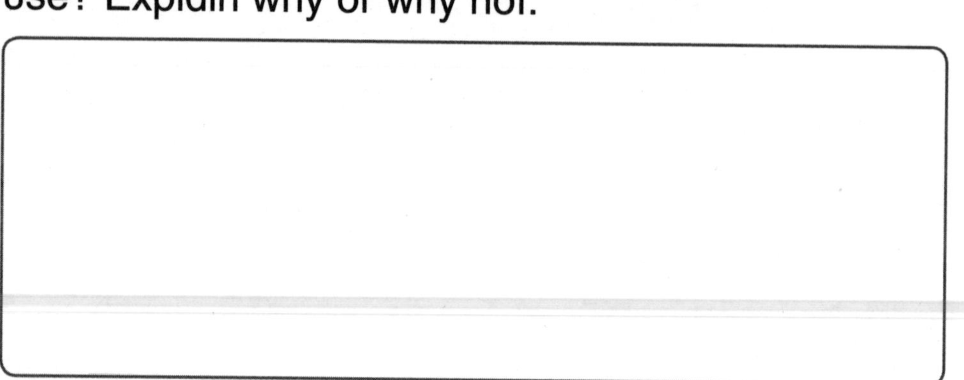

7. **Higher Order Thinking** Kristin found 562 − 399 = 163 using an open number line. She added up to subtract. First she added 1, then 100, and then 62.

Draw Kristin's number line. Do you think Kristin's strategy was helpful? Explain.

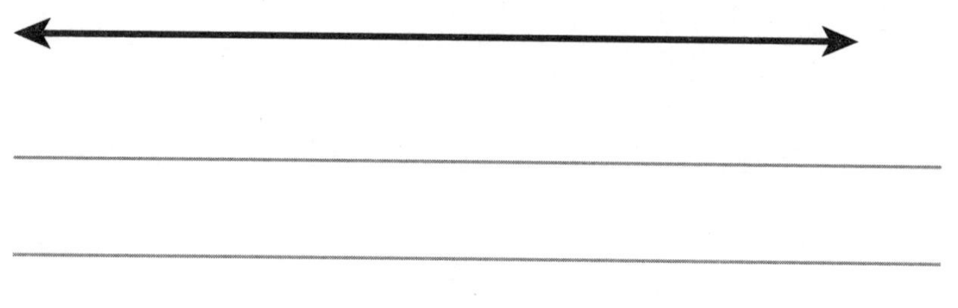

8. **Assessment Practice** Jeff counted back on this open number line to find 812 − 125.

Use the numbers on the cards to find the missing numbers in the open number line. Write the missing numbers.

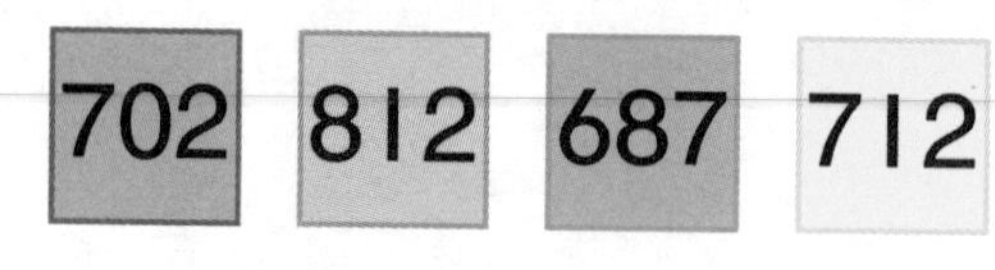

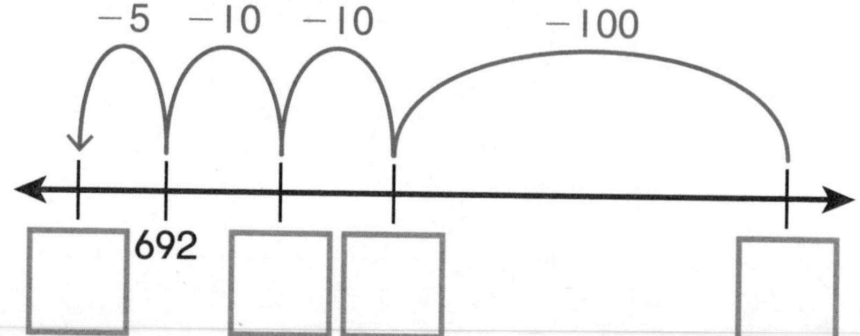

Name ______________________________

Jody wants to bake 350 muffins. She bakes one batch of 160 muffins and one batch of 145 muffins. How many more muffins does Jody need to bake?

Solve any way you choose. Show your work. Be prepared to explain why your way works.

Problem Solving

Lesson 11-6
Persevere

I can ...
solve problems that take more than one step.

I can also add and subtract three-digit numbers.

Thinking Habits

What do I know?

What do I need to find?

How can I check that my solution makes sense?

 Visual Learning  Glossary

Visual Learning Bridge

Grade 2 wants to sell 10 more tickets to the school play than Grade 1.

Grade 1 sold 476 tickets.
Grade 2 sold 439 tickets.

How many more tickets does Grade 2 have to sell to reach their goal?

How can I make sense of the problem?

I can see what I know.
I can find hidden questions.
I can choose a strategy to solve the problem.

An easy first step is to answer the hidden question.

What is the Grade 2 goal?

Grade 2 Goal

476 + 10 = 486 tickets

Now I can subtract the number of tickets Grade 2 sold from their goal.

486 − 439 = ?

Count up to subtract.
439 + 1 = 440
440 + 46 = 486
486 − 439 = 47

Grade 2 needs to sell 47 more tickets.

Convince Me! What questions can you ask yourself when you get stuck? Be ready to explain how questions can help.

Guided Practice Solve the problem. Remember to ask yourself questions to help. Show your work.

1. Kim had 455 shells. First, she gives 134 of the shells to a friend. Then she finds 54 more shells. How many shells does Kim have now?

What will you find first? Which operation will you use?

Name ____

Independent Practice

Use the table to solve each problem. Show your work.

Weights of Wild Animals (in pounds)					
Animal	Arctic Wolf	Black Bear	Grizzly Bear	Mule Deer	Polar Bear
Weight	176	270	990	198	945

2. How much heavier is a grizzly bear than an arctic wolf and a black bear together?

3. How much less does a black bear weigh than the weight of 2 mule deer?

4. How much more does a polar bear weigh than an arctic wolf, a black bear, and a mule deer together?

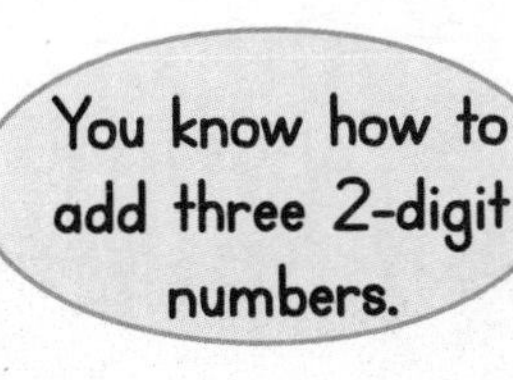

You know how to add three 2-digit numbers.
How can that help you add three 3-digit numbers?

Problem Solving

Performance Task

Big Truck
The picture at the right shows the height of a truck and the height of a smokestack on top of the truck. The height of a bridge is 144 inches.

Use the information at the right.
Can the truck travel under the bridge?

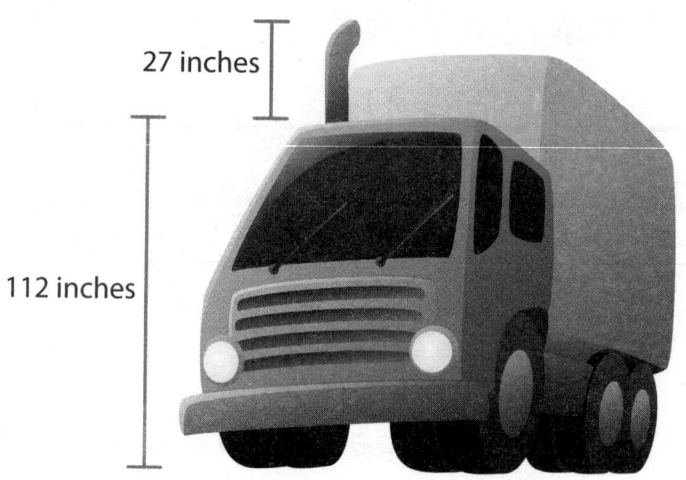

5. **Make Sense** What do you know? What are you trying to find?

____

____

____

____

____

6. **Make Sense** What hidden question do you need to answer first? Find the answer to the hidden question.

7. **Explain** Can the truck travel under the bridge? Show your work. Why does your solution make sense?

Name ____________________

Fluency Practice Activity

Color a path from **Start** to **Finish**. Follow the sums and differences that are even numbers. You can only move up, down, right, or left.

I can ... add and subtract within 20.

I can also be precise in my work.

Start

6 + 6	10 + 8	16 – 8	9 – 0	14 – 4	6 – 2	10 + 10	8 – 3	2 + 7
5 + 4	9 – 4	11 – 9	10 + 5	13 – 5	2 – 1	7 + 9	10 – 9	10 + 9
15 – 8	3 + 10	5 + 1	9 + 8	6 + 8	12 – 5	7 + 7	16 – 9	13 – 8
12 – 9	14 – 7	14 – 6	16 – 7	9 + 9	5 + 6	8 – 6	2 + 5	4 + 7
8 + 9	9 + 6	7 + 5	12 – 8	1 + 7	18 – 9	6 – 0	17 – 9	15 – 7

Finish

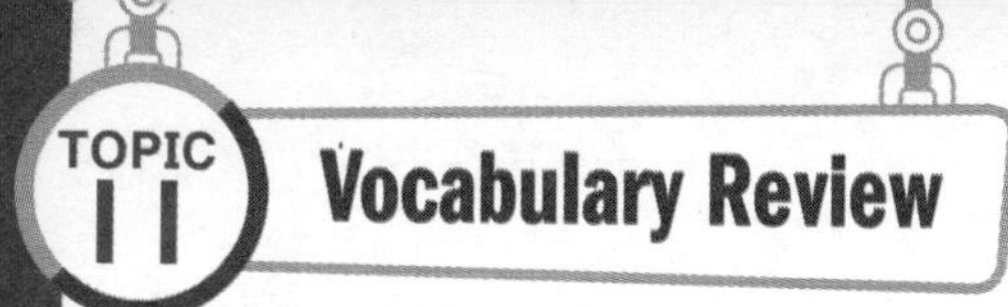

Word List
- difference
- hundreds
- mental math
- open number line
- partial differences
- regroup

Understand Vocabulary

Draw a line from each term to its example.

1. hundreds — 1 ten = 10 ones
2. open number line — 823 (8 underlined)
3. regroup — 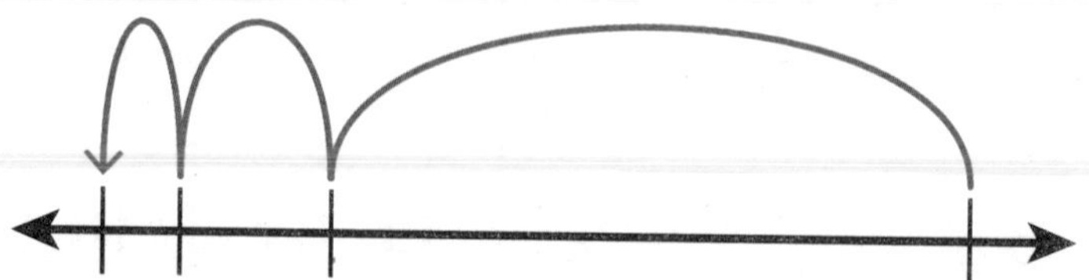

4. This open number line is incomplete. It needs to show counting back to find 538 – 115. Write in the missing numbers and labels.

Use Vocabulary in Writing

5. Find 235 – 127. Use terms from the Word List to explain your work.

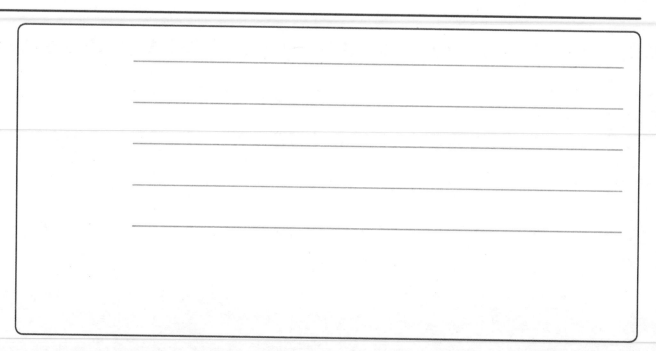

Name ______________________

Set A

You can subtract 10 or 100 mentally.

249 − 10 = ?

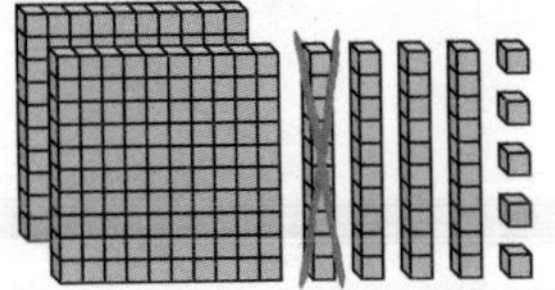

4 tens minus 1 ten is 3 tens.

249 − 10 = 239

249 − 100 = ?

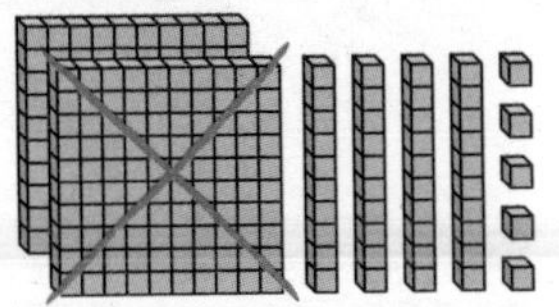

2 hundreds minus 1 hundred is 1 hundred.

249 − 100 = 149

Subtract using place-value blocks or mental math.

1. 426 − 10 = ______

2. 345 − 100 = ______

3. 287 − 100 = ______

4. 309 − 10 = ______

5. 800 − 10 = ______

6. 140 − 100 = ______

Set B

Find 213 − 108.

One Way

Start at 108 on an open number line. Add up to 213.

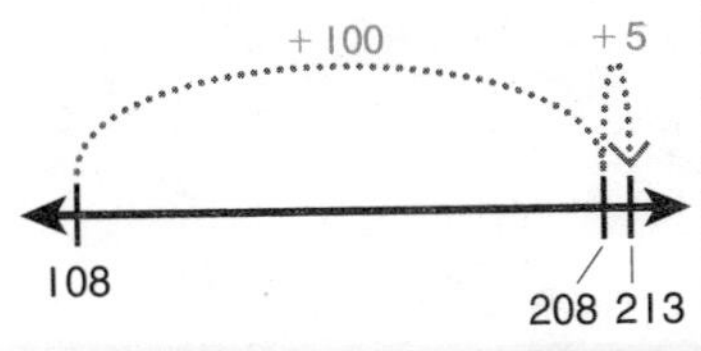

Another Way

Count back from 213 on an open number line.

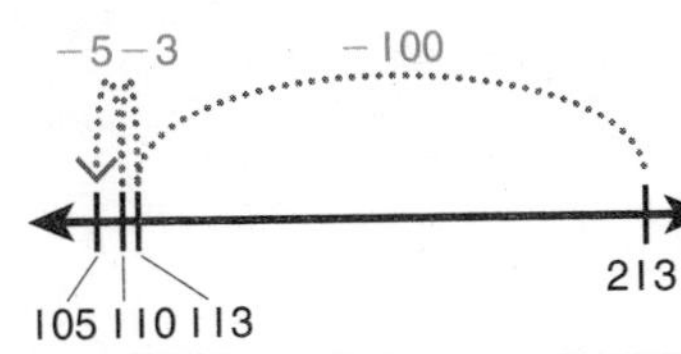

So, 213 − 108 = 105.

Use the open number line to subtract.

7. 449 − 217 = ______

8. 903 − 678 = ______

Set C

You can draw place-value blocks to show subtraction. Find 327 − 219.

327 − 219 = 108

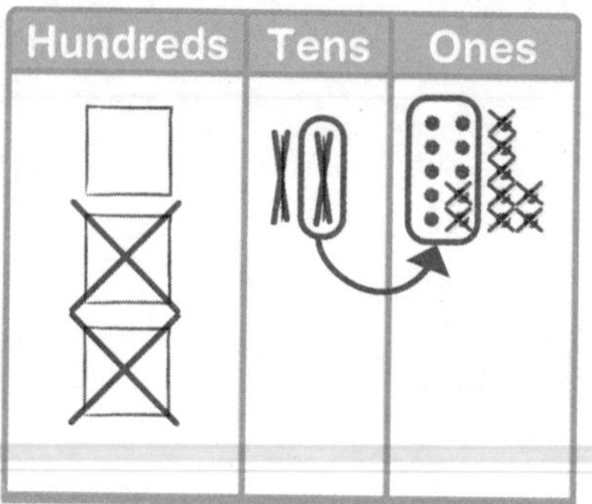

Draw blocks to find the partial differences. Record the partial differences to find the difference.

9. 653 − 427 = ______

Hundreds	Tens	Ones

Set D

Thinking Habits

Persevere

What do I know?

What do I need to find?

How can I check that my solution makes sense?

Solve the problem.
Ask yourself questions to help.

10. Marni has 354 pennies. First, she gives 149 pennies to her sister. Then, she gets 210 more pennies from her mother. How many pennies does Marni have now?

Name ______________________________

1. Which equals 100 less than 763?
Choose all that apply.

- ☐ 663
- ☐ 600 + 60 + 3
- ☐ 863
- ☐ 800 + 60 + 3
- ☐ 600 + 100 + 60

2. The open number line below shows subtraction.

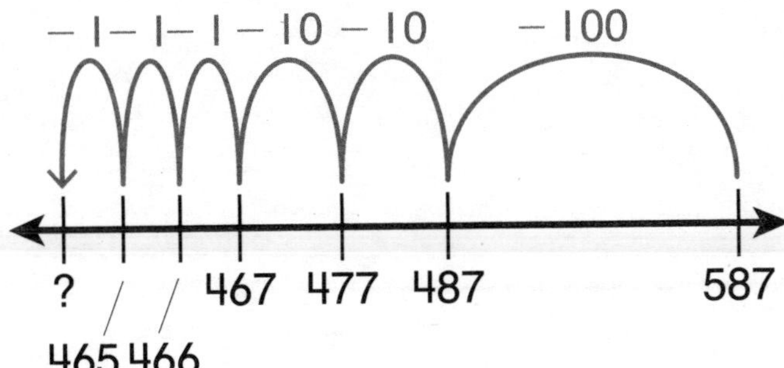

Complete the equation. Write the numbers being subtracted and the difference.

_____ – _____ = _____

3. Nico collected 235 coins. Amber collected 120 fewer coins than Nico. How many coins did they collect in all?

Ⓐ 350
Ⓑ 115
Ⓒ 500
Ⓓ 550

4. There are 537 boys and 438 girls at the concert. How many more boys than girls are at the concert?

Ⓐ 89
Ⓑ 99
Ⓒ 101
Ⓓ 109

5. Show how to add up on an open number line to find 740 – 490. Then write the difference below.

740 – 490 = _____

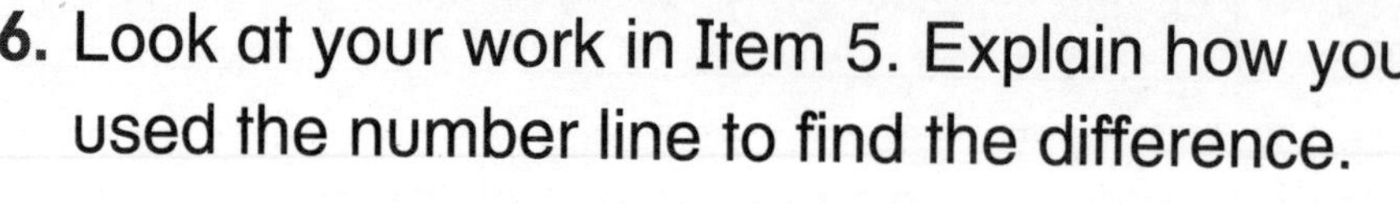

6. Look at your work in Item 5. Explain how you used the number line to find the difference.

____

____

____

____

____

____

____

7. Use place value and partial differences to find 374 – 157. Show your work.

374 – 157 = _____

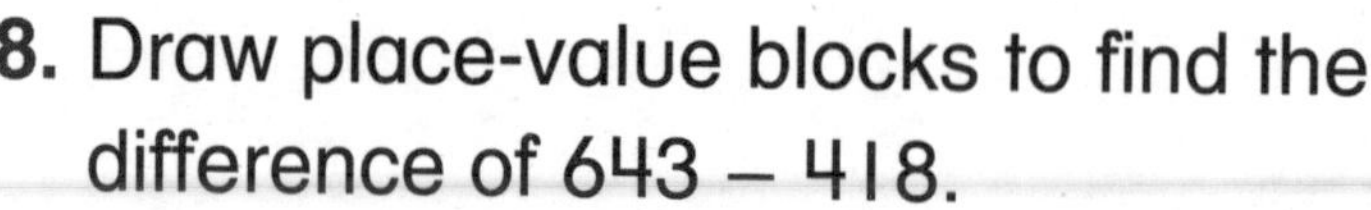

8. Draw place-value blocks to find the difference of 643 – 418.

Hundreds	Tens	Ones

643 – 418 = _____

Name ______________________________

Bead It!

The chart shows the number of beads sold at Betty's craft store for 4 weeks.

Number of Beads Sold	
Week 1	400
Week 2	536
Week 3	675
Week 4	289

1. How many more beads did Betty sell in Week 2 than in Week 1? Write the missing numbers in the equation. Then use any strategy to solve.

   _____ − _____ = _____

   _____ more beads

2. 458 glass beads were sold in Week 3. The other beads sold in Week 3 were plastic. How many plastic beads were sold in Week 3?

   Use the open number line to solve.

   _____ − _____ = _____

   Explain how you solved the problem. Tell how you know your answer is correct.

3. Dex buys 243 beads at Betty's store. He uses 118 of them to make a bracelet. How many beads does Dex have left?

Solve the problem. Show your work. Explain which strategy you used.

_____ − _____ = _____

_____ beads

Here are some strategies you can use.

Strategies

Use place value.
Use easier numbers.
Add up on a number line.
Count back on a number line.
Use models.
Use another strategy.

4. Ginny buys 958 beads. 245 beads are blue. 309 beads are orange. 153 beads are white. The rest are red. How many red beads does Ginny buy?

Part A

What is the hidden question in the problem?

____

____

Part B

Solve the problem. Show your work. Explain which strategy you used.

_____ red beads

TOPIC 12 Measuring Length

Essential Question: What are ways to measure length?

Digital Resources

Interactive Student Edition | Activity | Visual Learning | Video | Practice | Assessment | Games | Tools | Glossary

Look how tall sunflowers grow!
Sunlight and water help plants grow.
Wow! Let's do this project and learn more.

enVision® STEM Project: Growing and Measuring

Find Out Grow bean plants. Give them numbers. Put some in sunlight. Put some in a dark place. Water some of the plants. Do not water some of the plants. See how the plants in each group grow.

Journal: Make a Book Show what you learn in a book. In your book, also:

- Tell if plants need sunlight and water to grow.
- Find plants to measure. Draw pictures of the plants. Tell how tall each plant is.

Name ______________________________

Vocabulary

1. Draw a line under the bat to show its **length**.

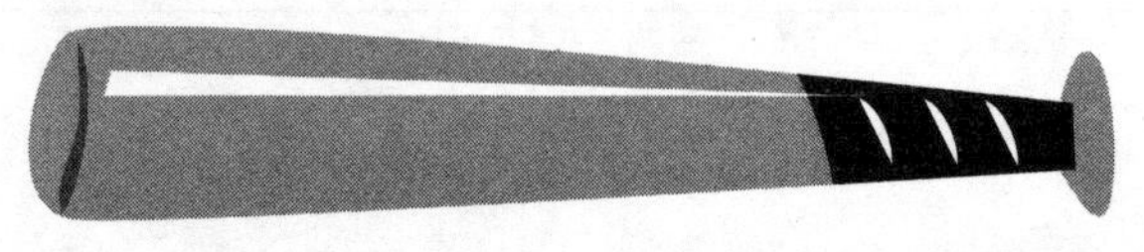

2. School is getting out. Circle **a.m.** or **p.m.**

a.m.

p.m.

3. Draw clock hands to show **quarter past** 10.

Estimating and Measuring Length

4. Use snap cubes.

Estimate the length.

about _____ cubes

Measure the length.

about _____ cubes

5. Use snap cubes.

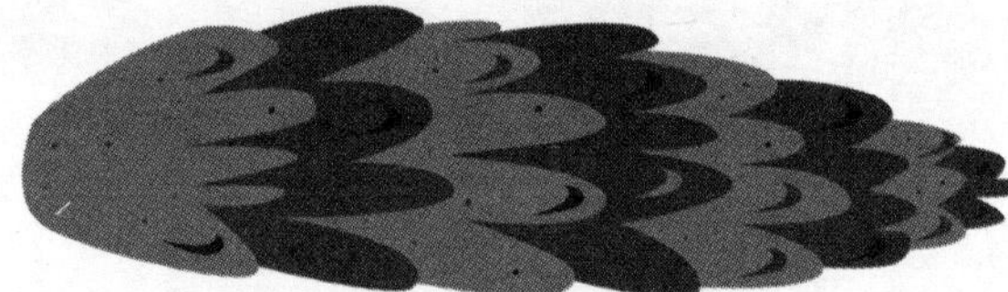

Estimate the length.

about _____ cubes

Measure the length.

about _____ cubes

Skip Counting

6. Write the missing numbers.

5, 10, _____, 20, _____

210, 220, _____, 240

400, _____, 600, 700

Look for a pattern.

Name ________________________________

Pick a Project

PROJECT 12A

How are measurements used to design clothing?

Project: Measure Feet and Create Sock Designs

PROJECT 12B

What units should you use to measure longer distances?

Project: Compare the Measurements of Sports Fields

PROJECT 12C

What can help you remember different measurement facts?

Project: Create a Booklet of Measurement Rhymes

PROJECT 12D

How long or how tall are some animals and insects?

Project: Make a Poster of Snake Lengths

Name ___________________________

Activity

Lesson 12-1
Estimating Length

I can ...
estimate the length of an object by relating the length of the object to a measurement I know.

I can also reason about math.

Solve & Share

Your thumb is about 1 inch long. Use your thumb to find three objects that are each about 1 inch long. Draw the objects.

From your elbow to your fingers is about 1 foot long. Use this part of your arm to find three objects that are each about 1 foot long. Draw the objects.

about 1 inch	about 1 foot

Visual Learning

Glossary

You can use the length of objects you know to **estimate** the length of other objects.

Some small paper clips are 1 inch (1 in.) long.

Use a small paper clip to estimate how long the eraser is.

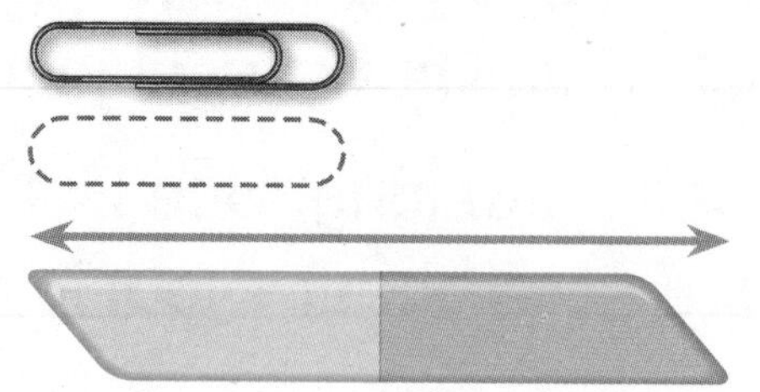

The eraser is about 2 paper clips long. So, it is about 2 inches long.

You can estimate with objects that are about 1 foot (ft) and 1 yard (yd) in length, too.
1 yd
1 ft

Convince Me! Is your height closer to 4 feet or 4 yards? How do you know?

Guided Practice Write the name and length of an object whose length you know. Then use that object to help you estimate the length of the object shown.

Object	Object Whose Length I Know	Estimate
1.	My paper clip is 1 inch long.	My pencil is about ______ long.
2.	My book is ______ long.	My desk is about ______ long.

Name ____________________

Tools
Assessment

Independent Practice Write the name and length of an object whose length you know. Then use that object to help you estimate the length of the object shown.

Object	Object Whose Length I Know	Estimate
3.	My ________ is ________ long.	My hand is about ________ long.
4.	My ________ is ________ long.	My chair is about ________ high.

5. **Higher Order Thinking** Would you estimate the distance from your classroom to the principal's office in inches, feet, or yards? How many units? Explain.

A giant step is about a yard.

____

____

____

____

____

Problem Solving Solve each problem.

6. **Vocabulary** Complete each sentence using one of the words below.

exact **estimated** **inch** **yard**

An __________ measurement is a good guess.

The height of a kitchen window is about 1 __________.

A small paper clip is about 1 __________ long.

7. **Reasoning** Joy and Kyle estimate the height of their classroom. Joy estimates the height to be 10 feet. Kyle estimates the height to be 10 yards. Who has the better estimate? Explain.

____

____

____

____

8. **Higher Order Thinking** A city wants to build a bridge over a river. Should they plan out an exact length of the bridge, or is an estimated length good enough? Explain.

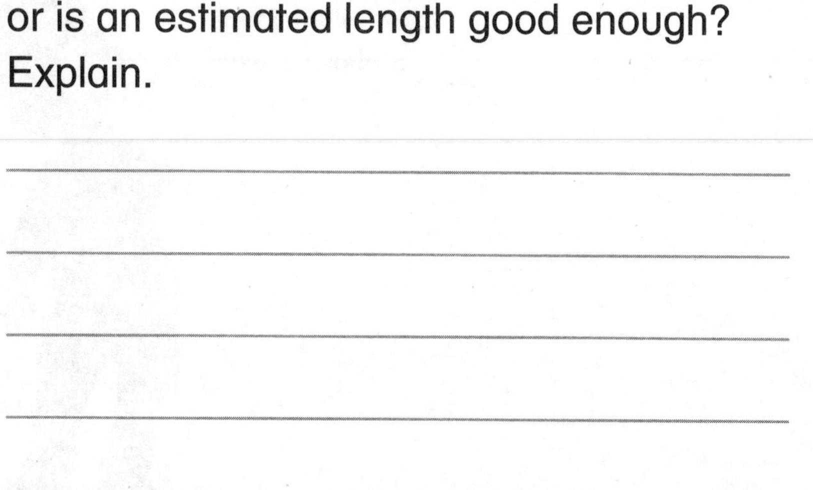

9. **Assessment Practice** Draw a line from each estimate to a matching object.

About 1 inch	About 1 foot	About 1 yard

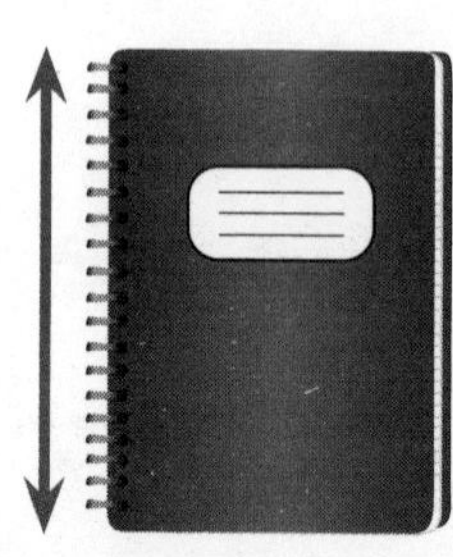

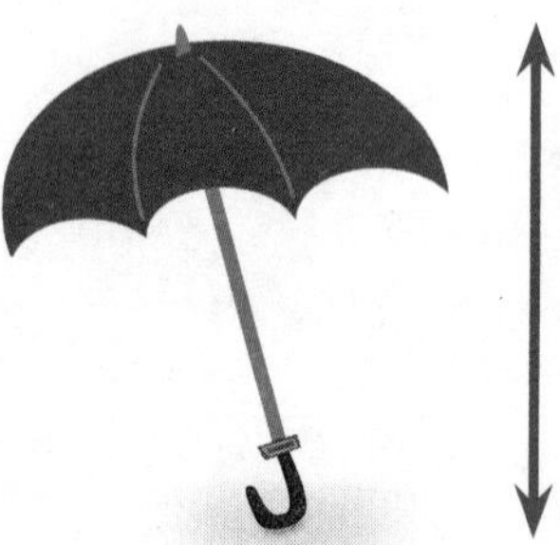

Name ______________________

Solve & Share

The orange square is 1 inch long. How can you use 1 inch squares to find the length of the line in inches? Measure the line and explain.

Lesson 12-2

Measure with Inches

I can ... estimate measures and use a ruler to measure length and height to the nearest inch.

I can also use math tools correctly.

1 inch

The line is about ____ inches long.

Visual Learning Bridge

You can measure the length and **height** of an object in inches (in.).

Start measuring from the 0 mark on the ruler.
0
1
2
INCHES

To measure to the **nearest inch**, look for the halfway mark.

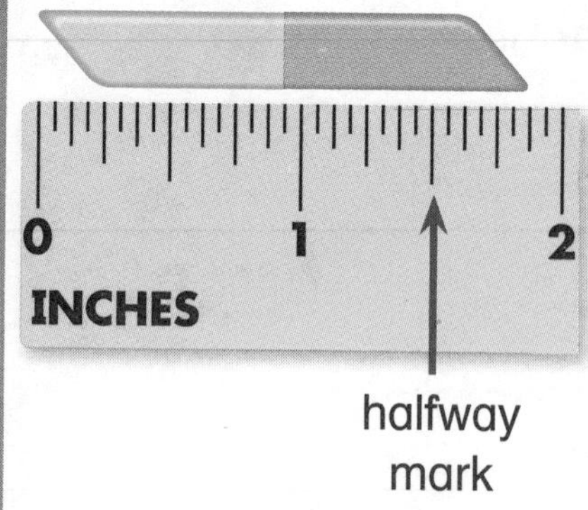

If the object is longer than the halfway mark, use the greater number.

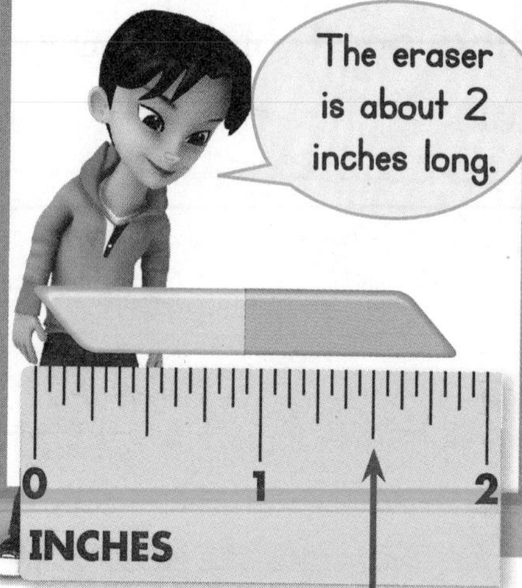

The eraser is about 2 inches long.
0
1
2
INCHES

If the object is shorter than the halfway mark, use the smaller number.

0
1
2
INCHES
The pine cone is about 1 inch long.

Convince Me! Use a ruler to measure. What classroom objects are about 12 inches long?

Guided Practice Estimate the height or length of each real object. Then use a ruler to measure to the nearest inch.

1. 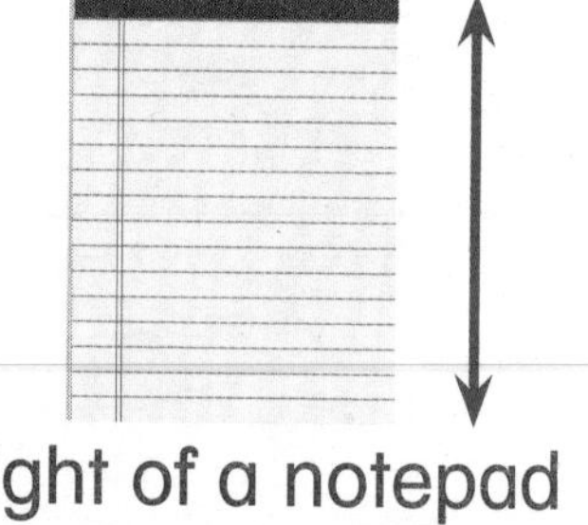

height of a notepad

2. 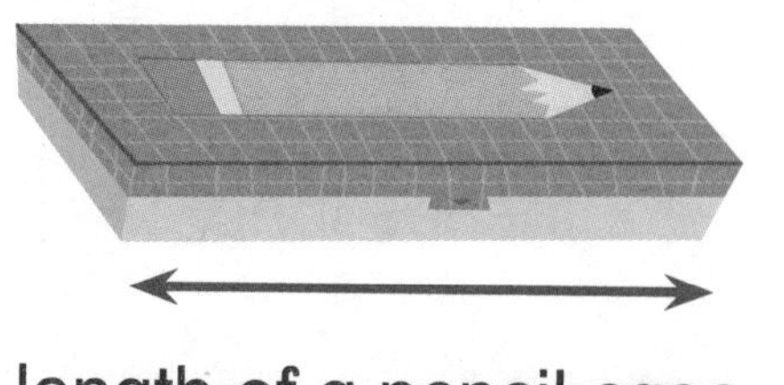

length of a pencil case

	Estimate	Measure
1.	about 12 inches	about 11 inches
2.	about ___ inches	about ___ inches

Name ____________________

Independent Practice Estimate the height or length of each real object. Then use a ruler to measure. Compare your estimate and measurement.

3. 

width of a book bag

4. 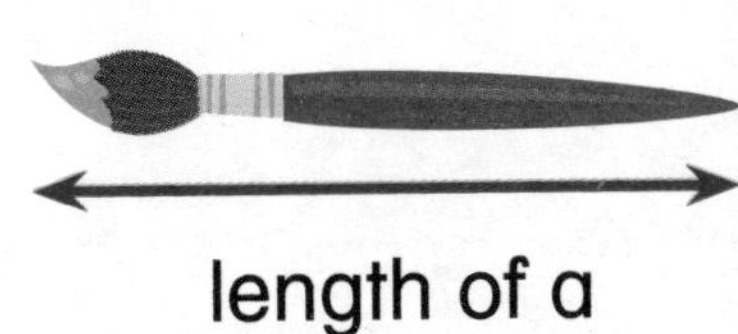

length of a paintbrush

	Estimate	Measure
3.	about ____ inches	about ____ inches
4.	about ____ inches	about ____ inches

5.  

height of a cup

6.

length of a crayon box

	Estimate	Measure
5.	about ____ inches	about ____ inches
6.	about ____ inches	about ____ inches

Higher Order Thinking Think about how to use a ruler to solve each problem.

7. Jason measures an object. The object is just shorter than the halfway mark between 8 and 9 on his inch ruler. How long is the object?

about ____ inches

8. Gina measures an object. The object is just longer than the halfway mark between 9 and 10 on her inch ruler. How long is the object?

about ____ inches

Problem Solving Solve each problem.

9. **Explain** Pam says that each cherry is about 1 inch wide. Is she correct? Explain.

10. **Vocabulary** Find an object in the classroom that measures about 6 inches. Write a sentence to describe the object. Use these words.

estimate **inches**

11. **Higher Order Thinking** Explain how to use an inch ruler to measure the length of an object.

12. **Assessment Practice** Use a ruler. About how many inches long are the two stamps together?

Ⓐ 4 inches

Ⓑ 3 inches

Ⓒ 2 inches

Ⓓ 1 inch

Name ______________________________

Activity

Lesson 12-3

Inches, Feet, and Yards

Solve & Share

Which objects in the classroom are about 1 inch, about 1 foot, and about 1 yard long? Show these objects below.

I can ...
estimate measures and use tools to measure the length and height of objects to the nearest inch, foot, and yard.

I can also reason about math.

about 1 inch

about 1 foot

about 1 yard

Visual Learning | A-Z Glossary

Visual Learning Bridge

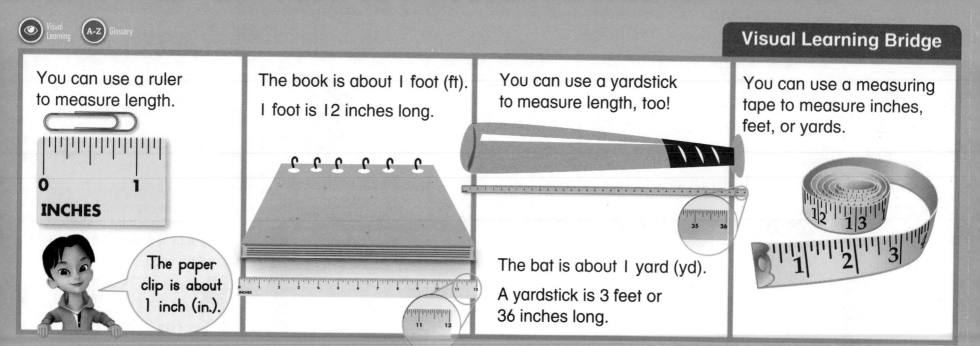

You can use a ruler to measure length.

The paper clip is about 1 inch (in.).

The book is about 1 foot (ft).

1 foot is 12 inches long.

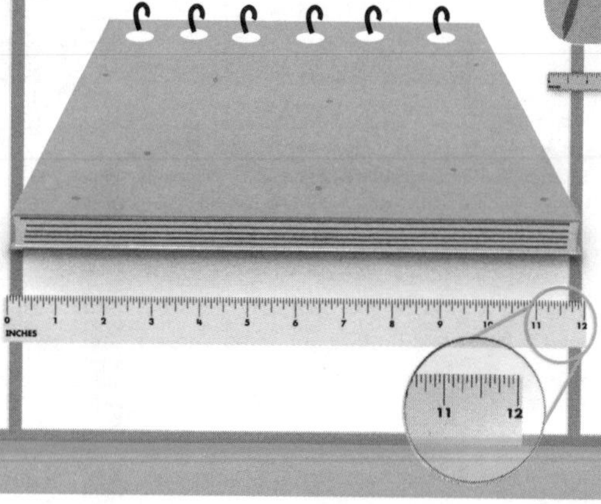

You can use a yardstick to measure length, too!

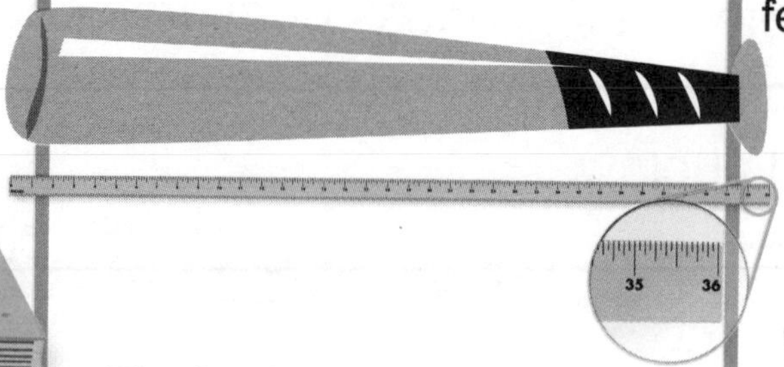

The bat is about 1 yard (yd).

A yardstick is 3 feet or 36 inches long.

You can use a measuring tape to measure inches, feet, or yards.

Convince Me! Would you measure the length of a school building in inches or yards? Why?

Match each object with a reasonable estimate of its length.

1. 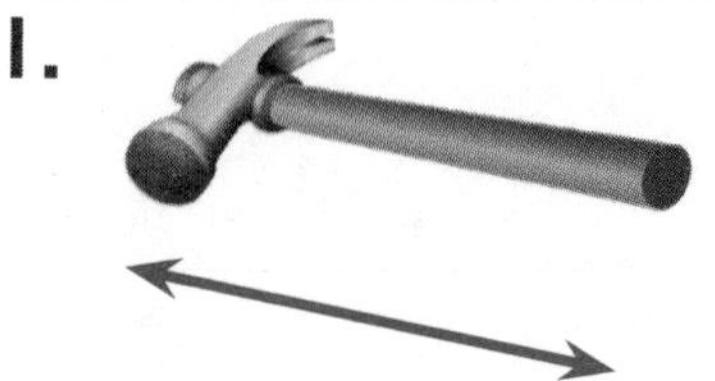

about 1 yard

2. 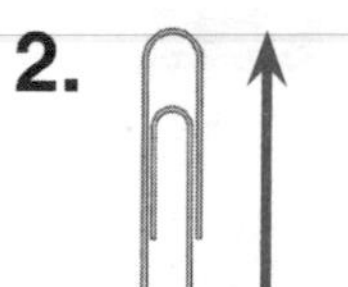

about 1 inch

3. 

about 1 foot

Be ready to tell which tool you would use to measure each object.

Name ______________________________

Independent Practice Estimate the length of each real object. Choose a ruler, yardstick, or measuring tape to measure. Write the tool you used.

	Estimate	Measure	Tool
4. 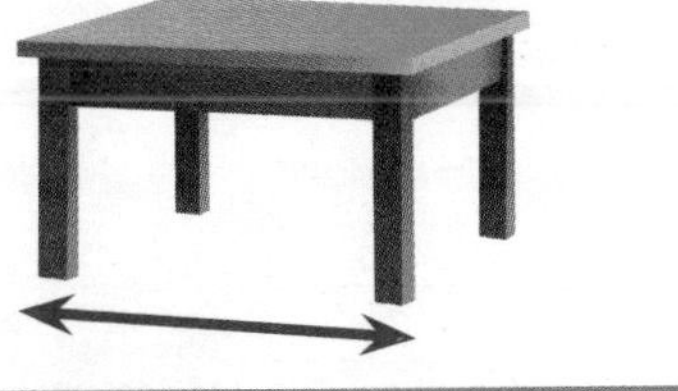	about ____ inches	about ____ inches	____________
5.	about ____ feet	about ____ feet	____________
6. 	about ____ yards	about ____ yards	____________

7. **Higher Order Thinking** Explain how you could use a foot ruler to measure the length of a room in feet.

____

____

____

____

Problem Solving Solve each problem.

8. **Generalize** Circle the real object that is about 4 feet in length.

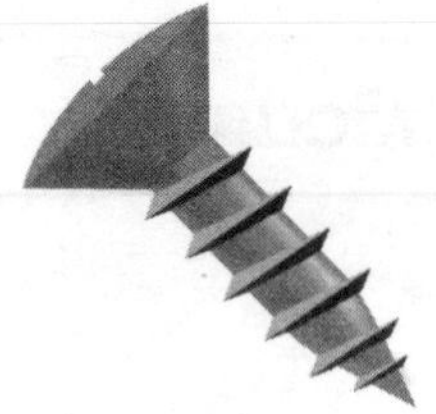

9. **Number Sense** Explain how to use a yardstick to measure the length of an object. Estimate the length of your classroom in yards. Then measure.

10. **Higher Order Thinking** Find an object in the classroom that you estimate measures about 2 feet. Draw the object.

What tool would you use to measure it? Explain why you chose the tool you did.

11. **Assessment Practice** Jon sets two of the same real objects next to each other. Together, they have a length of about 4 feet. Which is the object Jon uses?

Name ____________________

Activity

Lesson 12-4

Measure Length Using Different Customary Units

I can ...
estimate and measure the length and height of objects in inches, feet, and yards.

I can also be precise in my work.

Solve & Share

Choose an object. Measure your object in feet. Then measure it in inches.

Do you need more units of feet or inches to measure your object? Why?

about ____ feet long

about ____ inches long

____

____

Visual Learning A-Z Glossary

Visual Learning Bridge

You can use different units to measure objects.
Would you use more units of feet or yards to measure the length of the bookcase?

Measure the bookcase in feet.

It is about 3 feet long.

Measure the bookcase in yards.

It is about 1 yard long.
1

I used more units of feet than yards because a foot is a smaller unit than a yard.

Convince Me! Juan measures the height of a wall in his room. He lines the wall with one-foot rulers. He could find this height with yardsticks. Would Juan need more rulers or yardsticks? Explain.

Guided Practice Measure each real object using different units. Circle the unit you use *more* of to measure each object.

1. 

about _____ feet   about _____ yards

I use more units of:

feet   yards

2. 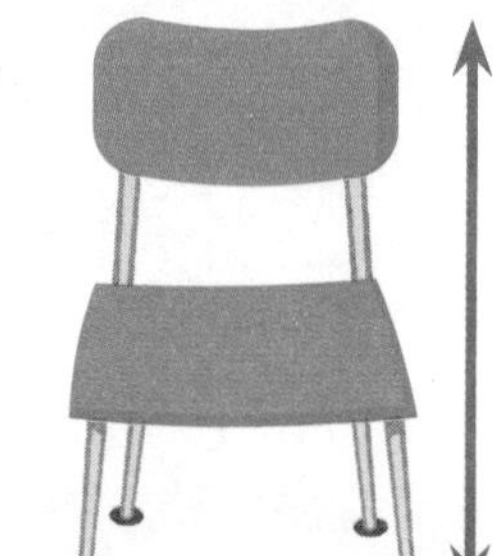

about _____ inches   about _____ feet

I use more units of:

inches   feet

Name ______________________________

Independent Practice

Measure each real object using different units.
Circle the unit you use *fewer* of to measure each object.

3. 

about _____ inches about _____ feet

I use fewer units of:

inches feet

4. 

about _____ feet about _____ yards

I use fewer units of:

feet yards

5. 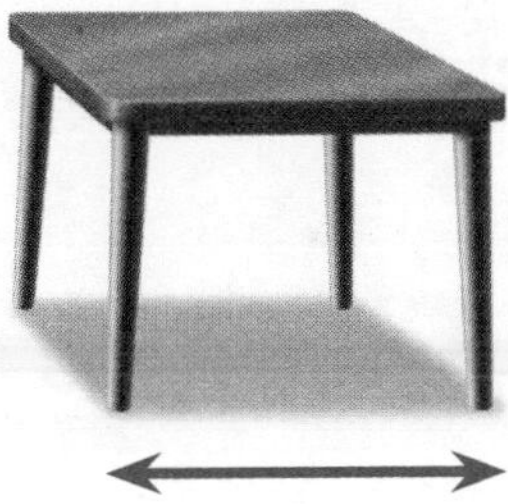

about _____ feet

about _____ yards

I use fewer units of:

feet yards

Number Sense Circle the best estimate for the length of each object.

6. About how long is a key?

2 inches 2 feet 2 yards

Which tool would you use to measure the length of a key?

____

7. About how long is a suitcase?

2 inches 2 feet 2 yards

Which tool would you use to measure the length of a suitcase?

____

Problem Solving Solve each problem.

8. **Use Tools** Measure the length of an object in your classroom using two different units.

Object: ______________________

about ____________ about ____________

Which unit did you use more of? ____________

Circle which tool you used.

ruler yardstick measuring tape

9. **Higher Order Thinking** Andrew wants to measure the length of a football field. Should he use feet or yards to measure it? Which tool should he use? Explain.

____

____

____

____

____

10. **Assessment Practice** Which unit would you need the fewest of to measure the length of the table?

Ⓐ inches Ⓒ yards

Ⓑ feet Ⓓ all the same

11. **Assessment Practice** Which is the best estimate for the length of a vegetable garden?

Ⓐ about 5 inches Ⓒ about 5 yards

Ⓑ about 1 foot Ⓓ about 20 inches

Name ______________________

Lesson 12-5

Measure with Centimeters

I can ...

estimate measures and use a ruler to measure length and height to the nearest centimeter.

I can also be precise in my work.

Solve & Share

The green cube is 1 centimeter long. How can you use 1 centimeter cubes to find the length of the line in centimeters? Measure the line and explain.

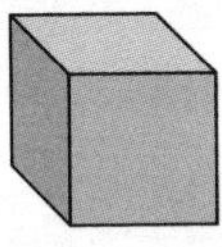

1 cm

The line is about _____ centimeters long.

 Visual Learning  Glossary

Visual Learning Bridge

1 **centimeter (cm)** is smaller than 1 inch.

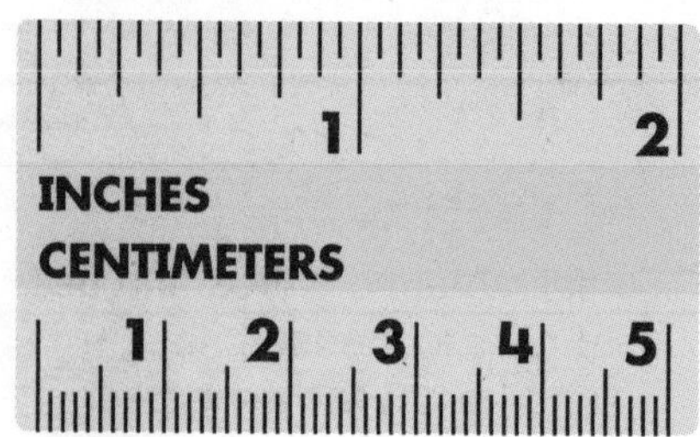

1 cm

Start measuring from the 0 mark. To measure to the **nearest centimeter**, look for the halfway mark.
If the object is longer than the halfway mark, use the greater number.

The cube is about 2 centimeters long.

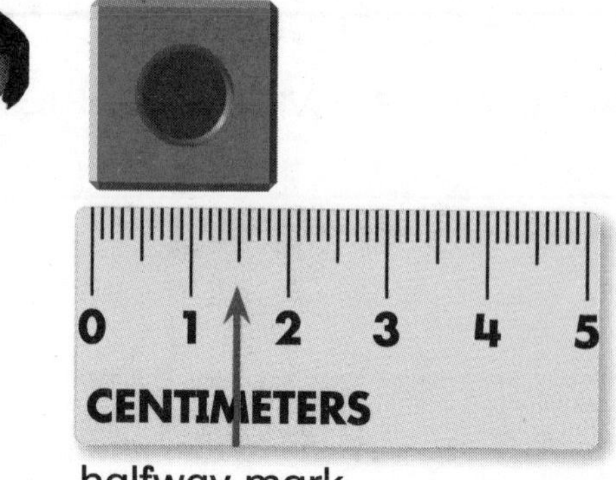

halfway mark

If the object is shorter than the halfway mark, use the smaller number.

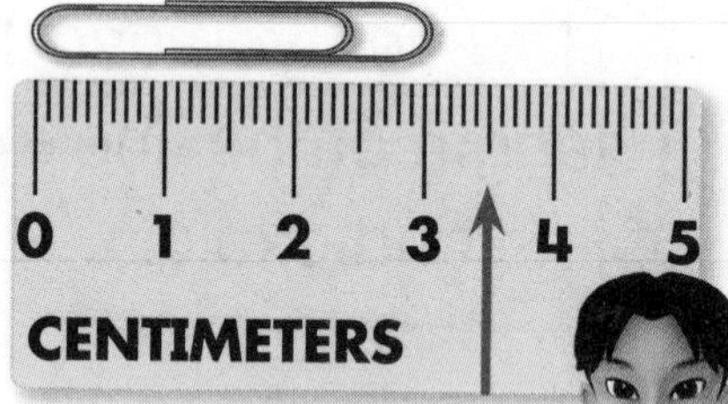

This paper clip is about 3 centimeters long.

Convince Me! Explain how you know the length of the paper clip above is about 3 centimeters long.

Guided Practice

Estimate the height or length of each real object. Use a ruler to measure to the nearest centimeter.

1\. 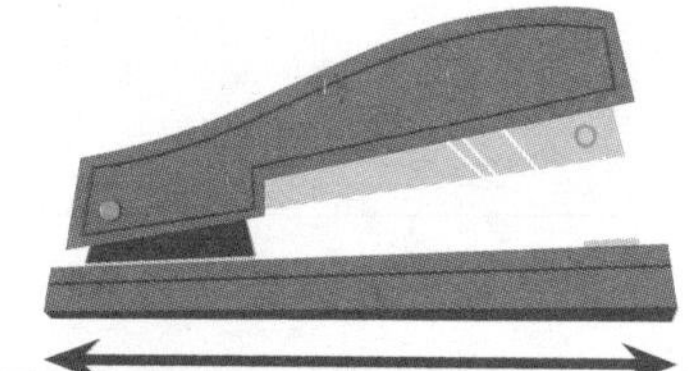

length of a stapler

2\. 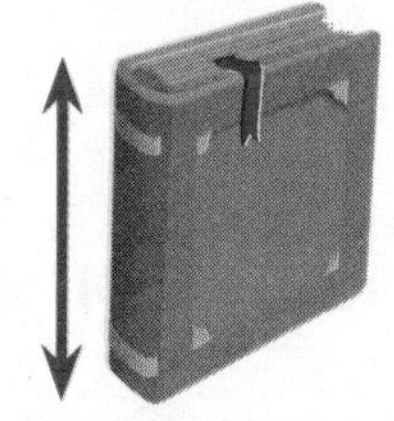

height of a book

Estimate	Measure
about 15 centimeters	about 18 centimeters
about ____ centimeters	about ____ centimeters

Name ______________________

Tools Assessment

Independent Practice Estimate the width, height, or length of each real object. Then use a ruler to measure. Compare your estimate and measurement.

3. 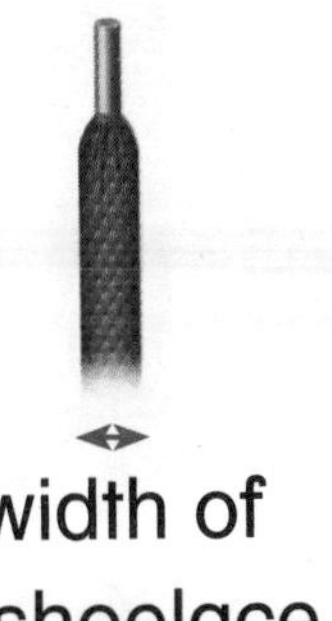
width of a shoelace

4. width of a chair

Estimate	Measure
about ____ centimeters	about ____ centimeters
about ____ centimeters	about ____ centimeters

5. length of a pencil

6. 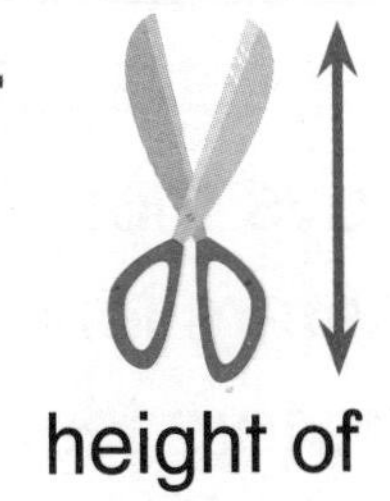
height of scissors

Estimate	Measure
about ____ centimeters	about ____ centimeters
about ____ centimeters	about ____ centimeters

Higher Order Thinking Explain whether each estimate is reasonable or not.

7. Josh estimated that the length of his reading book is about 6 centimeters.

____

____

8. Shae estimated that the height of her desk is about 10 centimeters.

____

____

Problem Solving Solve each problem.

9. **Vocabulary** Find an object that is about 10 centimeters long. Write a sentence to describe your object using these words.

centimeters **estimate**

____

____

____

10. **Look for Patterns** Nick wants to put another pen end to end with this one. About how long would the two pens be together?

about _____ centimeters

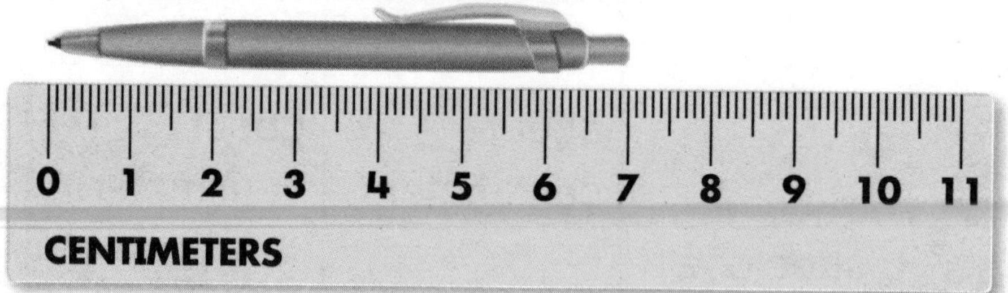

11. **Higher Order Thinking** Paul says that a toothbrush is about 19 centimeters long. Sarah says it is about 50 centimeters long. Who is correct? Explain.

12. **Assessment Practice** Mary measures the length of her eraser to the nearest centimeter. What is the length of her eraser to the nearest centimeter?

_____ centimeters

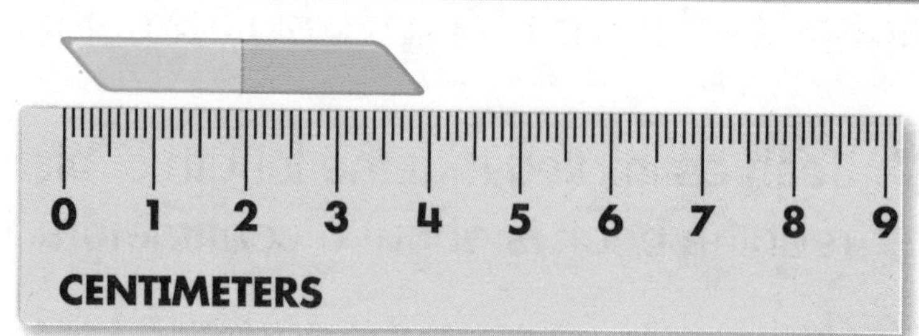

Name ______________________________

Lesson 12-6

Centimeters and Meters

I can ...
estimate measures and use a ruler, a meter stick, or a tape measure to measure length and height to the nearest centimeter or meter.

I can also use math tools correctly.

Solve & Share Which objects in the classroom are about 3 centimeters long?
Which objects are about 1 meter long?
Show these objects below.

about 3 centimeters

about 1 meter

Visual Learning Bridge

You can use a ruler or a meter stick to measure length.

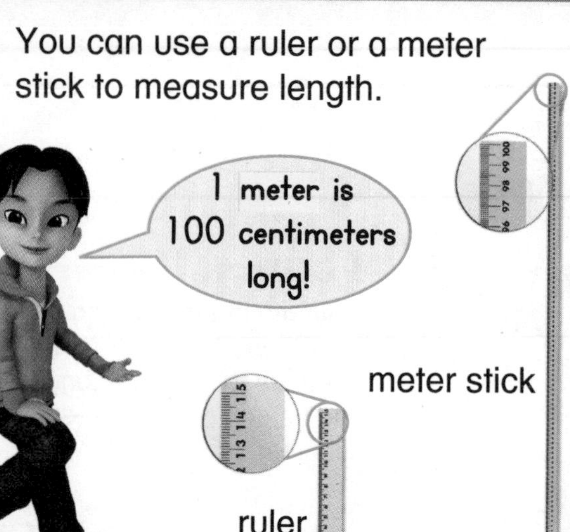

The button is about 1 centimeter (cm) long.

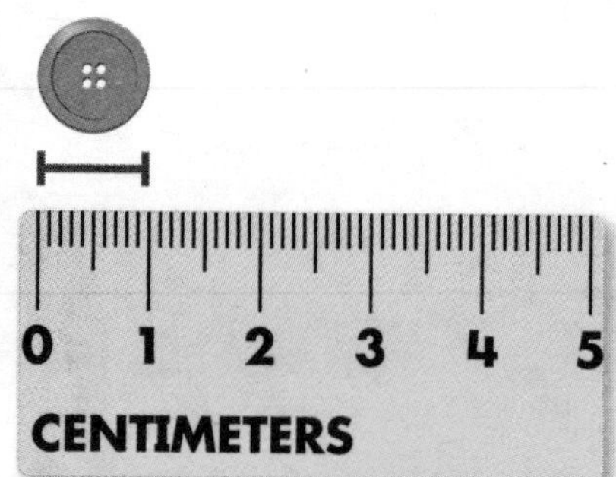

This table is about 1 meter (m) wide.

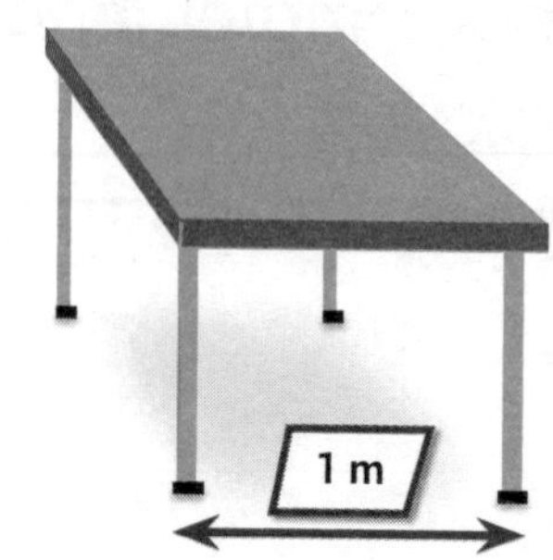

You can also use a measuring tape to measure centimeters and meters.

Convince Me! Would you measure the length of a house in centimeters or meters? Why?

☆ **Guided Practice** ☆ Match each object with a reasonable estimate of its length.

1. 

about 1 cm

2. 

about 10 cm

3. 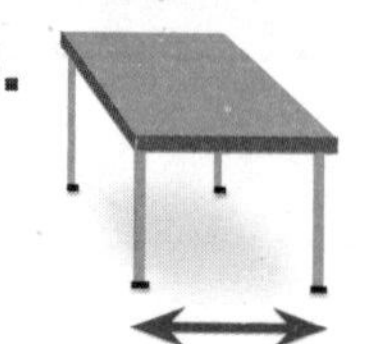

about 1 m

4. 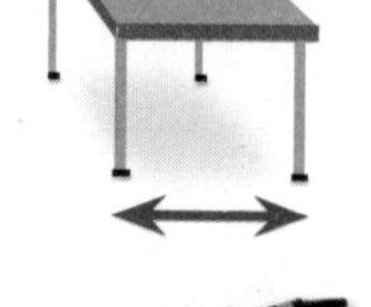

about 10 m

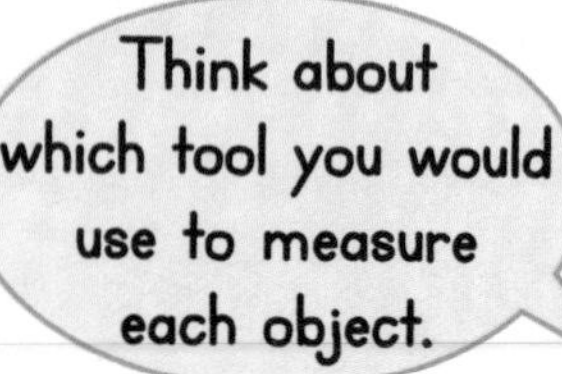

Think about which tool you would use to measure each object.

Name ______________________

Tools Assessment

Independent Practice

Estimate the length or height of each real object shown. Then choose a tool and measure. Compare your estimate and measurement.

	Estimate	Measure	Tool
5.	about _____ cm	about _____ cm	__________
6.	about _____ m	about _____ m	__________
7.	about _____ cm	about _____ cm	__________
8.	about _____ m	about _____ m	__________

9. Tom uses a meter stick to measure the length of a fence. He places the meter stick 5 times on the fence to measure from one end to the other end. How long is the fence?

_____ meters

10. **Higher Order Thinking** Debbie says that her doll is about 30 meters long. Do you think this is a good estimate? Why or why not?

____

____

Problem Solving Solve each problem.

11. **Be Precise** Choose an object to measure. Use metric units. Estimate first and then measure.
Draw the object and write your estimate and measurement. Was your estimate reasonable?

Remember to include the units.

12. Circle the real object that would be about 2 meters long.

13. **Higher Order Thinking** Each side of a place-value cube is 1 centimeter long. Use a place-value cube to draw a 5-centimeter ruler.

14. **Assessment Practice** Choose an appropriate tool. Measure each line. Which lines are at least 6 centimeters long? Choose all that apply.

- ☐
- ☐
- ☐
- ☐

Name ______________________________

Activity

Lesson 12-7

Measure Length Using Different Metric Units

I can ...
measure the length and height of objects using different metric units.

I can also be precise in my work.

Solve & Share

Measure this pencil in inches. Then measure it again in centimeters. Which measurement has more units?

about ____ inches about ____ centimeters

Which has more units? ______________________

Visual Learning A-Z Glossary

Visual Learning Bridge

You can use different units to measure the lengths of objects. Would you use more units of centimeters or meters to measure the desk?

Measure the length using centimeters.

Measure the length using meters.

It is about 1 meter long!

I used more units of centimeters than meters because a centimeter is a much smaller unit than a meter.

Convince Me! Tina measures the length of a room with centimeter rulers. She could find this length with meter sticks. Would Tina need fewer rulers or meter sticks? Explain.

Guided Practice

Measure each real object using different units. Circle the unit you use *more* of to measure each object.

1. 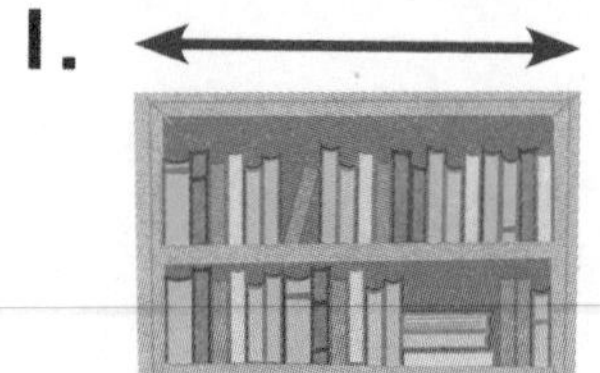

about _____ centimeters

about _____ meters

I use more units of: centimeters meters

2. 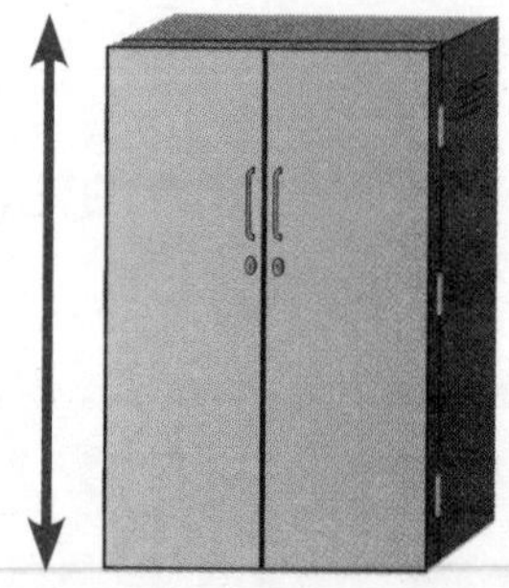

about _____ centimeters

about _____ meters

I use more units of: centimeters meters

Name ____________________

Tools Assessment

Independent Practice Measure each real object using different units. Circle the unit you use *fewer* of to measure each object.

3. 

about _____ meters about _____ centimeters

I use fewer units of: centimeters meters

4. 

about _____ meters about _____ centimeters

I use fewer units of: centimeters meters

5. Higher Order Thinking Jay measured the height of his bedroom in both centimeters and meters. Did he use fewer units of centimeters or meters? Explain.

____

____

____

____

Problem Solving Solve each problem.

6. **Explain** If you had to measure the length of the hallway outside of your classroom, would you use centimeters or meters? Explain.

____

____

____

____

7. **Higher Order Thinking** A meter stick is about 39 inches long. Is a meter longer or shorter than a yard? Explain.

____

____

____

____

____

8. **Assessment Practice** Estimate the length of a baseball bat in centimeters and meters.

_____ centimeters

_____ meters

Which number must be greater? Explain.

____

____

____

____

____

9. **Assessment Practice** Tina measures the length of a jump rope using different units. How will her measurements compare?

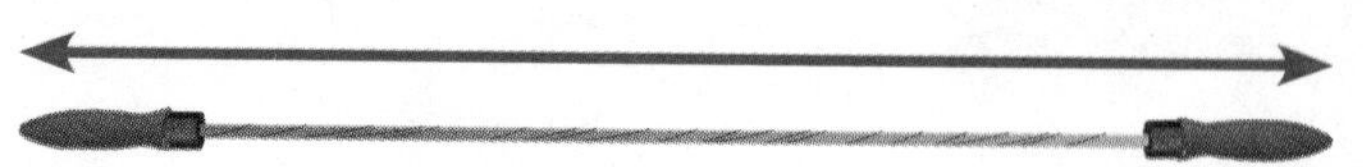

Choose Yes or No.

More units of meters than centimeters	○ Yes	○ No
More units of inches than feet	○ Yes	○ No
More units of yards than feet	○ Yes	○ No

Name ______________________

Activity

Lesson 12-8
Compare Lengths

I can ...
tell how much longer one object is than another.

I can also model with math.

Solve & Share

Circle two paths. Estimate which one is longer. How can you check if your estimate is correct?

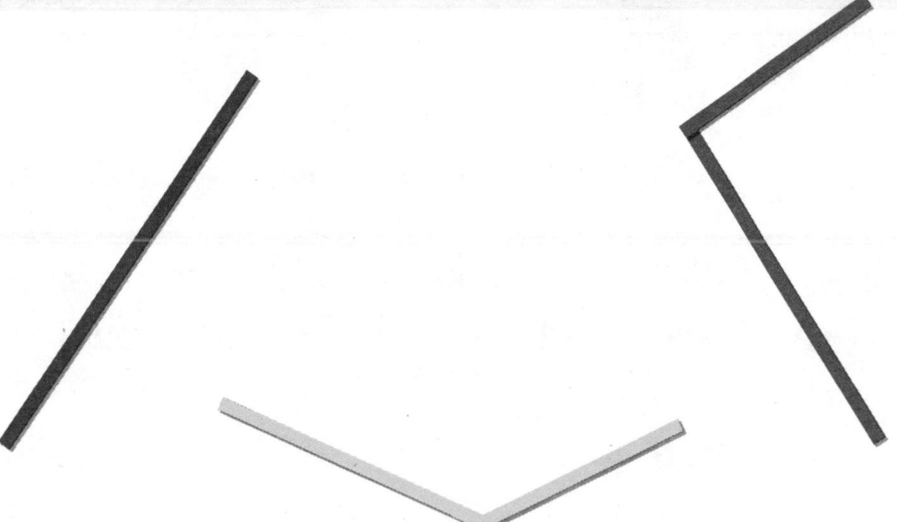

Estimate: The ____________ path is longer.

Measure: The ____________ path is longer.

Visual Learning Bridge

Which path is longer?
How much longer?

Think about both parts of the path when you estimate and measure.

Estimate: 5 cm

Estimate: 6 cm

One part of the blue path is about 2 cm. The other part is about 2 cm. Add to find the length.

2 + 2 = 4
The blue path is about 4 cm long.

0 1 2 3 4
CENTIMETERS

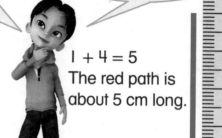

One part of the red path is about 1 cm. The other part is about 4 cm. Add to find the length.

1 + 4 = 5
The red path is about 5 cm long.

0 1 2 3 4
CENTIMETERS

Subtract to compare lengths.
5 − 4 = 1

The red path is about 1 cm longer than the blue path.

Convince Me! How can you find the length of a path that is not straight?

Guided Practice Estimate the length of each path. Then use a centimeter ruler to measure each path.

1. **Path A**

Estimate: about 9 cm
Measure: about 10 cm

2. **Path B**

Estimate: about ______ cm
Measure: about ______ cm

3. Which path is longer?

______

4. How much longer?

about ______ cm longer

Name ______________________________

Independent Practice

Estimate the length of each path. Then use a centimeter ruler to measure each path. Compare your estimate and measurement.

5. **Path C**

Estimate: about _____ centimeters

Measure: about _____ centimeters

6. **Path D**

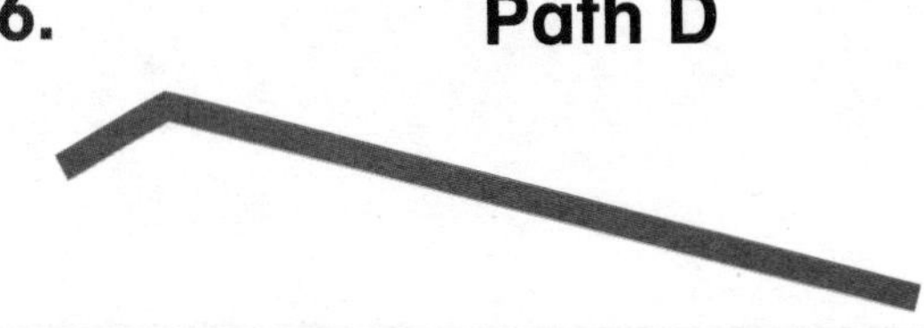

Estimate: about _____ centimeters

Measure: about _____ centimeters

7. Which path is longer?

____

8. How much longer?

about _____ centimeters longer

Higher Order Thinking Think about the length of each object. Circle the best estimate of its length.

9. a key

about 1 cm about 6 cm about 20 cm

Think about objects that are about 1 cm long to help.

10. a pen

about 2 cm about 4 cm about 15 cm

Use your estimates to complete:

A pen is about _____ cm

_________ than a key.

Problem Solving Solve each problem.

11. **Explain** A path has two parts. The total length of the path is 12 cm. If one part is 8 cm, how long is the other part? Explain.

_____ centimeters

12. **Higher Order Thinking** Draw a path with two parts. Measure the length to the nearest centimeter. Write an equation to show the length of your path.

13. **Higher Order Thinking** Beth drew a picture of a bike path. Use tools. Measure the length of the path below. Write the total length.

Beth's Path

about _____ centimeters

14. **Assessment Practice** Measure each path in centimeters.

Path A

Path B

How much longer is Path A than Path B? Show your work.

Name ______________________

Solve & Share

Zeke measures the snake and says it is about 4 inches long. Jay says it is about 5 inches long.

Who measures the snake more precisely? Measure and explain.

Problem Solving

Lesson 12-9

Precision

I can ...
choose tools, units, and methods that help me be precise when I measure.

I can also measure the length of straight or curved objects.

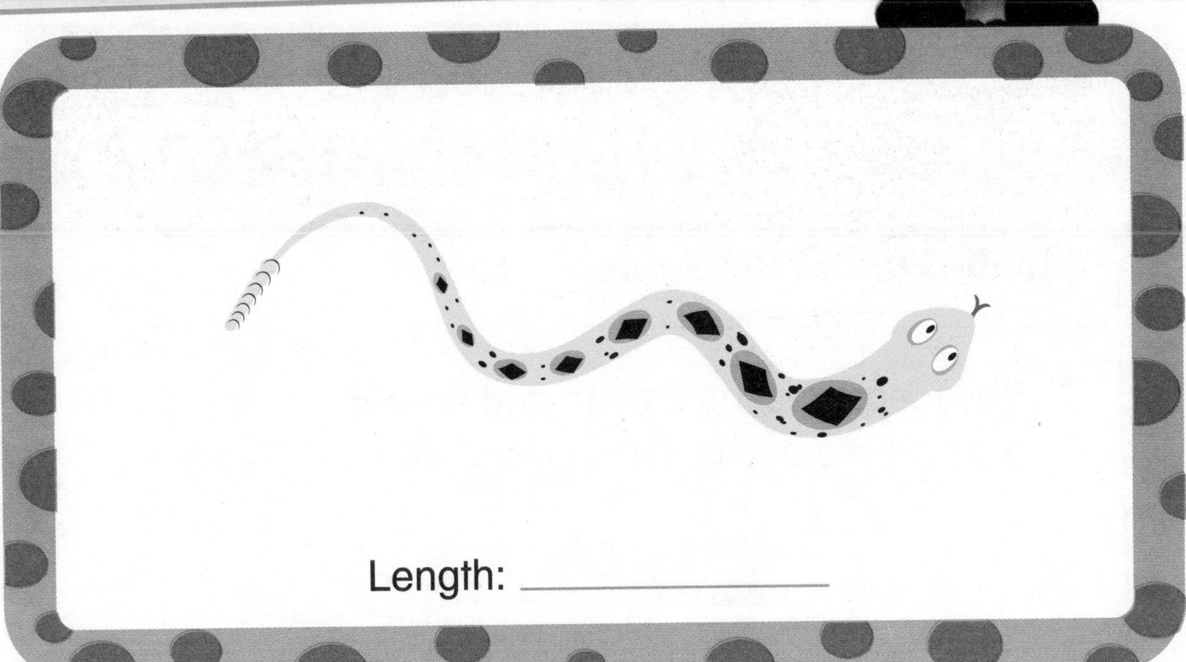

Length: ____________

____

____

____

____

Thinking Habits

Which unit of measure will I use?

Is my work precise?

Anna uses a string to help measure the worm.

Is her work precise? Why or why not?

What can I do to measure precisely?

I can choose units and tools that will help me measure precisely.

Measure Precisely
- Estimate first.
- Choose a tool.
- Start at 0.
- Measure twice.
- Write the unit.

Anna lines up the string along a ruler to measure the length.

Then Anna measures the worm again to check her work. Then she writes the length.

The worm is about 3 inches long.

Anna uses precision to measure and write the units.

Convince Me! How does using a string help Anna use precision to measure the worm?

Guided Practice Solve.

1. Bev measures the crayon and says it is 5 centimeters long. Is her work precise? Explain.

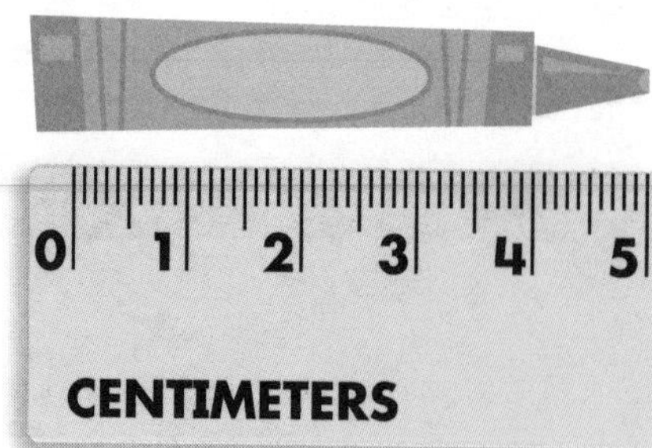

____

____

Tools Assessment

Name ______

Independent Practice

Solve each problem.

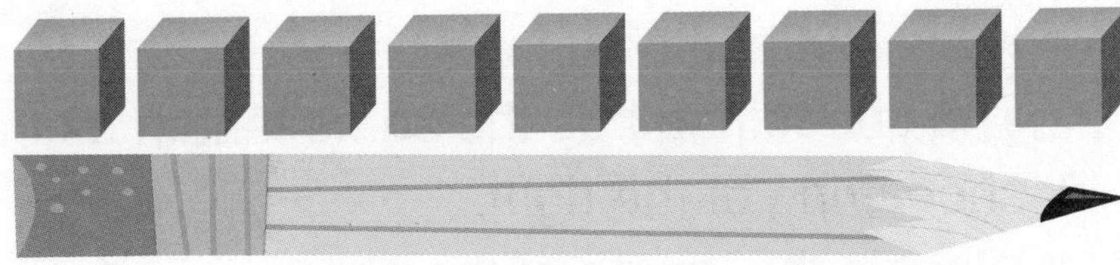

2. Steve uses centimeter cubes. He says the pencil is 9 centimeters long. Is his work precise? Explain.

3. Use a centimeter ruler to measure the pencil yourself. How long is the pencil? Explain what you did to make sure your work is precise.

4. Find the difference in the lengths of the paths in inches. Is your answer precise? Explain.

Problem Solving

Performance Task

Shoestring

Katie lost a shoestring.
The shoestring has the same length as the shoestring at the right.
What is the length of the shoestring Katie lost?

5. **Make Sense** Estimate the length of the shoestring in the picture. Explain how your estimate helps you measure.

____

____

____

____

6. **Use Tools** What tools can you use to measure the shoestring? Explain.

____

____

____

____

____

7. **Be Precise** Measure the shoestring. Tell why your work is precise.

____

____

____

Name ________________________________

Fluency Practice Activity

Find a partner. Point to a clue. Read the clue.

Look below the clues to find a match. Write the clue letter in the box next to the match.

Find a match for every clue.

I can ... add and subtract within 100.

I can also make math arguments.

Clues

A The sum is between 47 and 53.

B The difference equals 56 − 20.

C The sum equals 100.

D The difference equals 79 − 27.

E The difference is between 25 and 35.

F The sum equals 41 + 56.

G The difference is less than 20.

H The sum equals 26 + 19.

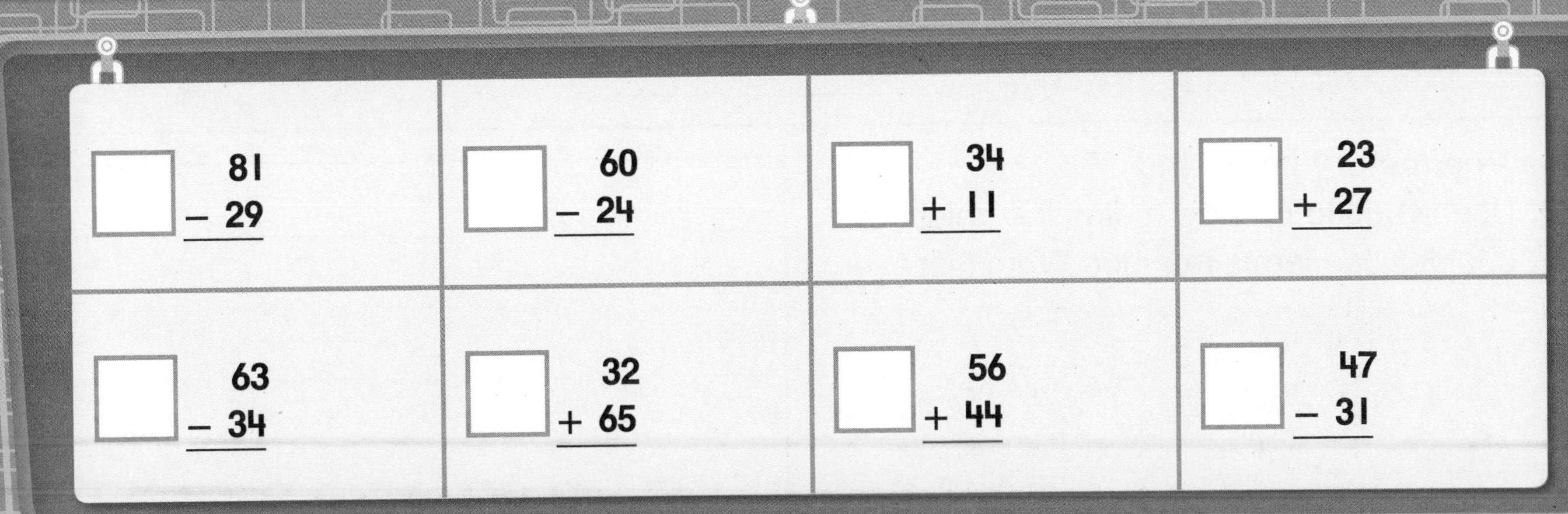

☐ $81 - 29$	☐ $60 - 24$	☐ $34 + 11$	☐ $23 + 27$
☐ $63 - 34$	☐ $32 + 65$	☐ $56 + 44$	☐ $47 - 31$

Vocabulary Review

Word List

- centimeter (cm)
- estimate
- foot (ft)
- height
- inch (in.)
- length
- meter (m)
- nearest centimeter
- nearest inch
- yard (yd)

Understand Vocabulary

1. Circle the unit that has the *greatest* length.

   foot   meter   inch

2. Circle the unit that has the *shortest* length.

   yard   inch   centimeter

3. Cross out the unit you would **NOT** use to measure the length of a book.

   inch   centimeter   yard

4. Cross out the unit you would **NOT** use to measure the height of a house.

   inch   foot   meter

Estimate the length of each item.

5. pencil ________

6. paper clip ________

7. school desk ________

Use Vocabulary in Writing

8. Use words to tell how to find the height of a table. Use terms from the Word List.

Name ______________________

Reteaching

Set A

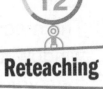

There are 12 inches in 1 foot.
There are 3 feet in 1 yard.
You can use lengths of objects you know to estimate lengths of other objects.

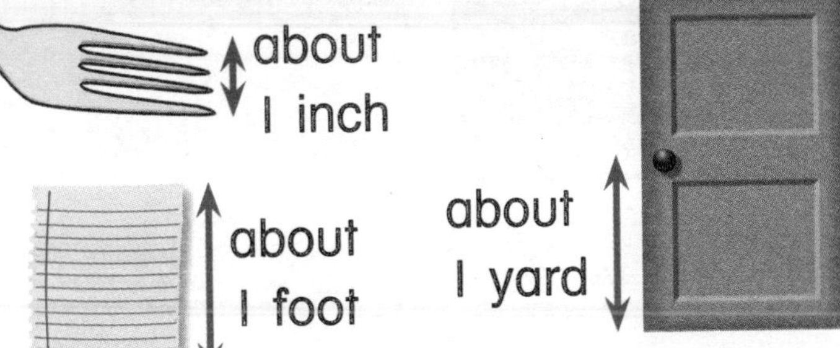

Estimate the lengths of two classroom objects in feet. Name each object and write your estimate.

1. Object: ______________________

   about ______ feet

2. Object: ______________________

   about ______ feet

Set B

You can measure the length of an object to the nearest inch.

The string is longer than halfway between 1 and 2.
So, use the greater number.
The string is about __2__ inches.

Find objects like the ones shown. Use a ruler to measure their lengths.

3. 

   about ______ inches

4. 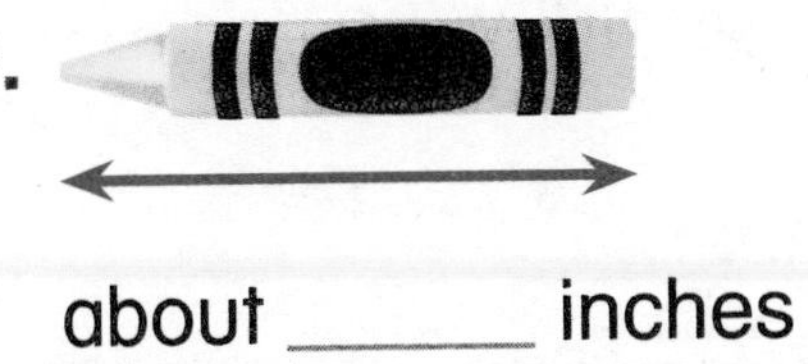

   about ______ inches

Set C

The measure of the height of a window takes *more* units of feet than yards.

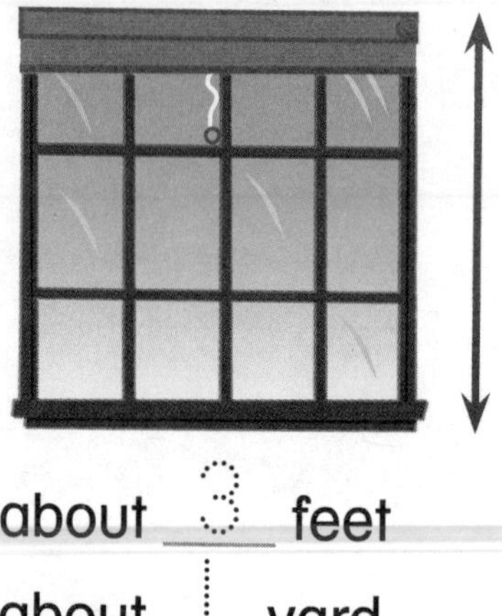

about 3 feet

about 1 yard

Measure the real object in inches and feet. Circle the unit you needed *more* of.

5.

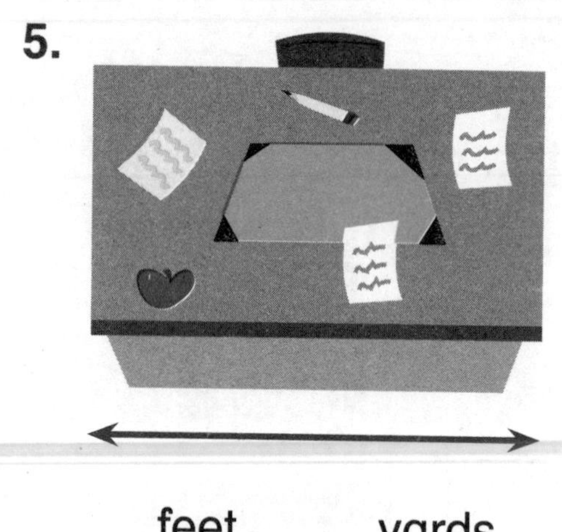

about ______ feet

about ______ yards

feet yards

Set D

You can measure the length of an object to the nearest centimeter.

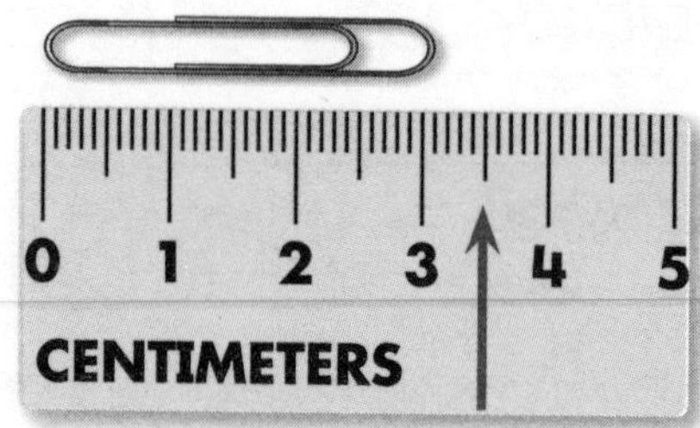

The paper clip is less than halfway between 3 and 4.

So, use the lesser number.

The paper clip is about 3 cm.

Find real objects like the ones shown. Use a ruler to measure their lengths.

6.

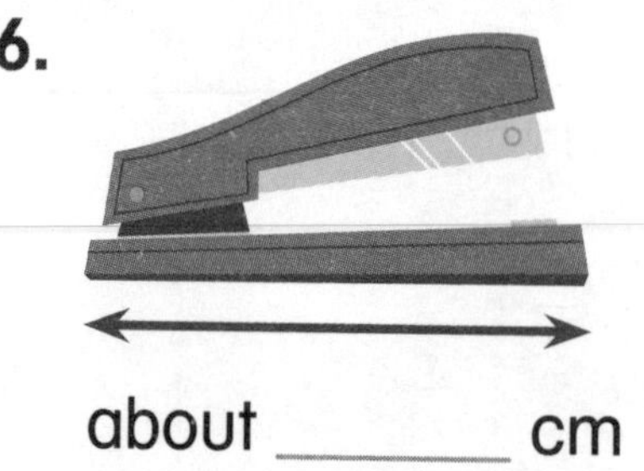

about ______ cm

7.

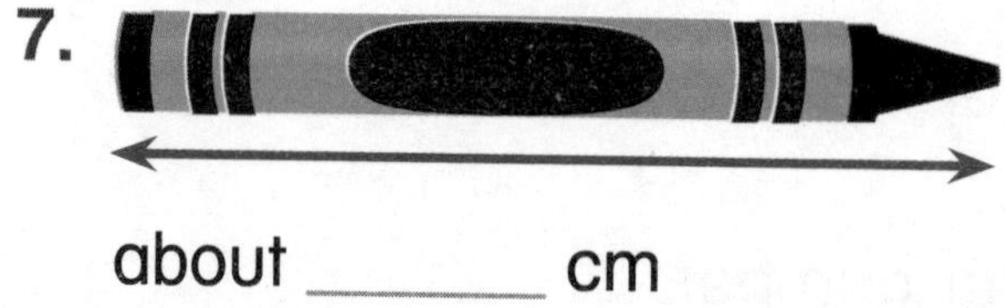

about ______ cm

Name ______________________

Set E

There are 100 centimeters in 1 meter.

about 1 centimeter

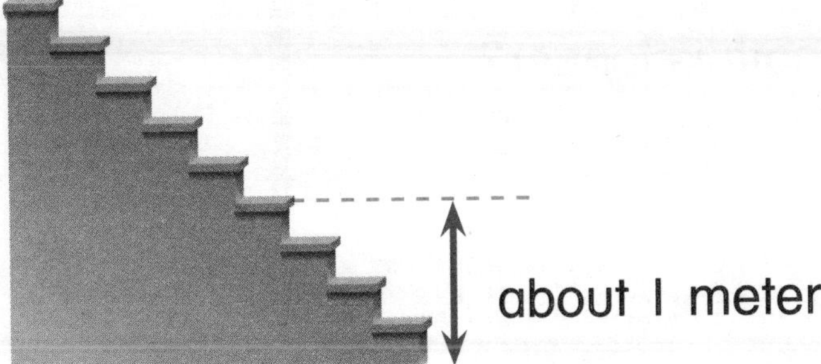

about 1 meter

Circle the picture of the real object that is about each length or height.

8. about 1 centimeter

9. about 1 meter

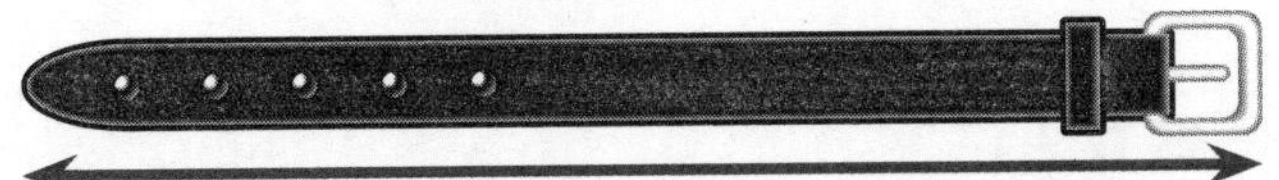

Set F

The measure of the height of this cart takes *fewer* units of meters than centimeters.

about 93 centimeters

about 1 meter

Measure the real object in centimeters and meters. Circle the unit you needed *fewer* of.

10.

about ______ centimeters

about ______ meters

centimeters

meters

Set G

Which path is longer? How much longer? Measure each part. Then add the lengths.

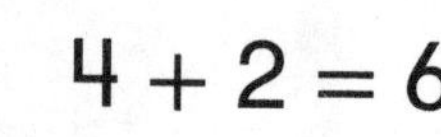

$4 + 2 = 6$
The purple path is 6 cm.

$2 + 3 = 5$
The green path is 5 cm.

Subtract the lengths to compare.

6 − 5 = 1

The purple path is about 1 centimeter longer.

Use a centimeter ruler. Measure each path.

11. Red path: _____ centimeters

12. Blue path: _____ centimeters

13. Which path is longer?

_____

How much longer is it?

about _____ centimeters longer

Set H

Thinking Habits

Attend to Precision

Which unit of measure will I use?

Is my work precise?

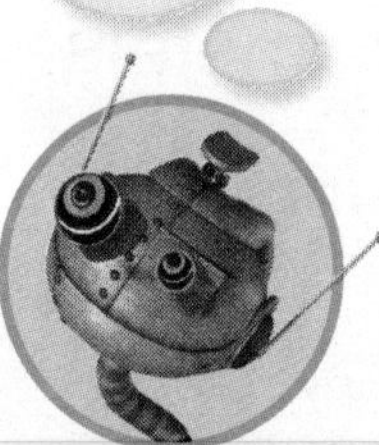

14. Measure the length of the bottom of this page in feet and in inches.

about _____ ft about _____ in.

15. Which measure in Item 14 is more precise? Explain.

_____

_____

_____

Name ______________________________

1. Estimate. About how tall is the flower?

Ⓐ about 5 cm

Ⓑ about 10 cm

Ⓒ about 15 cm

Ⓓ about 1 meter

2. Draw a line from each estimate to a matching object.

about 1 yard

about 1 foot

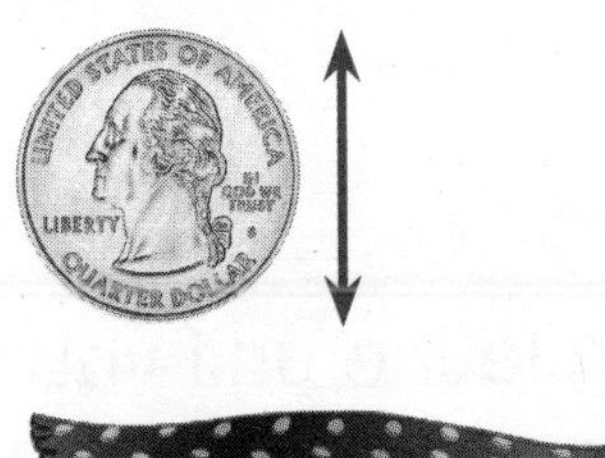

about 1 inch

3. Which units would you need the fewest of to measure the height of a fence?

Ⓐ inches

Ⓑ feet

Ⓒ yards

Ⓓ all the same

4. Dan measures the width of a window with a yardstick. He says it measures 3. Is his answer precise? Explain.

____

____

____

____

5. Use a ruler to measure each line to the nearest centimeter.
Which are about 3 centimeters long?
Choose all that apply.

- ☐ ————————
- ☐ ——————
- ☐ —————
- ☐ ——————
- ☐ none of them

6. Use a ruler to measure the length of the pencil in inches.
Which is the correct measurement?

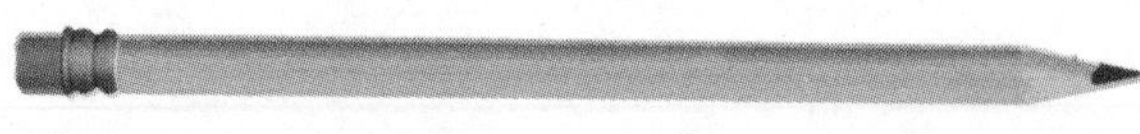

Ⓐ 2 inches
Ⓑ 3 inches
Ⓒ 4 inches
Ⓓ 5 inches

7. Circle the unit you need fewer of to measure the length of a kitchen.

centimeters meters

Circle the unit you need fewer of to measure the length of a table.

feet yards

8. Use a ruler. Measure each path to the nearest inch.

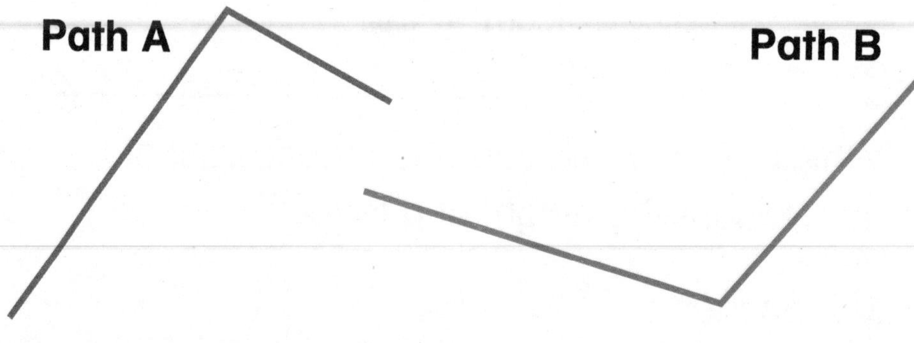

Which path is longer? ________

How much longer? about ________ longer

Name ____________________

9. Use a ruler. Measure the length of the marker to the nearest centimeter. How long is the marker?

Ⓐ 6 centimeters
Ⓑ 9 centimeters
Ⓒ 12 centimeters
Ⓓ 15 centimeters

10. A path has two parts.
The total length of the path is 15 cm.
One part of the path is 9 cm long.
How long is the other part?

Ⓐ 24 cm
Ⓑ 15 cm
Ⓒ 9 cm
Ⓓ 6 cm

11. Use a ruler. Measure each path to the nearest centimeter.

Path A 

Path B 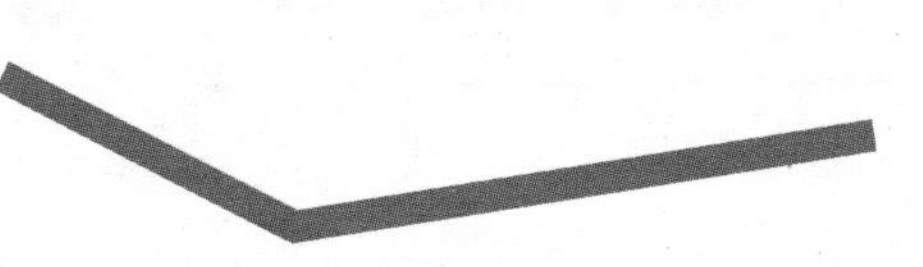

Which path is longer? ________

How much longer?

about ________________ longer

12. Measure the gray line with tools you need to be precise. Choose all the measurements that are precise.

☐ 4 centimeters
☐ 4 inches
☐ 10
☐ 10 centimeters
☐ 4

13. Juan uses different units to measure a jump rope. Compare the measurements. Choose all that apply.

- ☐ more inches than feet
- ☐ fewer inches than feet
- ☐ more centimeters than meters
- ☐ fewer centimeters than meters
- ☐ more yards than feet
- ☐ fewer yards than feet

14. What is the length of the crayon to the nearest centimeter? What would be the combined length of two crayons?

0 1 2 3 4 5 6 7 8 9
CENTIMETERS

The crayon is _____ centimeters.

Two crayons would measure _____ centimeters.

15. Kim's softball bat is 1 yard long. She uses 3 bats to measure the length of the classroom whiteboard. About how long is the whiteboard?

Ⓐ 3 inches
Ⓑ 3 feet
Ⓒ 1 yard
Ⓓ 3 yards

16. Kevin measured the length of a car in inches and in feet. Why is the number of feet less than the number of inches?

96 inches or 8 feet

____

____

____

____

Name ______________________

Happy Hiking!

The Torres family loves to hike.
They use this map to plan their hiking trip.

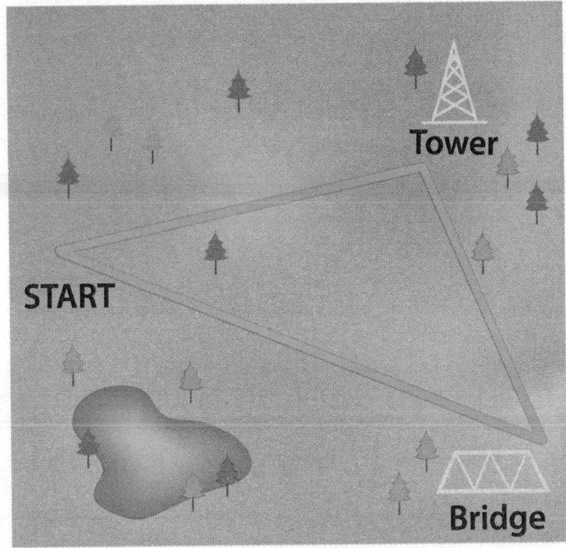

1. Use a centimeter ruler.
Find the total length of the triangle hiking path shown on the map.

about ____ centimeters

Explain how you found the length.

____

____

____

____

2. Debbie Torres uses a backpack for hiking.
She wants to measure its width.
She wants to be precise. Should she use inches, feet, or yards?
Explain your answer.

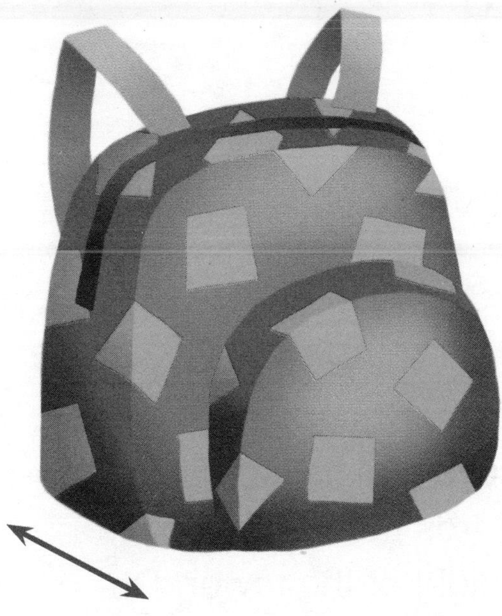

Width of a backpack

____

____

____

____

3. Daniel Torres estimates the height of his water bottle. Is his estimate reasonable? Explain.

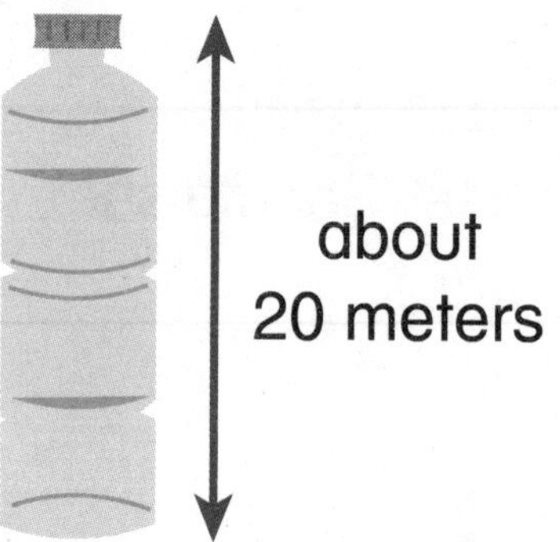

4. Maria Torres says that it would take more units of yards than feet to measure the height of the tower. Do you agree? Circle Yes or No. Explain.

Yes No

5. On the hike, the Torres family sees a caterpillar. Use the picture below to answer the questions.

Part A

To be precise, which unit would you choose to measure the length of the caterpillar? Explain.

Part B

Estimate and then measure the length of the caterpillar. Then explain how you measured.

Estimate: ______

Measurement: ______

Shapes and Their Attributes

Essential Question: How can shapes be described, compared, and broken into parts?

Different tools have different shapes!

How does the shape of a tool help it work?

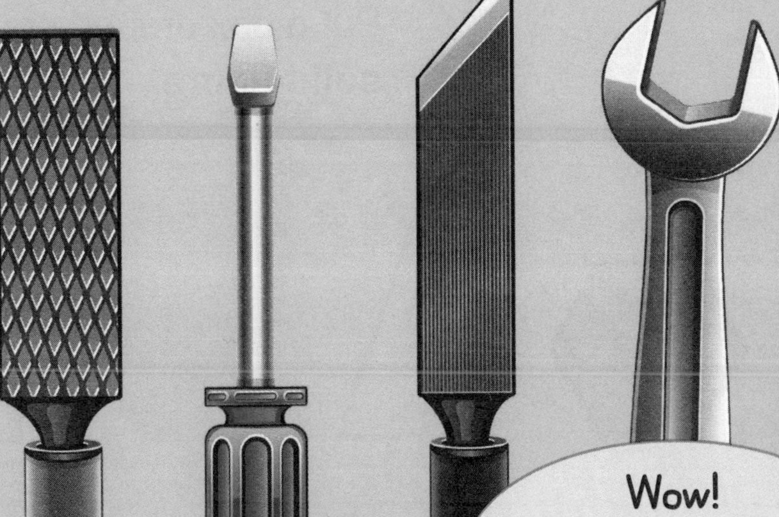

Wow! Let's do this project and learn more.

enVision® STEM Project: All About Shape

Find Out Draw pictures of tools used for gardening, cooking, or fixing. Describe the shape of each tool. Tell how the shape of each tool helps it work.

Journal: Make a Book Show your work in a book. In your book, also:

- Choose a tool that you use at school. Tell how the shape of the tool helps it work.
- Draw and describe polygon shapes.

Name ______________________

Review What You Know

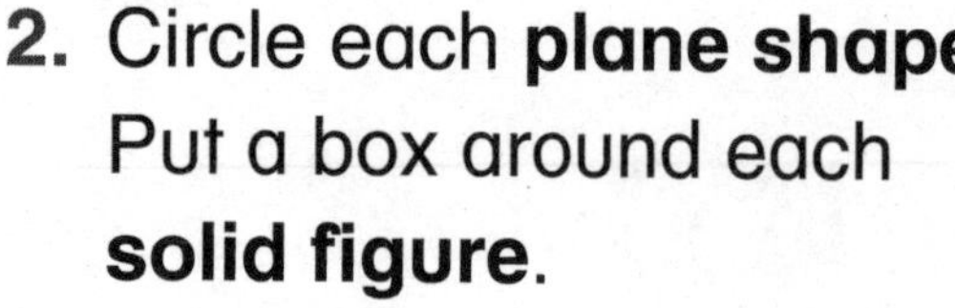

Vocabulary

1. Circle the shape that has 6 **sides**.

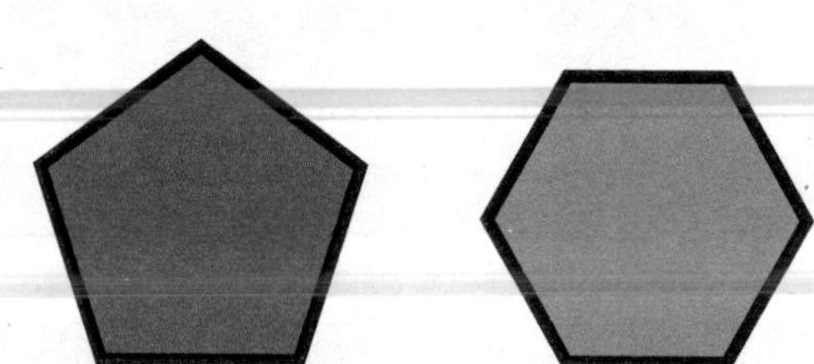

2. Circle each **plane shape**. Put a box around each **solid figure**.

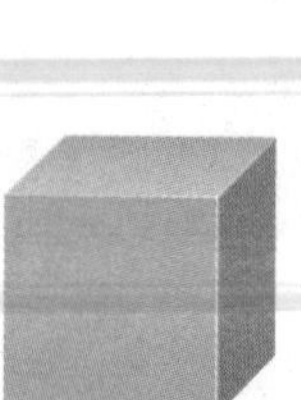

3. Put a box around the circle that shows **fourths**.

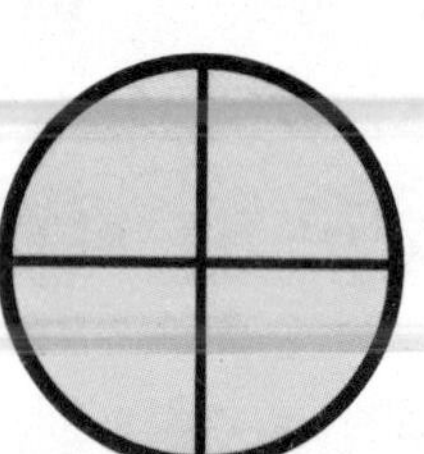

Basic Facts

4. Write each sum.

$$\begin{array}{r} 5 \\ +8 \\ \hline \end{array} \qquad \begin{array}{r} 7 \\ +7 \\ \hline \end{array} \qquad \begin{array}{r} 10 \\ +10 \\ \hline \end{array}$$

5. Write each difference.

$$\begin{array}{r} 17 \\ -9 \\ \hline \end{array} \qquad \begin{array}{r} 15 \\ -6 \\ \hline \end{array} \qquad \begin{array}{r} 12 \\ -8 \\ \hline \end{array}$$

Math Story

6. Edna has a bookcase with 5 shelves. She places 5 books in a row on each shelf. Write an equation that shows how many books Edna has in all.

____

____

Name ______________________________

Pick a Project

PROJECT 13A

What shapes can you find in a tile design?

Project: Create a Tile Design

PROJECT 13B

How do architects design a house?

Project: Draw Your Dream Building

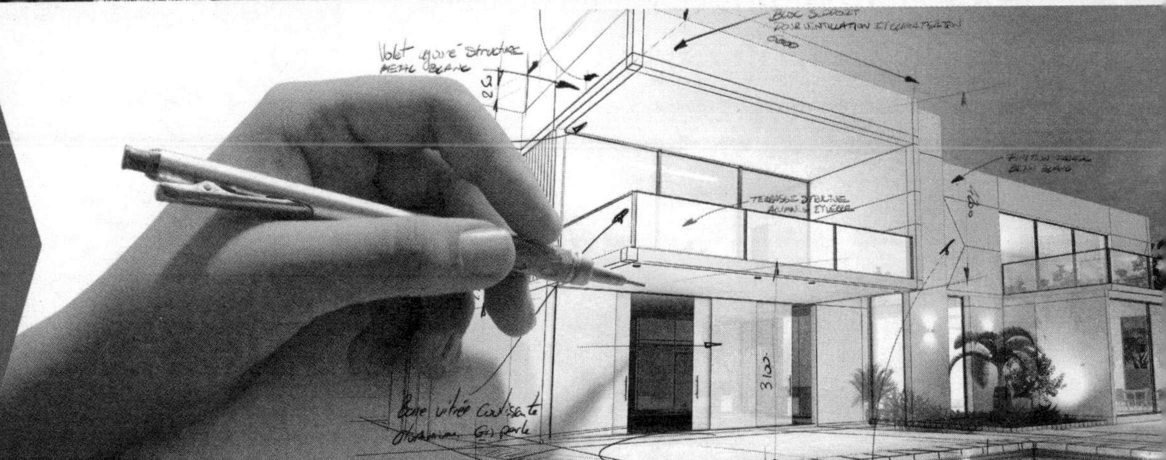

PROJECT 13C

What national landmarks are in your state?

Project: Build a Landmark

3-ACT MATH PREVIEW

Math Modeling

Straw Shaped

Before watching the video, think:

What can you build with straws? What kind of shapes? How can you compare those shapes?

I can ...

model with math to solve a problem that involves using properties of 2-D shapes and measurements.

Name ______________________

Activity

Lesson 13-1

2-Dimensional Shapes

I can ...

recognize shapes by how they look.

I can also make math arguments.

Solve & Share

Look at the picture.
How many triangles can you find?
Trace each triangle.
Be ready to explain how you know you have found them all.

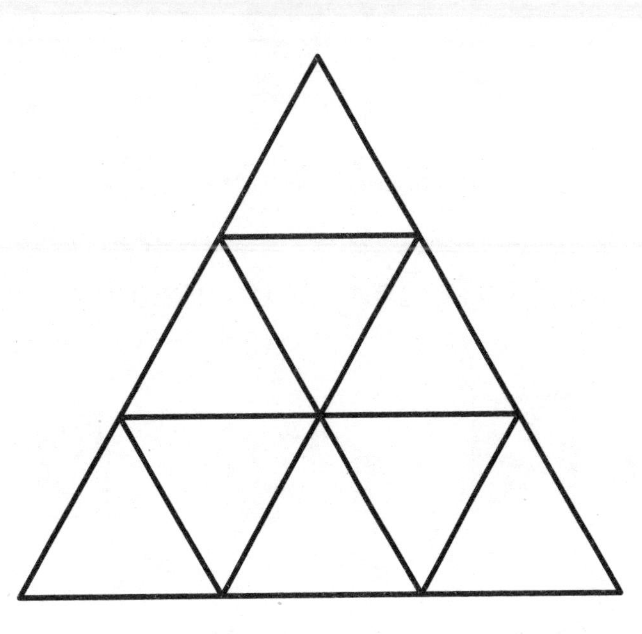

_____ triangles

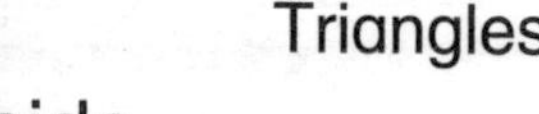

Visual Learning Bridge

Triangles	**Quadrilaterals**	**Pentagons**	**Hexagons**
	  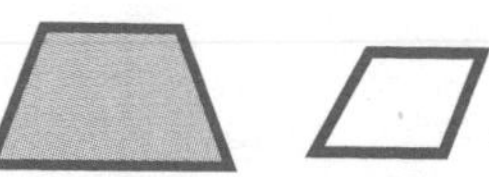		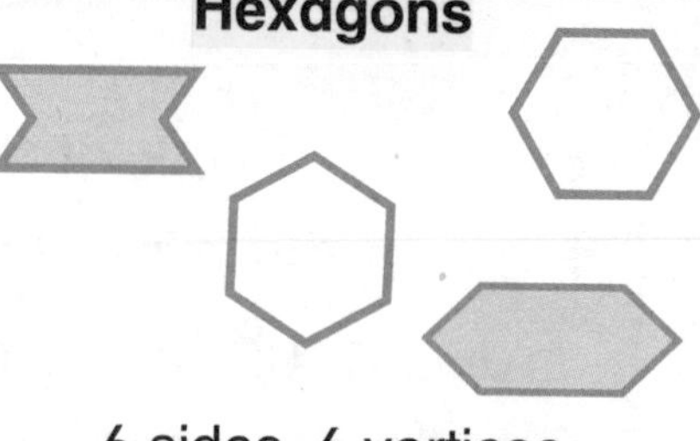
3 sides, 3 **vertices**	4 sides, 4 vertices	5 sides, 5 vertices	6 sides, 6 vertices
Not Triangles	Not Quadrilaterals	Not Pentagons	Not Hexagons
	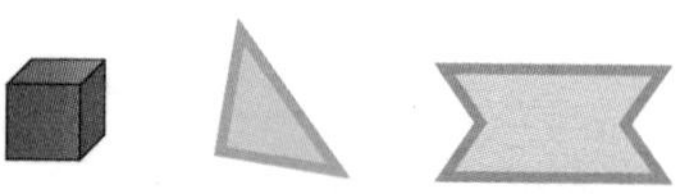		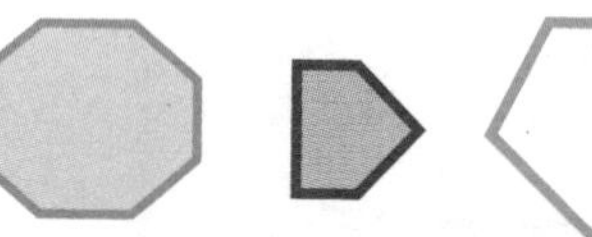

side

vertex

Convince Me! How do sides and vertices help you name a plane shape?

Guided Practice

Match each shape to its name.

1.

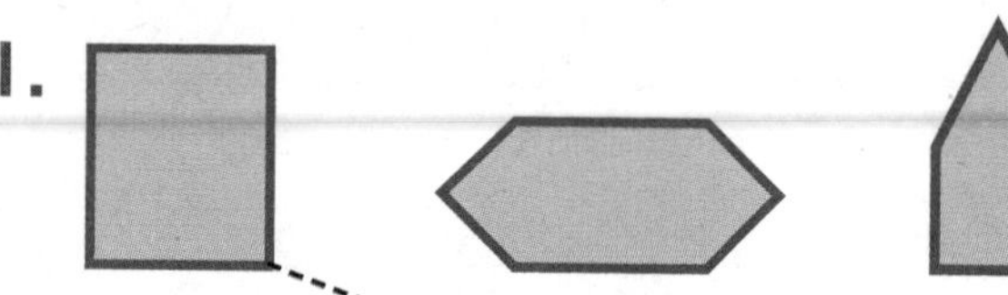

triangle quadrilateral pentagon hexagon

Tell how many sides and vertices. Name each shape.

2.

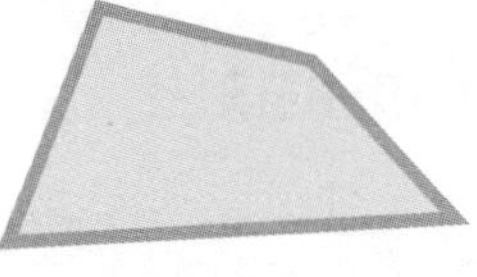

____ sides

____ vertices

Shape: __________

3.

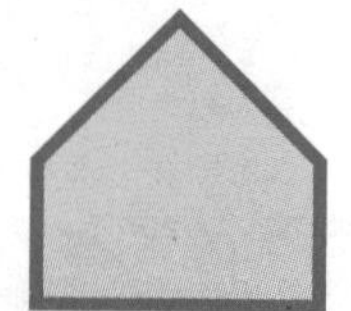

____ sides

____ vertices

Shape: __________

Name ______________________

Tools Assessment

Independent Practice

Match each shape to its name.

4. 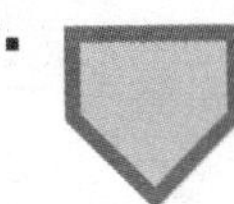   

triangle quadrilateral pentagon hexagon

5. 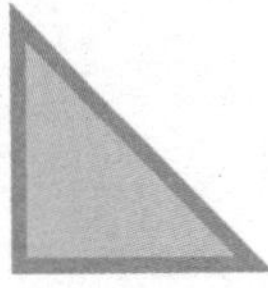   

triangle quadrilateral pentagon hexagon

Draw the shape. Tell how many sides and vertices.

6. Quadrilateral

_____ sides

_____ vertices

7. Hexagon

_____ sides

_____ vertices

8. Triangle

_____ sides

_____ vertices

9. Higher Order Thinking Bianca drew a triangle and a pentagon. How many sides and vertices did she draw in all? Draw the shapes.

_____ sides _____ vertices

Problem Solving Solve each problem.

10. Model Marcos has 4 toothpicks. He places them as shown. What shape can Marcos make if he adds one more toothpick?

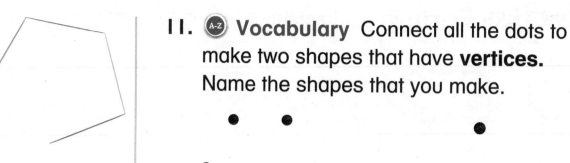

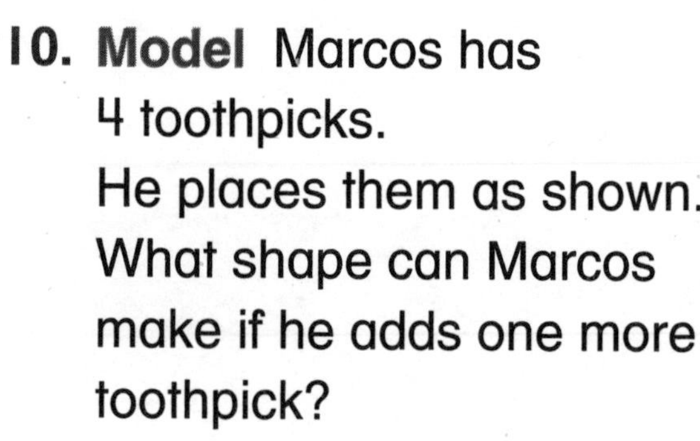

____

11. Vocabulary Connect all the dots to make two shapes that have **vertices.** Name the shapes that you make.

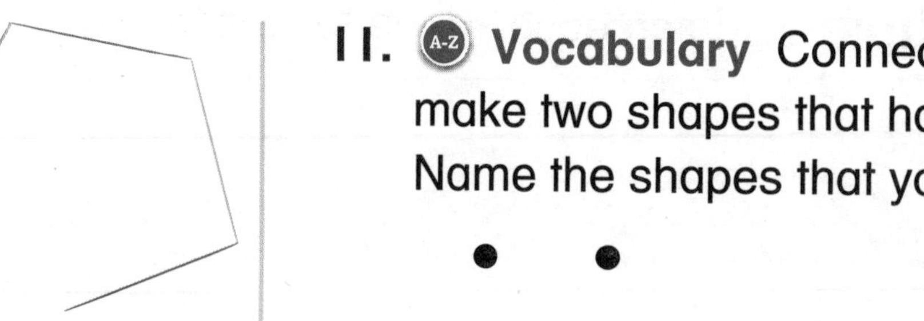

_______________ _______________

12. Higher Order Thinking Randall said that a square is a quadrilateral. Susan said that a square is a square, so it is not a quadrilateral. Who is correct? Explain.

____
____
____
____
____
____

13. Assessment Practice Which shape is **NOT** a hexagon?

Ⓐ

Ⓑ

Ⓒ

Ⓓ

Think: What do I know about hexagons?

Name ______________________________

Activity

Lesson 13-2

Polygons and Angles

I can ...
describe plane shapes by how they look.

I can also look for patterns.

Solve & Share

Look at the three plane shapes below. How are they alike? How are they different?

Measure the length of the sides to help describe them. Name each shape.

______ ______ ______

 Visual Learning  Glossary

Visual Learning Bridge

Polygon

A closed plane shape with 3 or more sides is called a polygon.

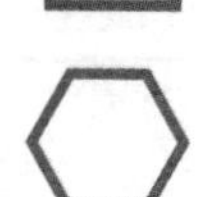

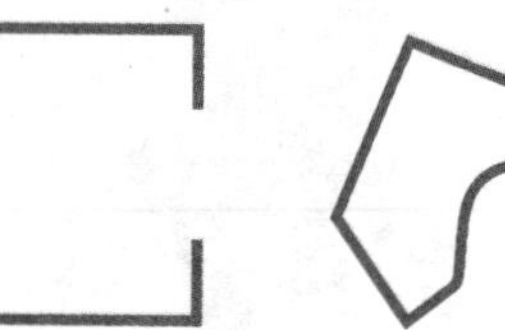

You know the names of these polygons.

Not Polygons

Polygons are not open shapes. Polygons do not have curved sides.

A circle is not a polygon.

Angle

Polygons have angles. They have the same number of angles as sides and vertices.

A triangle has 3 angles.

Right Angle

A right angle forms a square corner. A square has 4 right angles. The pentagon below has 3 right angles.

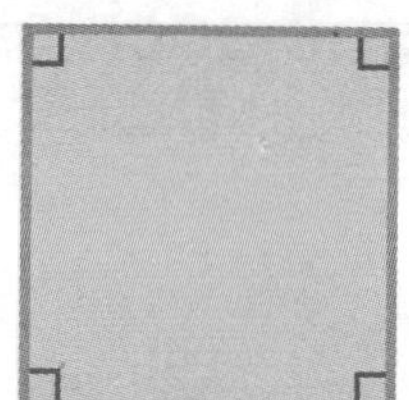

Convince Me! How many angles does this shape have? How many right angles? Name the shape.

Guided Practice Write the number of angles and then name the shape.

1.  ____ angles

Shape: ____________

2. 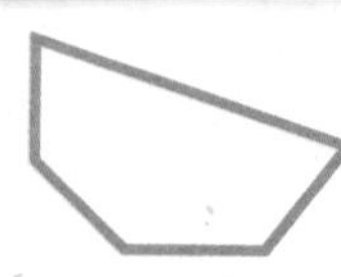 ____ angles

Shape: ____________

3. 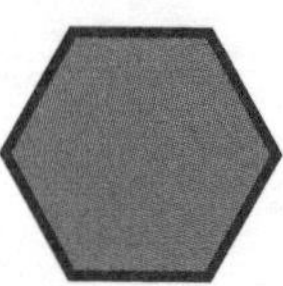 ____ angles

Shape: ____________

4. 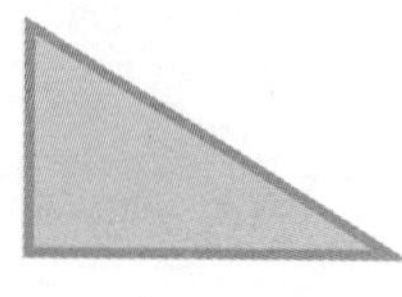 ____ angles

Shape: ____________

Name ____________________

Tools Assessment

Independent Practice

Write the number of angles and then name the shape.

5. ____ angles

Shape: ____________

6. ____ angles

Shape: ____________

7. ____ angles

Shape: ____________

8. ____ angles

Shape: ____________

9. ____ angles

Shape: ____________

10. ____ angles

Shape: ____________

11. **Higher Order Thinking** Draw a polygon with 2 right angles and 2 angles that are not right angles. Name the shape you draw.

How many angles will your polygon have in all?

Problem Solving Solve each problem.

12. **Be Precise** Which plane shapes are sewn together in the soccer ball?

13. **enVision® STEM** Bees make honeycomb. The honeycomb shape uses less wax than other shapes. Name the shape. Tell how many angles the shape has.

14. **Higher Order Thinking** Draw a polygon shape that has 7 angles. How many sides does the polygon have? How many vertices does it have?

15. **Assessment Practice** Name the shape of the sign below. Write 3 things that describe the shape.

Name ______________________________

Activity

Lesson 13-3

Draw 2-Dimensional Shapes

I can ...
draw polygon shapes.

I can also be precise in my work.

Solve & Share

Draw a polygon with 3 sides that are the same length. Then draw a polygon with 3 sides that are different lengths.

Measure the lengths of the sides you drew. Tell 4 ways the shapes are alike.

Sides: Same Length **Sides: Different Lengths**

____

____

____

____

Visual Learning Bridge

Draw a polygon with 5 vertices.

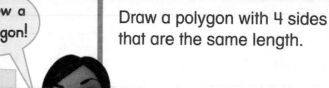

My polygon will have 5 vertices. That means it will have 5 sides, too!

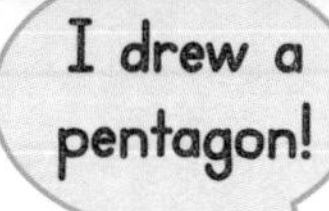

I drew a pentagon!

Draw a polygon with 4 sides that are the same length.

My next polygon will have 4 sides. A polygon with 4 sides is called a quadrilateral!

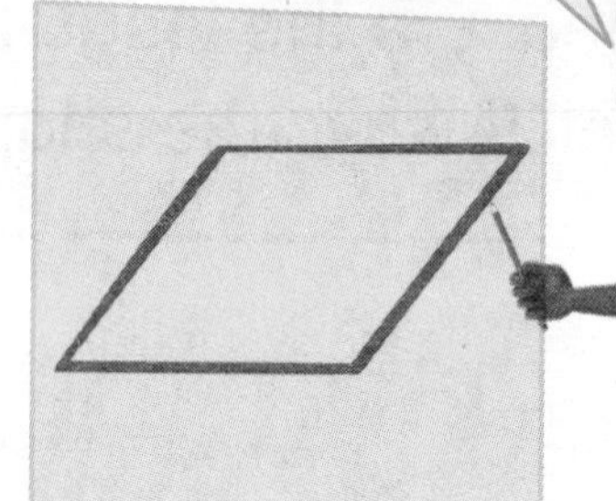

I drew a special kind of quadrilateral, called a rhombus. A rhombus has 4 sides that are all the same length.

Convince Me! Draw a quadrilateral with 4 sides that are the same length and with 4 right angles. Write 2 names for the quadrilateral.

☆ **Guided Practice** ☆ Draw each shape. Complete the sentences.

1. Draw a polygon with 3 vertices.

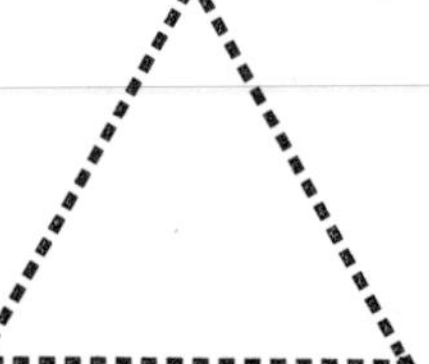

The polygon also has _____ sides.

The polygon is a _______________.

2. Draw a polygon with 6 sides.

The polygon also has _____ angles.

The polygon is a _______________.

Name ______________________________

Tools Assessment

Independent Practice

Draw each shape. Complete the sentences.

3. Draw a polygon with 3 vertices and 1 right angle.

The polygon also has

_____ sides.

The polygon is

a ____________________.

4. Draw a quadrilateral with opposite sides that are the same length.

The polygon also has

_____ vertices.

The polygon is

a ____________________.

5. Draw a polygon with 4 sides that are the same length.

The polygon also has

_____ angles.

The polygon is

a ____________________.

6. Draw a polygon with 4 sides that are different lengths.

The polygon also has

_____ angles.

The polygon is

a ____________________.

7. Draw a polygon with 5 vertices and 3 sides that are the same length.

The polygon also has

_____ sides in all.

The polygon is

a ____________________.

8. **Higher Order Thinking** Can you draw a polygon with 3 vertices and 4 sides? Explain.

Problem Solving Solve the problems below.

9. Be Precise Draw a rectangle with 4 equal sides.

What is another name for this shape?

____

10. Draw 3 shapes. The first shape is a quadrilateral. The number of vertices in each shape increases by one.

Name the third shape. _______________

11. Higher Order Thinking The owner of Joe's Fish Market wants a new sign. He wants the sign to have curved sides. Draw a sign for Joe's Fish Market.

Is the sign a polygon? Explain.

____

____

12. Assessment Practice David drew two different polygons. One of the polygons was a square. If David drew 9 sides and 9 vertices in all, what other polygon did David draw?

Ⓐ Ⓒ

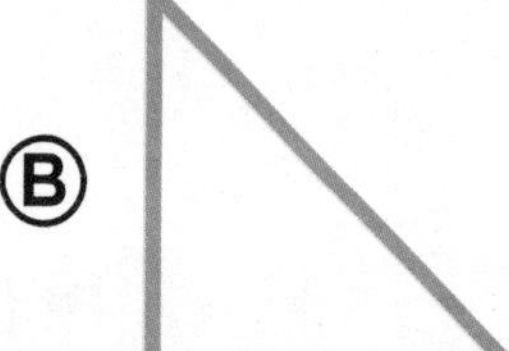

Ⓑ

Ⓓ

Name ____________________

Activity

Lesson 13-4
Cubes

I can ...
draw cubes and describe how they look.

I can also look for patterns.

Solve & Share

Describe the two shapes in 4 or more ways. Tell how they are different and how they are the same. Use a tool to include measurements in your description.

A **cube** is a solid figure with 6 equal **faces**, 12 **edges**, and 8 vertices.

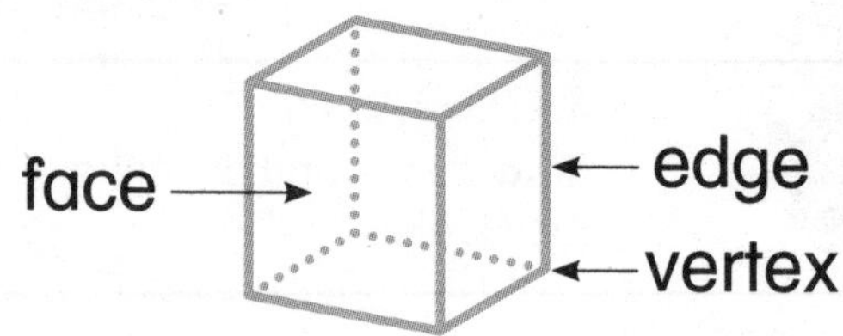

Each face is a square, with 4 equal edges and 4 right angles.

These are cubes.

These are **NOT** cubes.

You can use dot paper to draw a cube. The dashed lines show the edges that you can't see when you look at a solid cube.

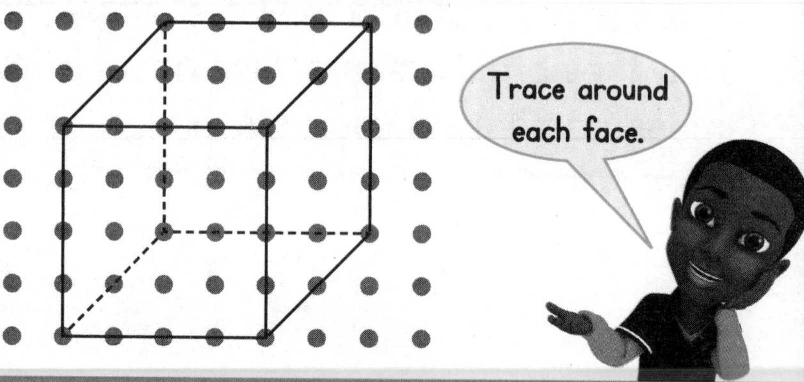

Convince Me! What solid figure has 6 equal faces?

____

What is the shape of each face?

____

Guided Practice Circle the cubes in the group of shapes. Be ready to explain how you know they are cubes.

1.   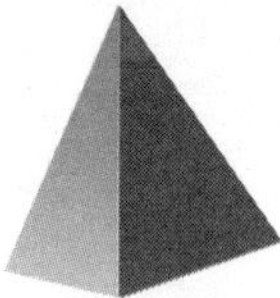 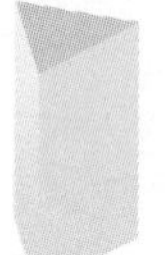 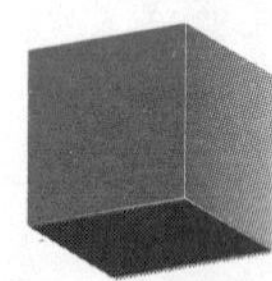

2. Use the dot paper. Draw a cube.

You can use the cube you traced as an example.

Name ______________________________

Independent Practice

Decide if the shape is a cube. Then draw a line from each shape to *cube* or ***NOT** a cube*.

3.

cube

NOT a cube

4. Trace the cube shown below.

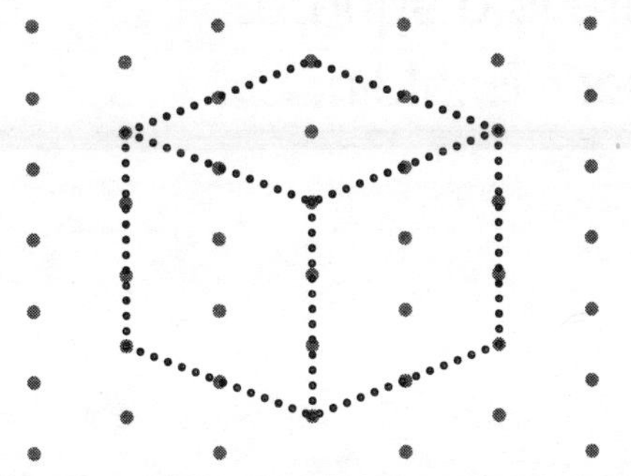

How many faces can you see?

____ faces

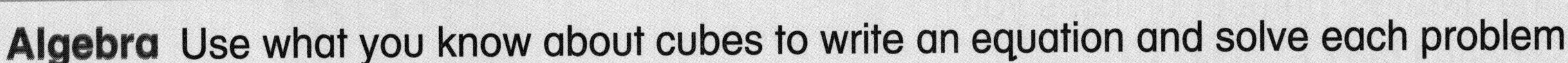

Algebra Use what you know about cubes to write an equation and solve each problem.

5. How many vertices do these two cubes have in all?

____ + ____ = ____

____ vertices

6. How many faces do these two cubes have in all?

____ + ____ = ____

____ faces

Problem Solving

Use what you know about cubes to solve each problem.

7. **Explain** Scott is holding a solid figure with 6 equal faces, 12 edges, and 8 vertices. Scott says the figure is a cube. Carmen says the figure is a square. Who is correct? Explain.

____

____

____

8. **Vocabulary** Circle the vocabulary word that completes the sentence.

vertices **faces** **edges**

A cube has 6 ____________.

9. **Higher Order Thinking** Use a place-value ones cube or another solid cube. Look at the cube as you turn it. Turn the cube in any direction.

What is the greatest number of faces you can see at one time? Explain.

____

____

____

10. **Assessment Practice** Complete the sentences about a cube.

A cube is a solid ____________.

A cube has _____ equal faces,

_____ vertices, and _____ edges.

Name ______________________

Activity

Lesson 13-5

Equal Shares

Solve & Share

How many equal squares cover this rectangle? How could you show this with an addition equation?

I can ...
cover rectangles with equal-size squares and count to find the total number of them.

I can also model with math.

Columns

Rows

_____ equal squares

Equation: ______________________

 Visual Learning A-Z Glossary

Visual Learning Bridge

How many red squares can cover this rectangle?

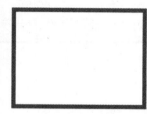

Begin like this:

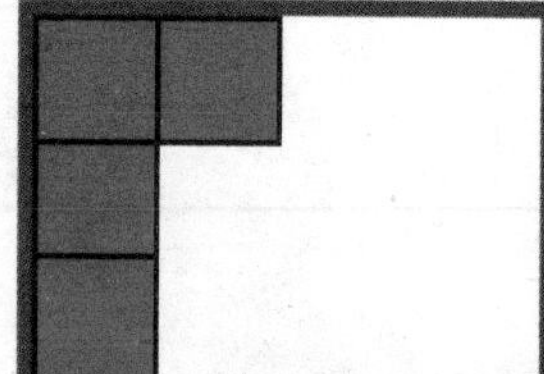

NOT like this:

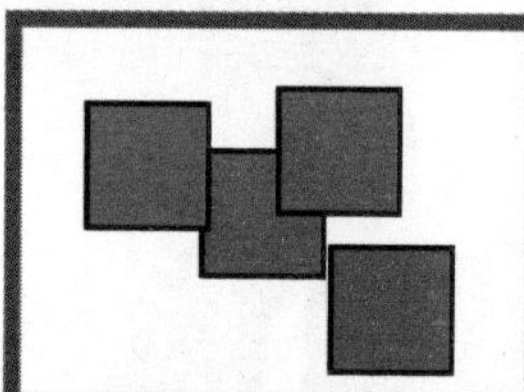

Count. Each row has 4 squares. You can add the squares by rows.

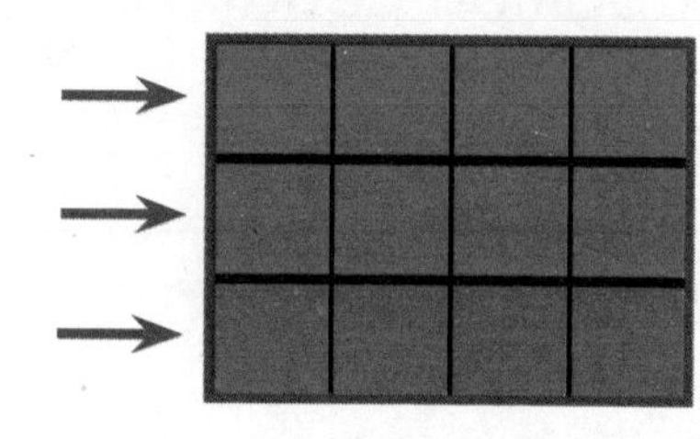

4 + 4 + 4 = 12

Count. Each column has 3 squares. You can add the squares by columns.

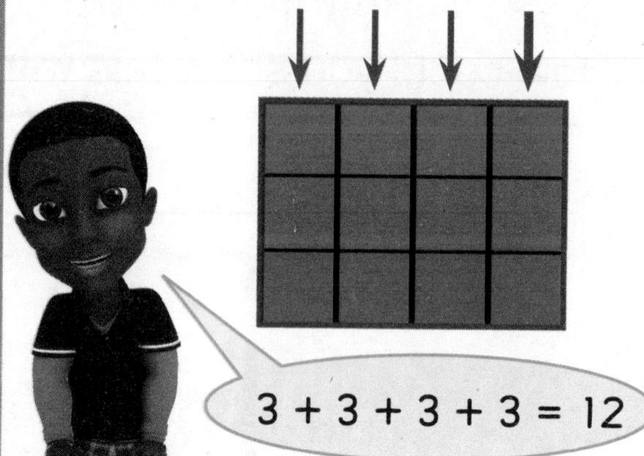

3 + 3 + 3 + 3 = 12

Convince Me! Explain how you can cover a rectangle with equal-sized squares to help you find the total number of them.

Guided Practice Solve.

1. Use square tiles to cover the rectangle. Trace the tiles. Column 1 is done for you.

2. Count and add. How many squares cover the rectangle?

Add by rows: ____ + ____ + ____ = ____

Add by columns:

____ + ____ + ____ + ____ + ____ + ____ = ____

Name ______________________

Tools Assessment

Independent Practice

Use square tiles to cover each rectangle. Trace the tiles. Count the squares.

3. 

Add by rows:

___ + ___ + ___ + ___ = ___

Add by columns:

___ + ___ + ___ + ___ + ___ = ___

4. 

Add by rows:

___ + ___ + ___ + ___ = ___

Add by columns:

___ + ___ + ___ + ___ = ___

5. **Number Sense** Draw a rectangle that is made up of 6 equal squares.

Problem Solving Solve each problem.

6. **Look for Patterns** Lisa bakes cornbread. She cuts it into equal square pieces. How many equal squares do you see? Write two equations to show the total number of square pieces.

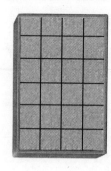

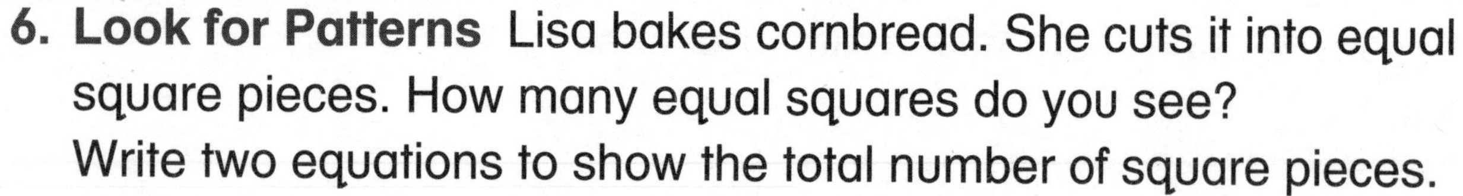

Rows: ____ + ____ + ____ + ____ + ____ + ____ = ____ pieces

Columns: ____ + ____ + ____ + ____ = ____ pieces

---

7. **Vocabulary** Label the **columns** and the **rows** for the large square below.

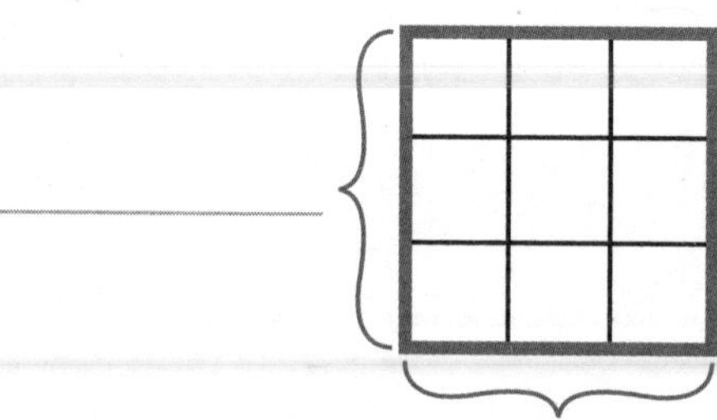

8. **Higher Order Thinking** Look at the large square in Item 7. What do you notice about the number of rows and the number of columns? Explain.

____

____

____

____

---

9. **Assessment Practice** Count the equal squares in the rows and columns of the rectangle. Then use the numbers on the cards to write the missing numbers in the equations.

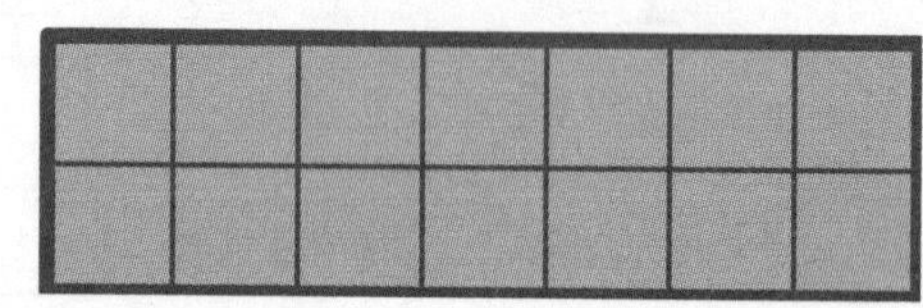

14 2 7

Rows: ____ + ____ = ____

Columns: ____ + ____ + ____ + ____ + ____ + ____ + ____ = ____

Name ______________________________

Lesson 13-6
Partition Shapes

I can ... show circles and rectangles in halves, thirds, and fourths.

I can also reason about math.

Solve & Share

Fold a paper square one time to make equal shares. How many equal shares are there?

Fold a different square 2 times to make equal shares. How many equal shares are there?

Draw your fold lines on the squares below. What can you say about the number of folds and the number of equal shares?

1 Fold	2 Folds
____ equal shares	____ equal shares

Visual Learning | A-Z Glossary

Visual Learning Bridge

Are these shares equal?

2 **equal shares**

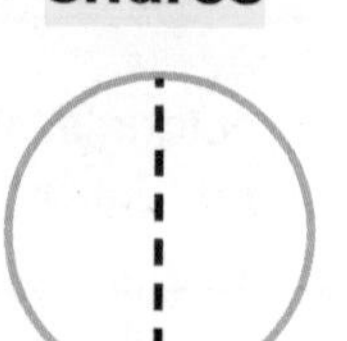

These shares are **halves**.

NOT equal shares

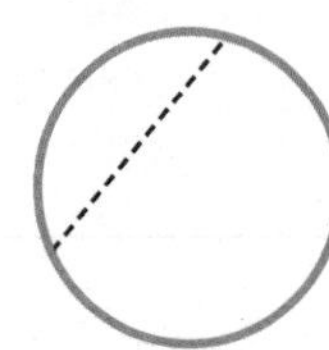

These shares are not halves.

Are these shares equal?

3 equal shares

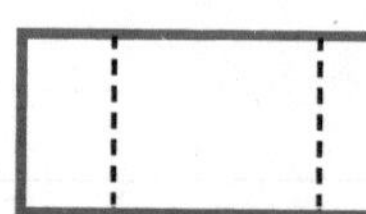

These shares are **thirds**.

NOT equal shares

These shares are not thirds.

Are these shares equal?

4 equal shares

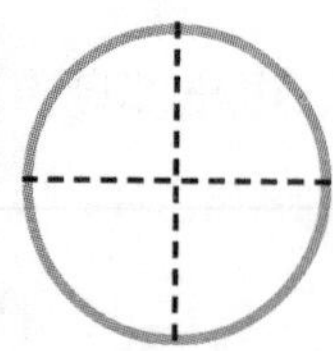

These shares are **fourths**.

NOT equal shares

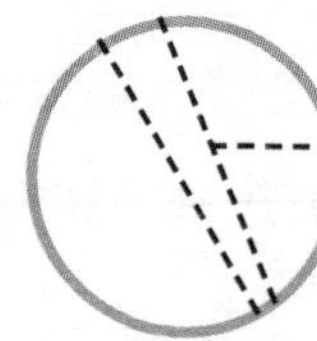

These shares are not fourths.

You can show equal shares in different ways.

Each share is a fourth of the whole.

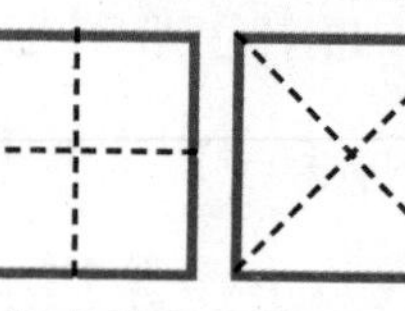

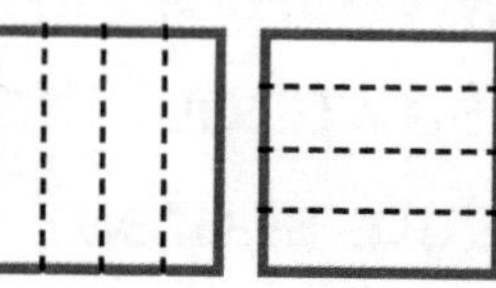

Convince Me! Show this rectangle with three equal shares. How many thirds is one share? How many thirds is the whole rectangle?

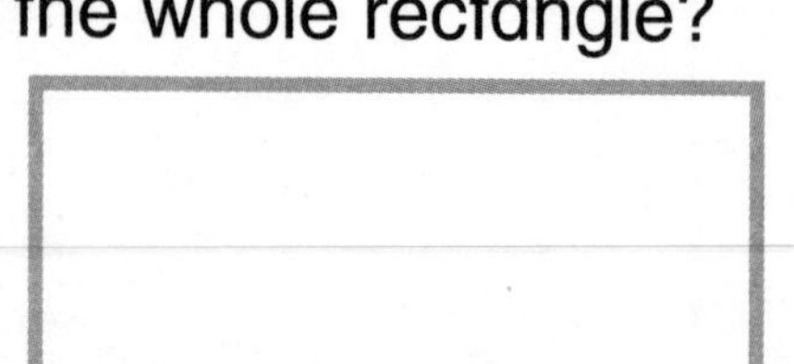

Guided Practice

Solve each problem.

1. Show each square in halves. Show four different ways.

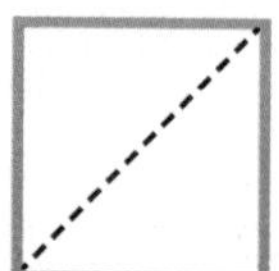 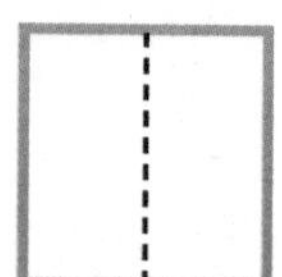 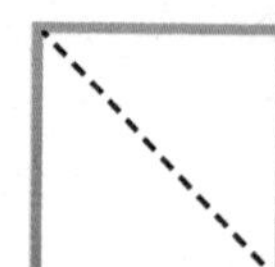 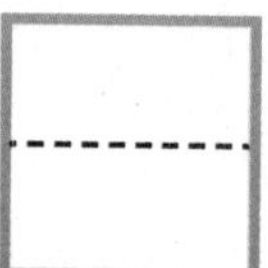

2. Tell what part of the whole each equal share is. Write *a half of, a third of,* or *a fourth of.*

  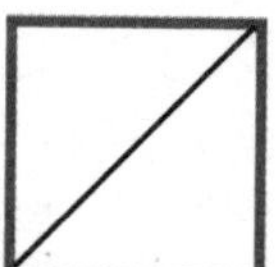

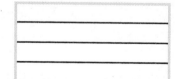

______ ______ ______

Name ____

Independent Practice Show each shape with the number of equal shares given. Show 2 ways. Then complete the sentences.

3. 3 equal shares

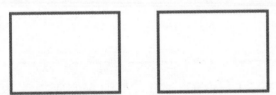

Each share is ______________ the whole.

Each whole is ______________.

4. 4 equal shares

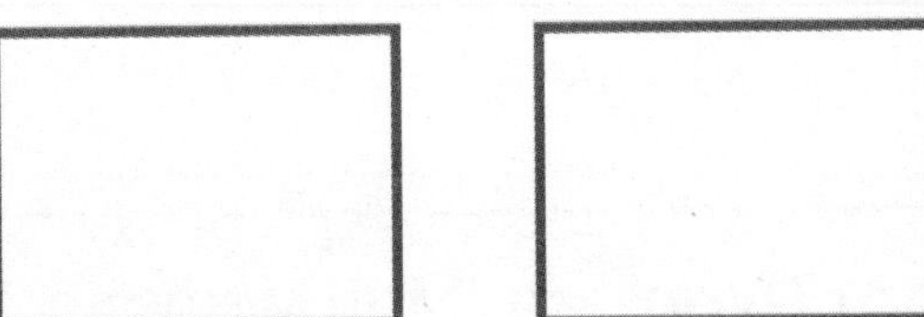

Each share is ______________ the whole.

Each whole is ______________.

5. 2 equal shares

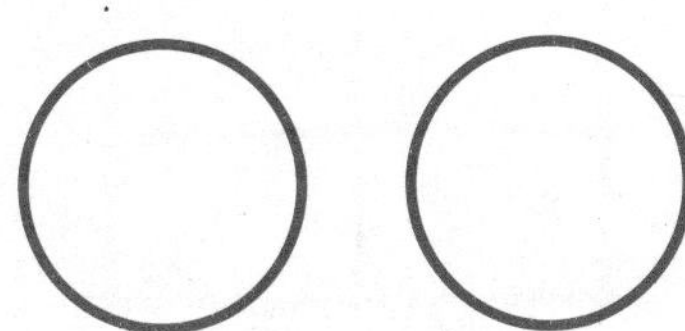

Each share is ______________ the whole.

Each whole is ______________.

6. Higher Order Thinking Draw what comes next.

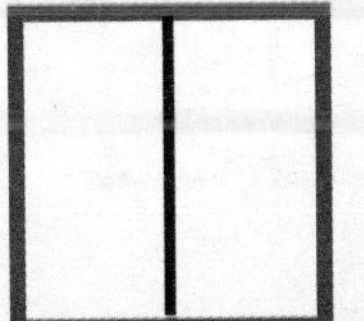      

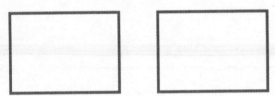

Problem Solving Solve each problem.

7. **Model** Leon cut a waffle into halves. Draw lines to show 3 different ways he could have cut the waffle.

8. **enVision® STEM** Tina is planting a garden. She wants to have equal parts for beans, for tomatoes, and for peppers. Draw a picture of how she could plant her garden.

9. **Higher Order Thinking** Draw lines on the picture to solve the problem.

4 friends want to share a watermelon. How could they cut the watermelon so each friend gets an equal share?

Each friend will get ______________.

10. **Assessment Practice** Matt wants a flag that shows fourths. Which flags could Matt use? Choose all that apply.

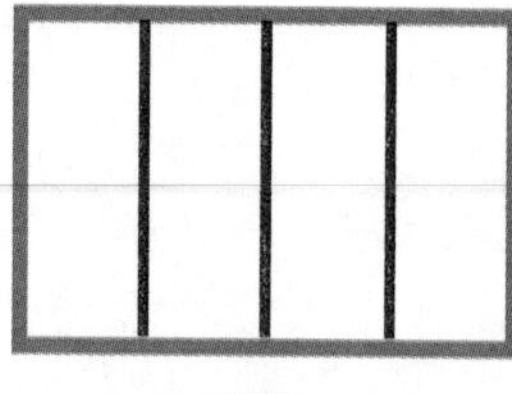 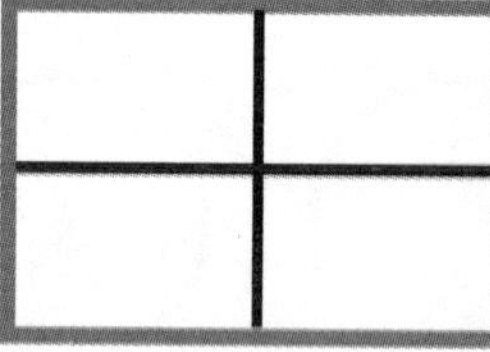

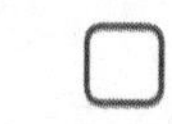 ☐

 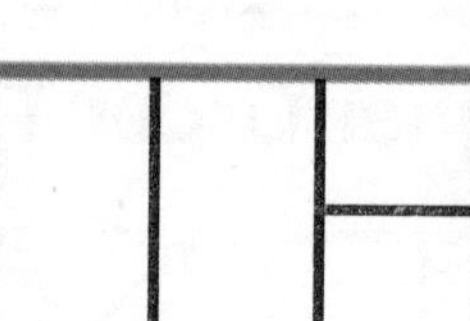 

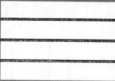

☐ ☐

Name ______________________________

Lesson 13-7

Equal Shares, Different Shapes

I can ...
make equal shares that do not have the same shape.

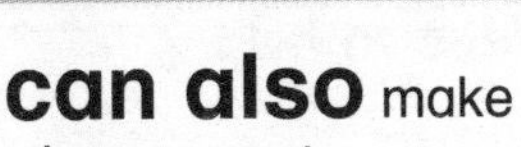

I can also make math arguments.

Solve & Share Use a crayon to show 4 equal shares of this pizza. Compare your answer with a partner. Did you both make 4 equal shares? Do your shares look the same?

Visual Learning A-Z Glossary

Visual Learning Bridge

How can this square be shown with 3 equal shares?

You can use the smaller squares to help.

You can draw lines to make 3 columns or 3 rows.

These show equal shares that are all the same shape.

This shows equal shares that are **NOT** all the same shape.

Each share is 3 squares. The shares are equal.

Equal shares can be different shapes.

Each way shows 3 equal shares.

Convince Me! How can you check to make sure all of the shares are equal?

Guided Practice Draw lines to show 2 equal shares. Each way should be different.

1.  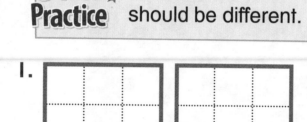

2. How many squares are in each equal share of the rectangles?

____

3. Describe the equal shares and the whole.

Each share is a half of the whole.

Each whole is two halves.

Name ______________________

Tools Assessment

Independent Practice

Draw lines in each rectangle to show 4 equal shares. Each way should be different. Then answer the questions.

4. Show equal shares that are the **same shape**.

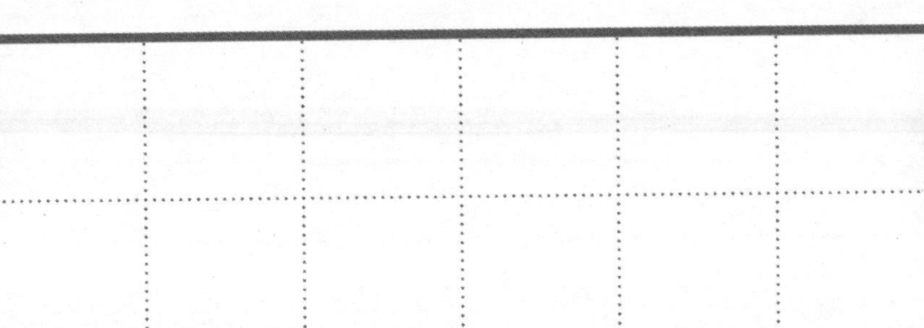

Show equal shares that are **different shapes**.

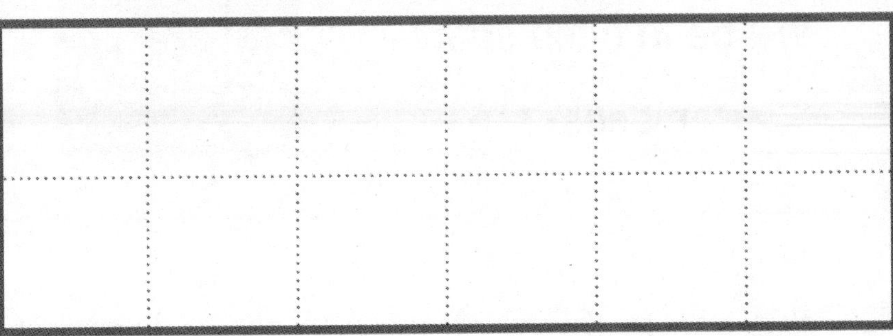

5. How many squares are in each equal share in Item 4? _____

6. Describe the equal shares and the whole in Item 4.

Each share is ______________ the whole.

Each whole is ______________.

Draw lines to show 3 equal shares in two different ways.

7.

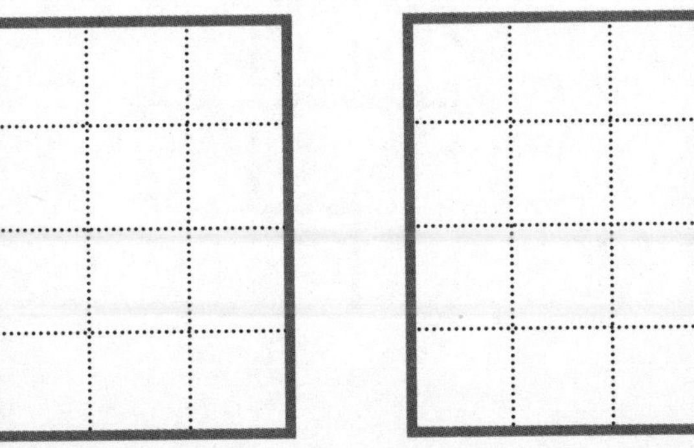

8. Higher Order Thinking How can equal shares in a rectangle have different shapes?

____

____

____

Problem Solving Solve each problem.

9. Allen wants to share this pan of corn bread with 3 friends. Allen and his friends will each get an equal share.

How many pieces will be in each share?

_____ pieces

10. **Explain** Greg says that equal shares can be different in shape and size. Is Greg correct? Explain.

____

____

____

11. **Higher Order Thinking** Donna drew the line in this rectangle to make 2 equal shares. Are the shares equal? Why or why not?

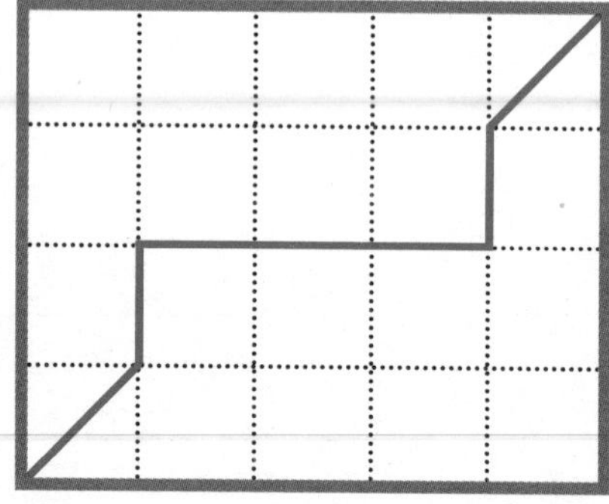

____

____

____

____

12. **Assessment Practice** Meg shows a rectangle with 3 equal shares that are **NOT** the same shape. Which could be Meg's rectangle?

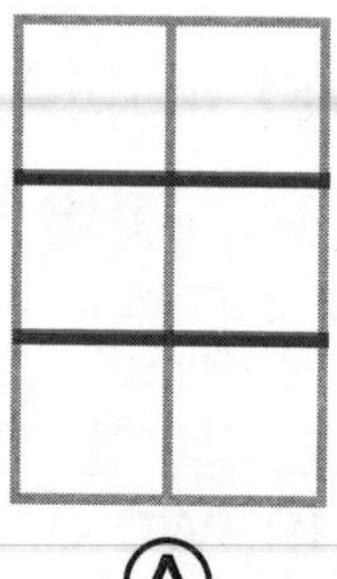

Ⓐ

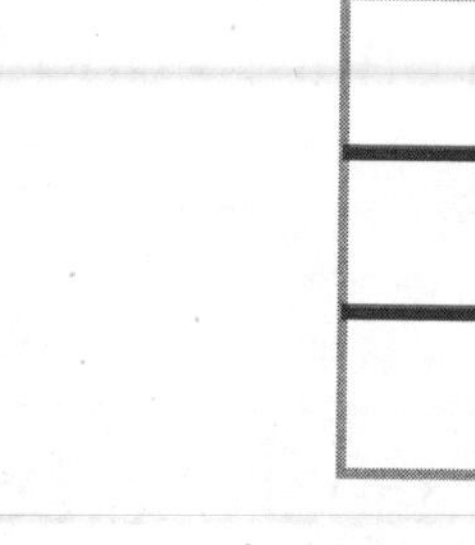

Ⓒ

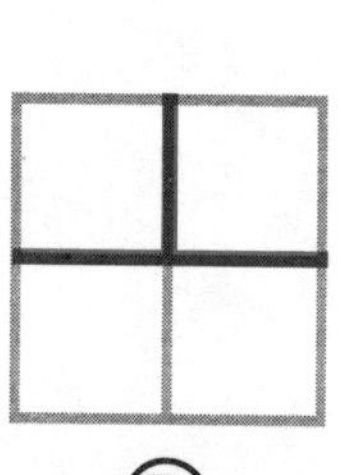

Ⓑ

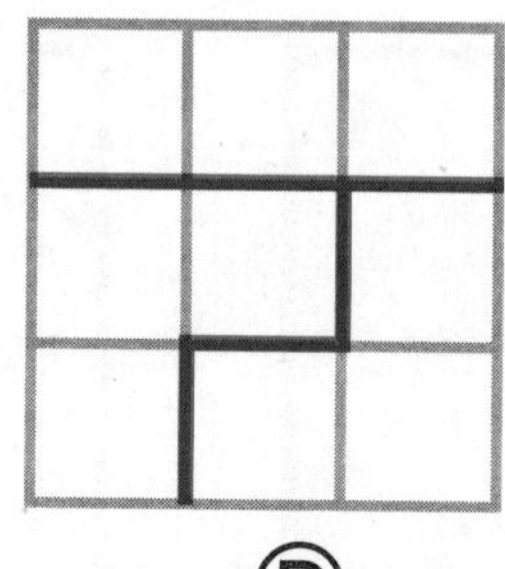

Ⓓ

Name ______________________________

Activity

Problem Solving

Lesson 13-8
Repeated Reasoning

I can ...
use repeated reasoning to show rectangles with rows and columns and create designs with equal shares.

I can also show equal shares in shapes.

Solve & Share

Design two different flags. Draw 15 equal-size squares in each flag. Use rows and columns.

Make three equal shares of different colors in each flag. Then write an equation for each flag to show the total number of squares.

My Flag Designs

Equation: ______________________

Equation: ______________________

Thinking Habits
Does something repeat in the problem?
How can the solution help me solve another problem?

Visual Learning Bridge

Sam is designing a square quilt. The quilt must have 4 colors with an equal share for each color.

Help Sam make two designs.

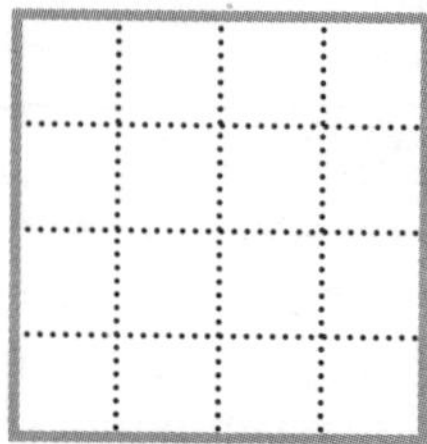

How can I look for things that repeat in the problem?

Each share has 4 small squares. So, any shape with 4 small squares is an equal share.

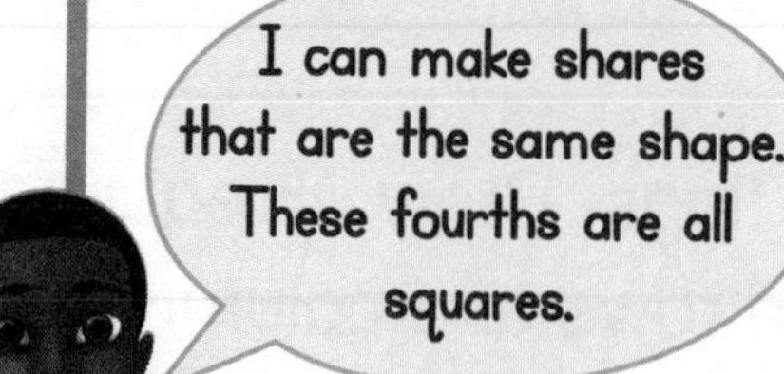

I can make shares that are the same shape. These fourths are all squares.

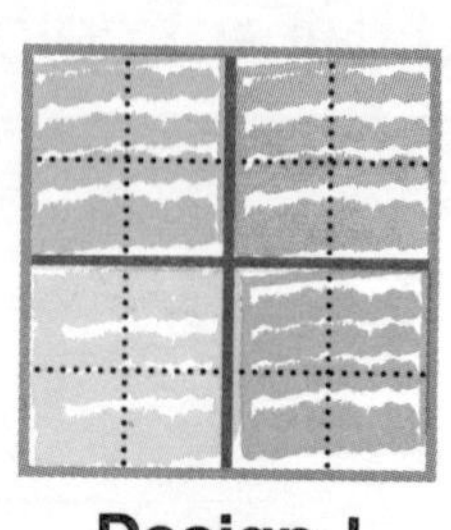

Design 1

In both designs, the fourths are equal in size.

Here, I used different shapes for the shares.

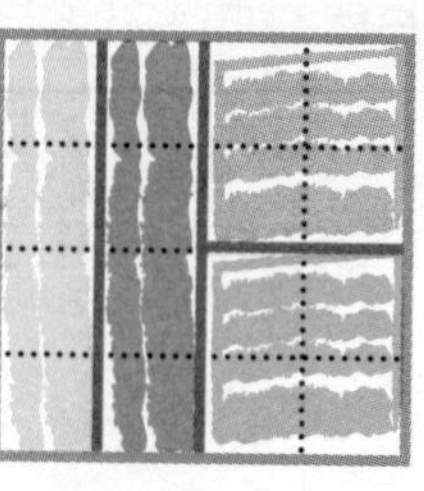

Design 2

Convince Me! How do you know each share in Design 2 is a fourth of the whole square?

Guided Practice Solve the problem. Use crayons to color.

1. Hamal is painting a design. The design must have 3 colors with an equal share for each color. Create two possible designs for Hamal.

Design 1

Design 2

Be ready to explain how you used repeated reasoning to help you solve the problem.

Name ______________________

Tools Assessment

Independent Practice Solve each problem. Use crayons to color. Explain your work.

2. Marie wants to put a rectangular design on a T-shirt. The design must have 4 colors with an equal share for each color. Create two possible designs for Marie.

Design 1

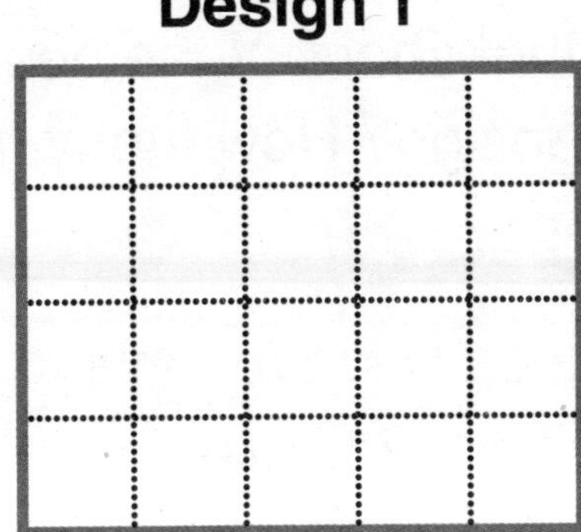

Design 2

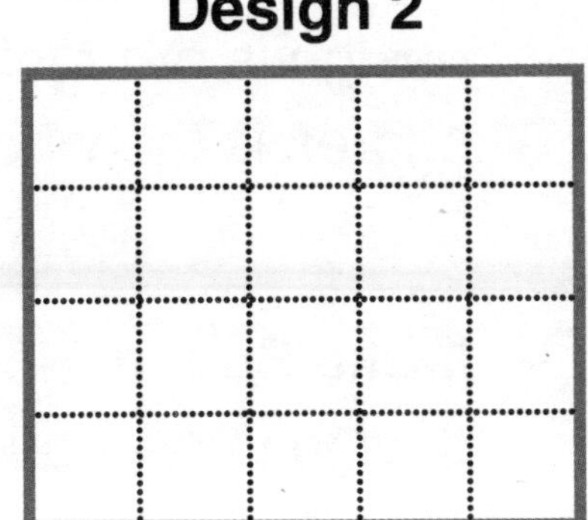

____

____

____

____

____

3. Grant wants to put a circle design on his toy car. The design must have 3 colors with an equal share for each color. Create two possible designs for Grant.

Design 1

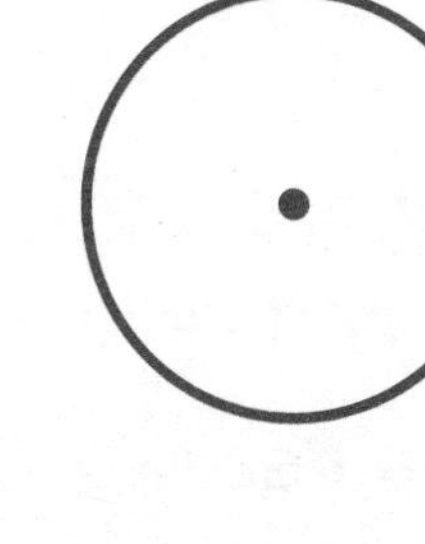

Design 2

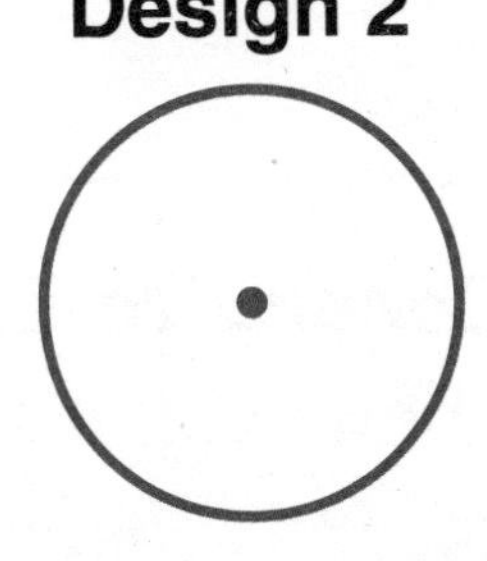

____

____

____

____

____

Problem Solving

Performance Task

Tile Design

Ms. Walton created this rectangular tile design. What share of the design is orange? What share of the design is yellow? How many shares is the whole design? How many thirds is the whole?

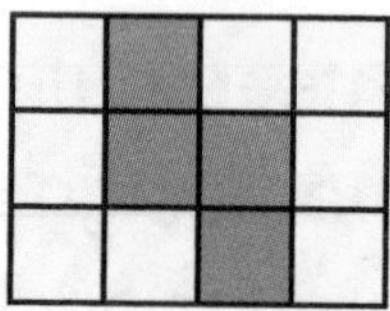

4. **Make Sense** How does Ms. Walton's design show equal shares? Explain.

5. **Reasoning** What share of the design is orange? What share of the design is yellow? How many shares is the whole design? How many thirds is the whole?

6. **Generalize** Copy the tile design above onto this grid. Then color it orange and yellow to match the design shown above.

How did you copy the design? Describe one or two shortcuts you used.

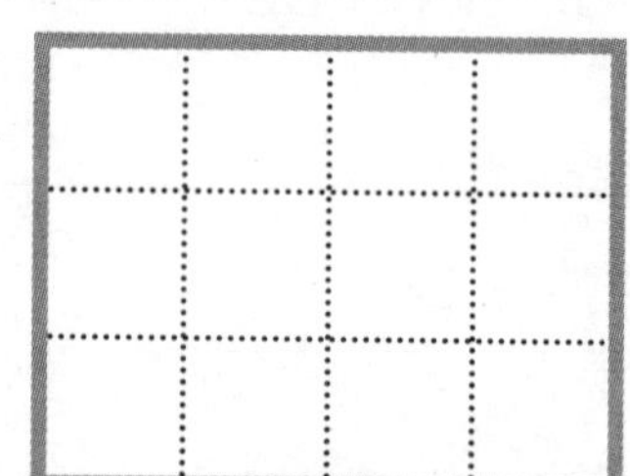

Name ______________________________

Fluency Practice Activity

Find each sum or difference. Then color a path from **Start** to **Finish**. Follow the sums and differences that are even numbers. You can only move up, down, right, or left.

I can ...
add and subtract within 100.

I can also be precise in my work.

Start

69 − 23	31 + 25	78 − 47	97 − 49	72 + 12	76 − 38	67 − 47	48 + 24	46 + 37
84 − 61	73 − 55	68 + 29	11 + 17	37 + 58	86 − 51	21 + 38	82 − 18	81 − 62
43 + 42	27 + 49	35 + 48	46 − 32	73 − 26	30 + 31	46 − 28	47 + 41	62 − 39
25 + 16	60 − 36	50 − 29	39 + 43	60 − 45	64 + 23	29 + 35	56 + 41	94 − 61
35 + 42	85 − 23	24 + 56	58 + 36	97 − 38	25 − 16	38 + 62	79 − 49	59 + 23

Finish

Vocabulary Review

Word List

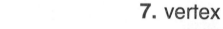

- angle
- cube
- edge
- equal shares
- face
- fourths
- halves
- hexagon
- pentagon
- polygon
- quadrilateral
- right angle
- thirds
- vertex

Understand Vocabulary

Write *always*, *sometimes*, or *never*.

1. A cube has exactly 4 faces. __________

2. A right angle forms a square corner. __________

3. Quadrilaterals are squares. __________

4. A solid figure with faces has edges. __________

Draw a line from each term to its example.

5. hexagon

6. pentagon

7. vertex

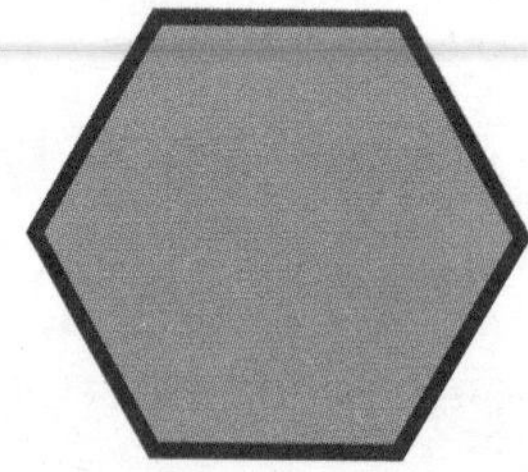

Use Vocabulary in Writing

8. Tell how you can divide a square into two equal shares. Then tell how you can divide that same square into 3 equal shares. Use terms from the Word List.

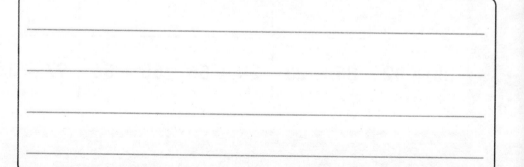

Name ______________________

TOPIC 13

Reteaching

Set A

You can name a plane shape by its number of sides and vertices.

vertex

side

3 sides

3 vertices

Shape: triangle

4 sides

4 vertices

Shape: quadrilateral

Write the number of sides and vertices. Name the shape.

1. ____ sides

____ vertices

Shape: ________

2. ____ sides

____ vertices

Shape: ________

Set B

You can name a polygon by the number of its angles.

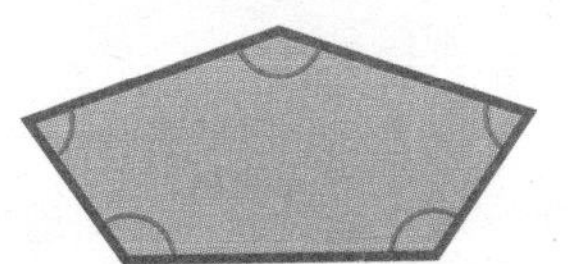

5 angles

pentagon

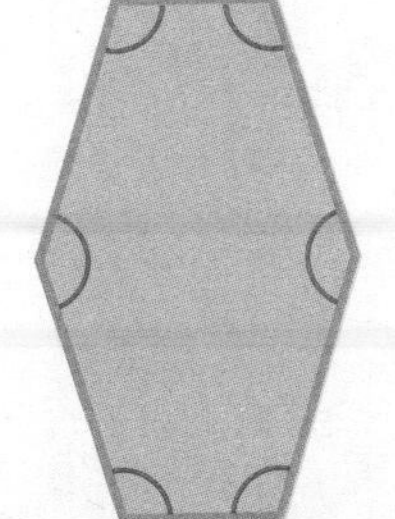

6 angles

hexagon

Write the number of angles. Then name the shape.

3. ____ angles

Shape: ________

4. ____ angles

Shape: ________

Set C

You can draw a polygon with a given number of sides, vertices, or angles.

Draw a polygon with 4 sides. Two sides have different lengths.

Draw a polygon with 5 vertices.

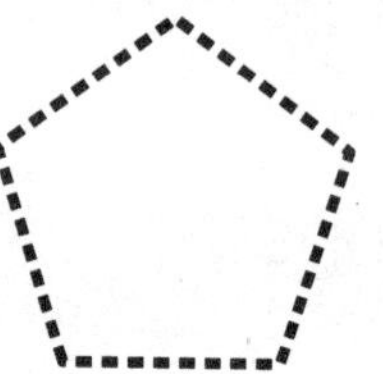

Draw a polygon with 3 angles. One angle is a right angle.

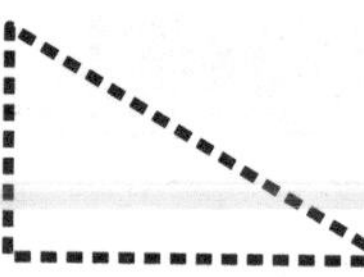

Draw each polygon described.

5. 6 sides

6. 3 vertices

7. 5 sides and 2 right angles

8. 8 angles

Set D

You can describe and draw cubes.

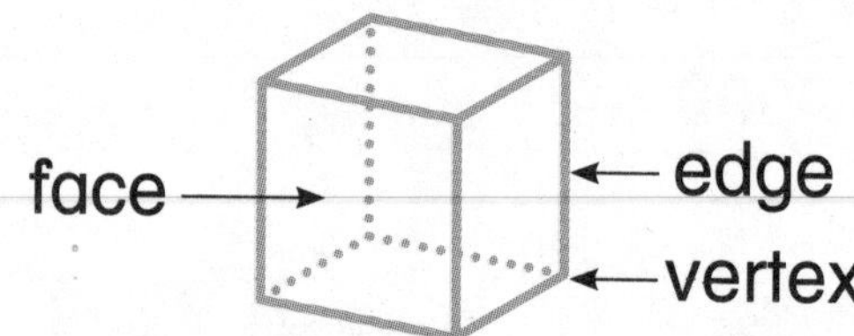

Every cube has 6 faces, 12 edges, and 8 vertices.

9. Cross out the shapes that are **NOT** cubes.

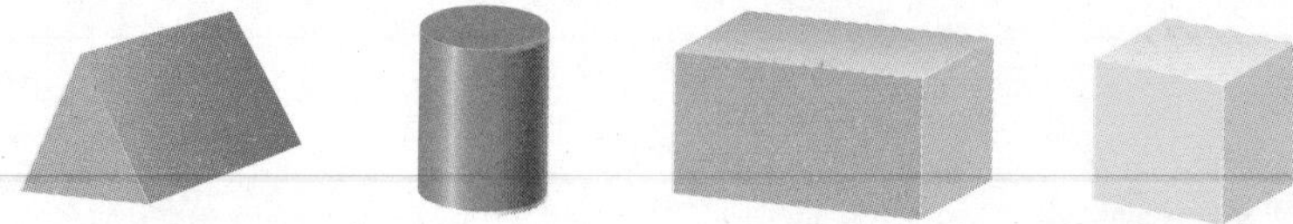

10. Draw a cube. Use the dots to help you.

Name ____________________

TOPIC 13

Reteaching
Continued

Set E

You can cover a rectangle with squares.

column

row →

Count by rows: 3 + 3 = 6

Count by columns: 2 + 2 + 2 = 6

6 squares cover the rectangle.

Use square tiles to cover the rectangle. Trace the tiles. Then count the squares.

11.

____ squares cover the rectangle.

Set F

You can show circles and rectangles with equal shares.

2 equal shares are **halves**.

3 equal shares are **thirds**.

4 equal shares are **fourths**.

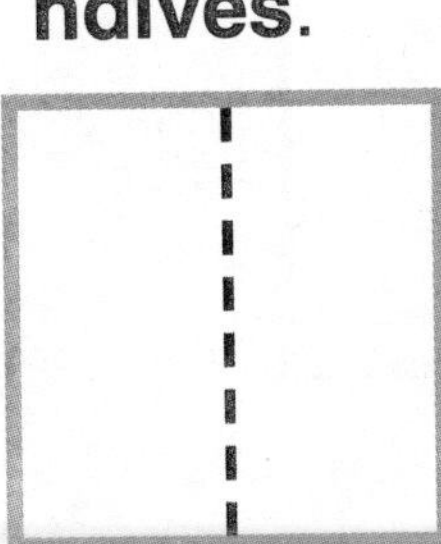

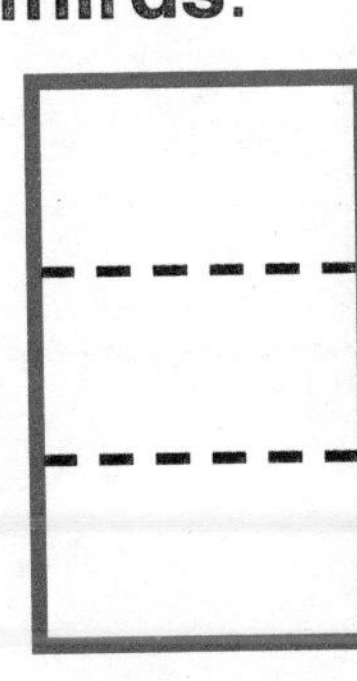

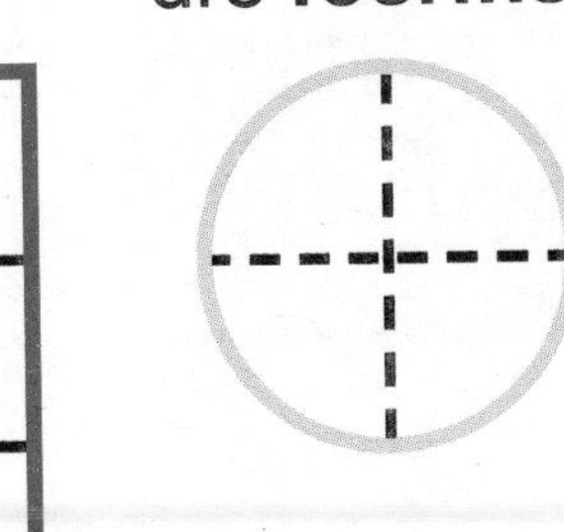

Show each shape with the given number of equal shares. Show 2 ways.

12. halves

13. thirds

14. fourths

Set G

Equal shares can be different shapes.

This is one way to show this rectangle with 3 equal shares.

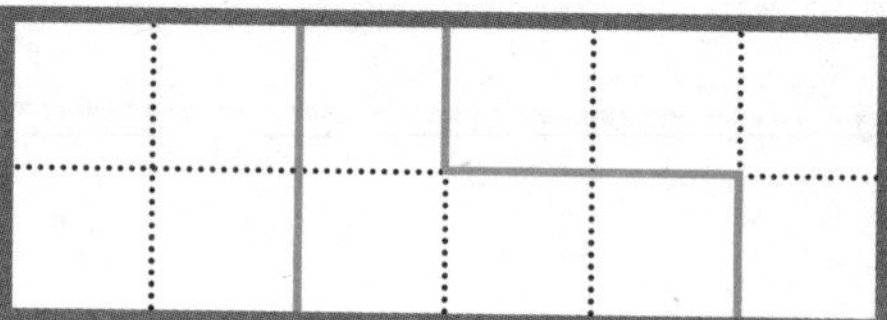

Each equal share is 4 squares.

Draw lines to show 2 more ways these rectangles can have 3 equal shares.

15. equal shares that are **NOT** all the same shape

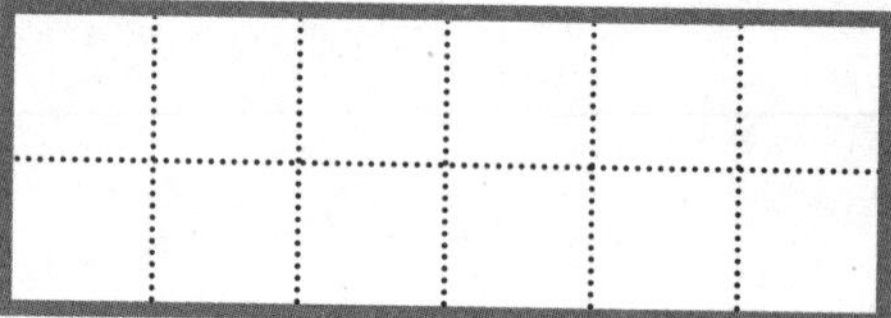

16. equal shares that are all the same shape

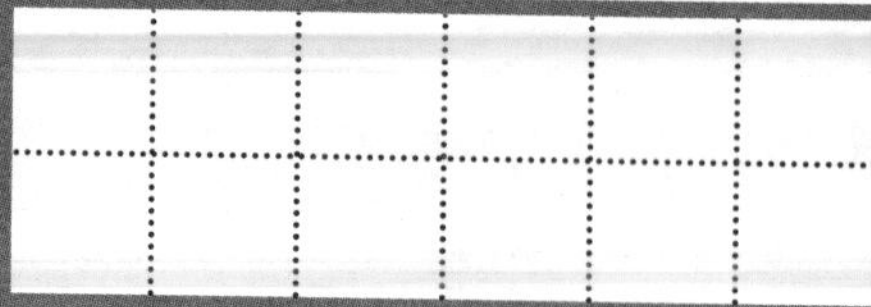

Set H

Thinking Habits

Repeated Reasoning

Does something repeat in the problem?

How can the solution help me solve another problem?

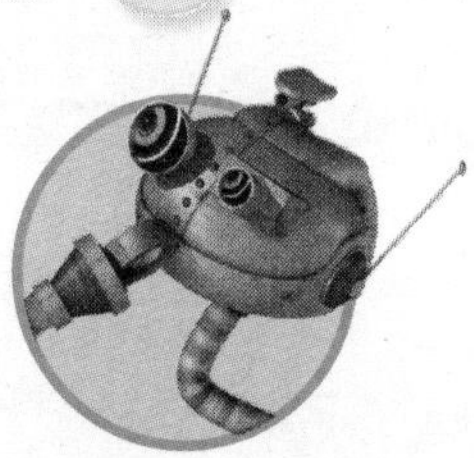

Use the design shown. Create a different design with 3 equal shares.

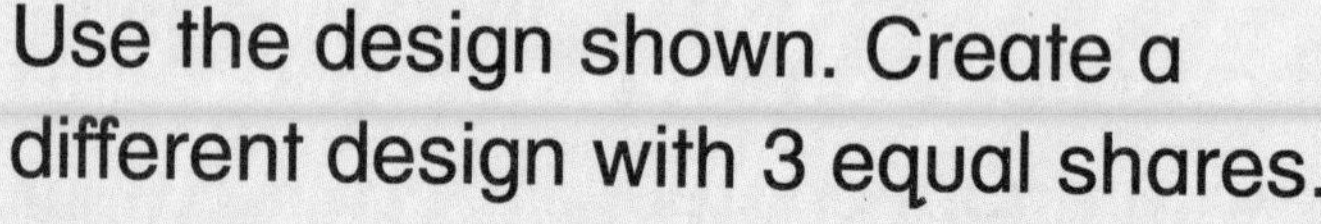

17.

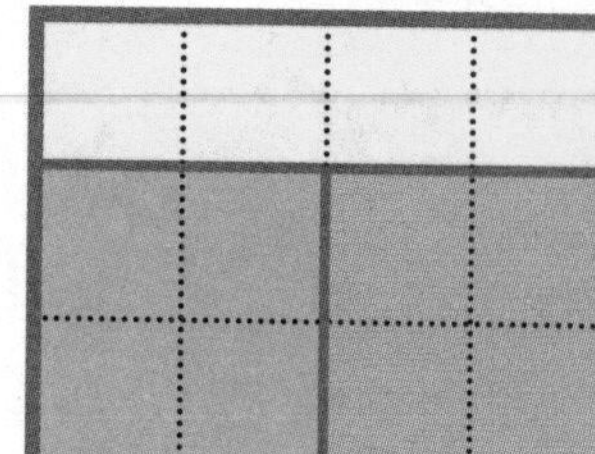

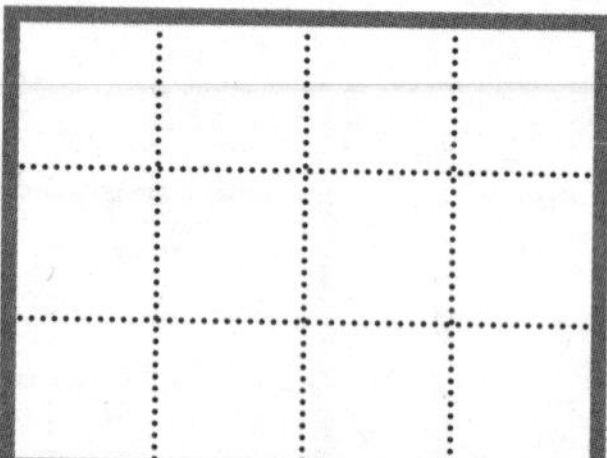

Name ______________________________

1. Which polygons are pentagons?

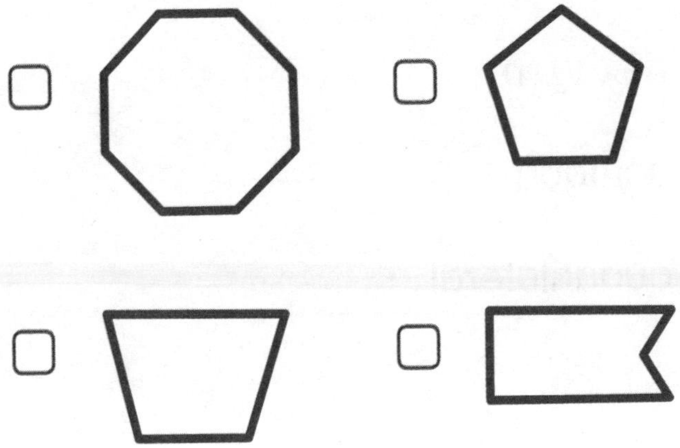

☐ ☐

☐ ☐

2. Rita draws a polygon. It has fewer than 8 sides and more angles than a square. Which shape did Rita draw?

Ⓐ triangle

Ⓑ rectangle

Ⓒ hexagon

Ⓓ quadrilateral

3. Which rectangles are shown in fourths?
Choose all that apply.

☐ ☐ ☐ ☐ ☐

4. Draw a polygon with 4 angles.
Make one angle a right angle.
Then name the polygon.

Name: ______________________________

5. Is the polygon a quadrilateral? Choose Yes or No.

I have 3 sides and 3 angles.	○ Yes	○ No
I have 4 sides and 4 angles.	○ Yes	○ No
I am a square.	○ Yes	○ No
I am a rectangle.	○ Yes	○ No

6. Mandy draws a polygon with 6 sides and 6 angles. Which shape did she draw?

Ⓐ pentagon

Ⓑ hexagon

Ⓒ octagon

Ⓓ quadrilateral

7. Name the shape below. Write 3 things that describe the shape.

____

____

____

____

8. Draw the polygon described below. Then complete the sentence.

I have 2 fewer sides than a pentagon.
I have 1 less angle than a square.
I have one right angle.

The shape is a ________________.

9. Complete the sentence to name and describe the solid figure below.

A ______ has ____ faces, ____ vertices, and ____ edges.

10. Show this circle with 2 equal shares. Then complete the sentences.

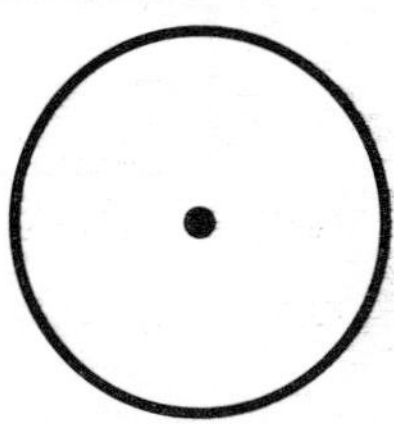

Each share is a ______ of the whole.

The whole is ____ halves.

11. Brad says there are only two ways to divide the same rectangle below into 3 equal shares. Do you agree? Use words and pictures to explain.

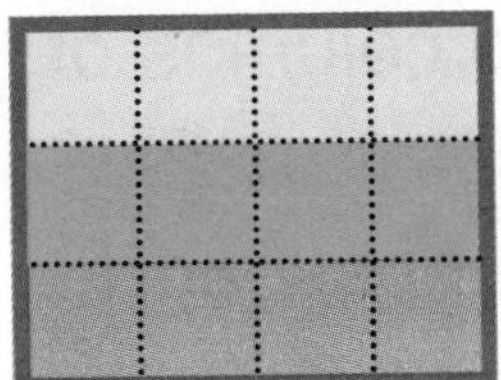
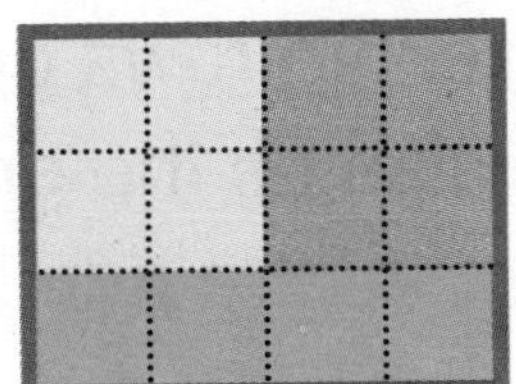

12. Count the number of squares in the rows and columns of the rectangle. Use the numbers on the cards to write the missing numbers in the equations.

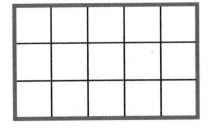

15 3 5

Rows: ____ + ____ + ____ = ____ squares

Columns: ____ + ____ + ____ + ____ + ____ = ____ squares

13. Kerry wants a design that shows thirds. Which designs could Kerry use? Choose all that apply.

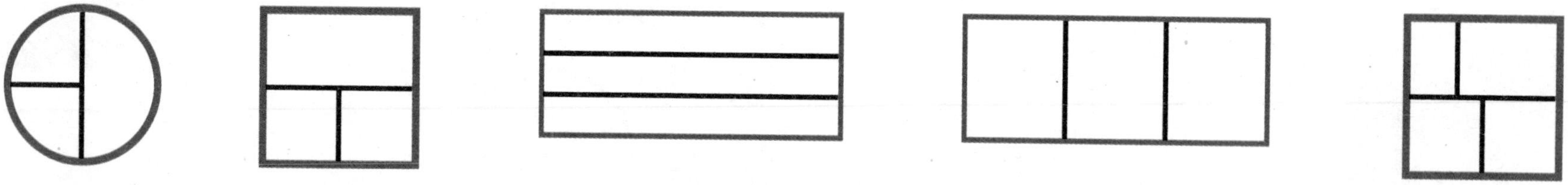

☐ ☐ ☐ ☐ ☐

14. Is the solid figure a cube? Choose Yes or No.

☐ Yes ☐ No ☐ Yes ☐ No ☐ Yes ☐ No ☐ Yes ☐ No

15. Use the dot paper. Draw a cube.

16. Divide the rectangle into rows and columns of squares the same size as the green square. Then count and record the number of squares.

_____ squares

Name ______________________________

Happy Home

Tina and her family moved into a new home. They bought different things for each room.

1. They hang pictures on the wall. Name the shape of each picture frame.

____

____

2. The rug in the kitchen has 5 sides and 5 vertices. Draw the shape of the rug.

Name the shape. ____________________

3. The wallpaper uses this pattern.

Name the shape in the pattern.

____

Write the number of sides, vertices, and angles in the shape.

_____ sides _____ vertices _____ angles

4. The living room has 2 end tables.

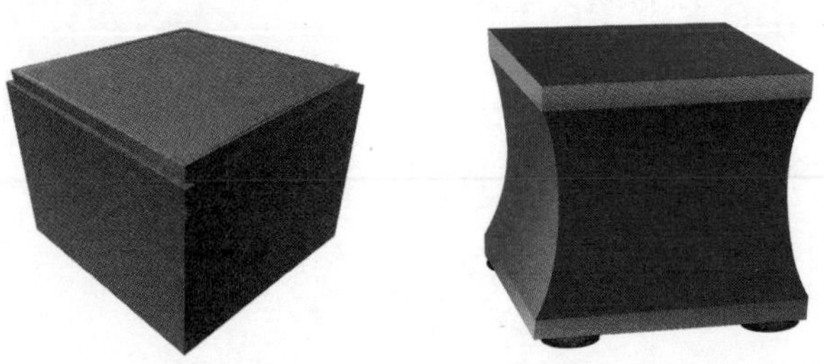

Circle the table that is a cube. Explain.

____

____

____

____

____

5. Tina has a new quilt for her bed. Her quilt has this design.

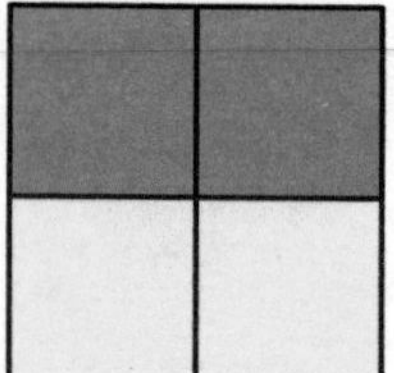

What share is green? __________

What share is yellow? __________

6. Tina's mother is making a quilt with smaller squares. She wants the quilt to have 4 colors. Each color has an equal share.

Part A

Use 4 colors to make a quilt design below. Make the equal shares the same shape.

Design 1

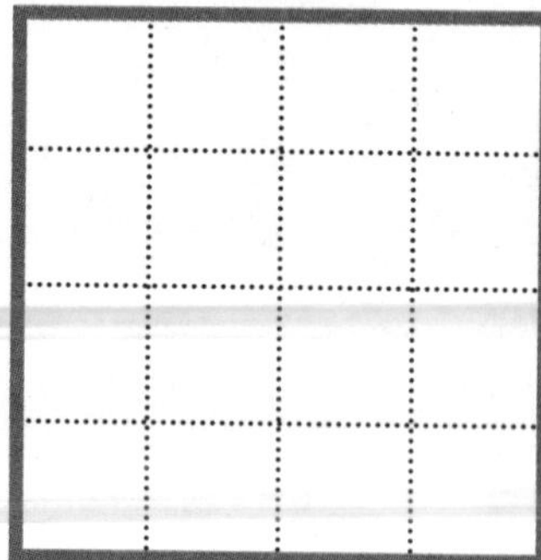

Part B

Use 4 colors to make a different quilt design below. Make equal shares that are not all the same shape.

Design 2

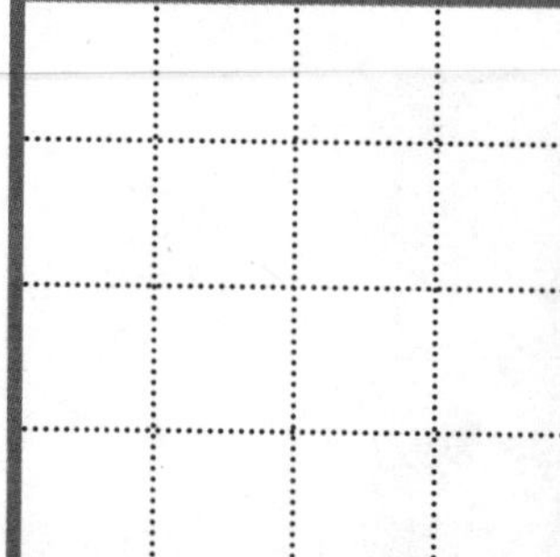

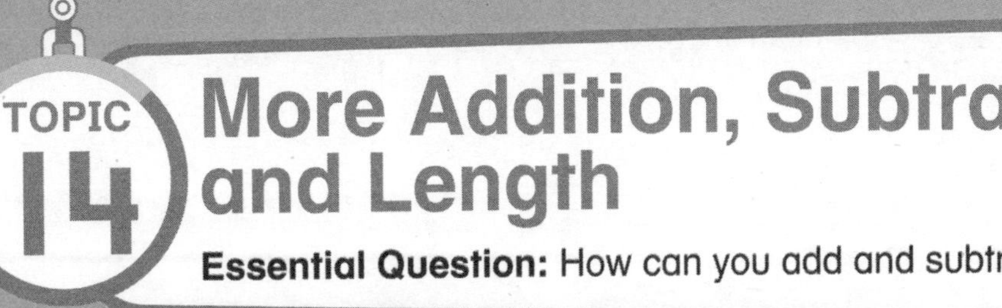

TOPIC 14 More Addition, Subtraction, and Length

Essential Question: How can you add and subtract lengths?

Look at the big waves! Look at the big rock!

Water and land in an area can have different sizes and shapes.

Wow! Let's do this project and learn more.

enVision® STEM Project: Modeling Land, Water, and Length

Find Out Find and share books and other sources that show the shapes and kinds of land and water in an area. Draw a picture or make a model to show the land or water in an area.

Journal: Make a Book Show what you learn in a book. In your book, also:

- Draw a picture to show the shape of some land or water in your area.
- Make up a math story about lengths. Draw a picture to show how to solve the problem in your story.

Name ___________________________________

Vocabulary

1. Circle the measuring unit that is better to **estimate** the **length** of a room.

meter

centimeter

2. Circle the number of feet in 1 **yard**.

2 feet

3 feet

4 feet

12 feet

3. The clock shows the time a math class begins. Circle **a.m.** or **p.m.**

a.m.

p.m.

Estimate

4. **Estimate** the length of the eraser in centimeters.

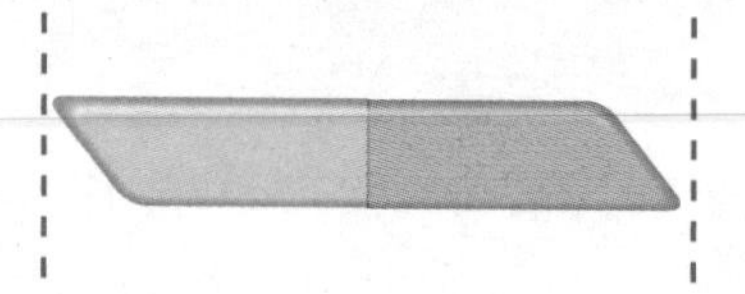

About ______ centimeters

Compare

5. A sidewalk is 632 yards long. A jogging trail is 640 yards long.

Use <, >, or = to compare the lengths.

632 ◯ 640

Rectangles

6. Label the 2 missing lengths of the sides of the rectangle.

4 cm

______ cm

3 cm

______ cm

Name ____

How tall are Ferris wheels?

Project: Write a Ferris Wheel Story

How big are insects?

Project: Make Insect Drawings

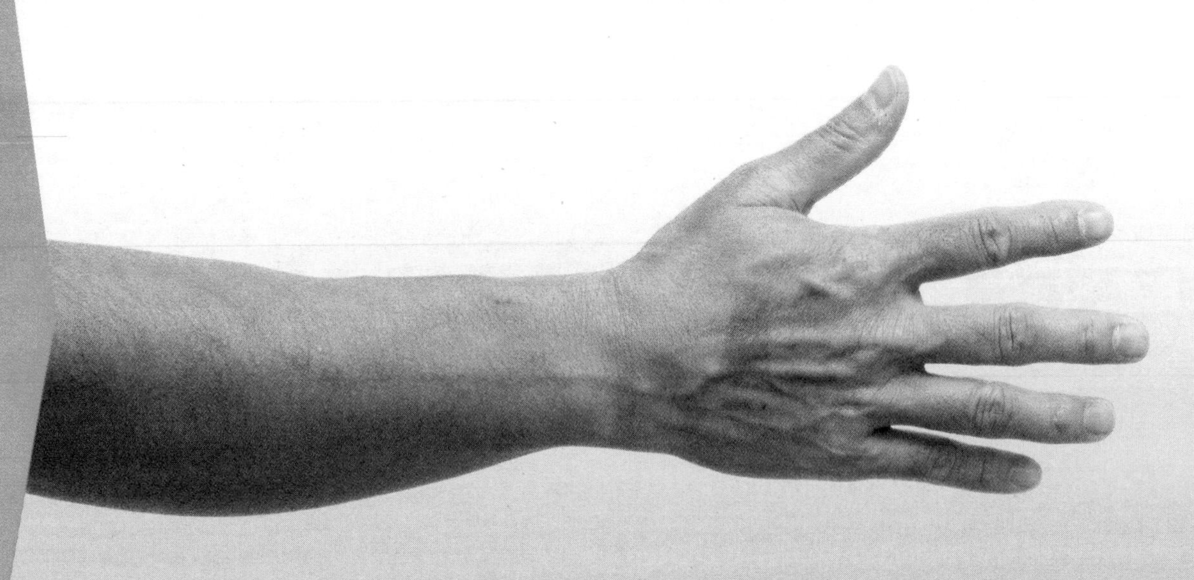

How can you measure if you do not have tools?

Project: Make a Measurement Poster

PROJECT
14D

How is some food grown?

Project: Draw a Garden Plan

Name ______________________

Solve & Share

The ant crawled along the edge of this blue rectangle. Measure the total distance the ant crawled. Show your work and be ready to explain it.

Activity

Lesson 14-1

Add and Subtract with Measurements

I can ...
solve problems by adding or subtracting length measurements.

I can also reason about math.

 Visual Learning A-Z Glossary

Visual Learning Bridge

The book is 9 inches long and 6 inches wide.

What is the distance around the front cover of the book?

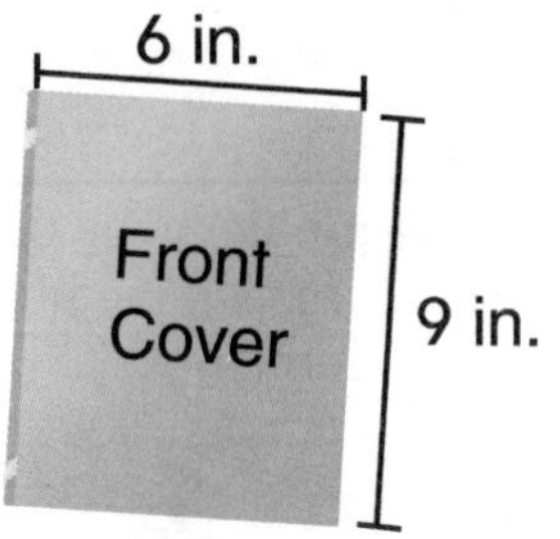

Add the lengths of all four sides to find the distance around the cover.

$9 + 6 + 9 + 6 = ?$

$18 + 12 =$

$10 + 10 + 8 + 2 =$

$20 + 10 = 30$

The distance around the cover is 30 inches.

How much longer is the teacher's arm than the child's arm?

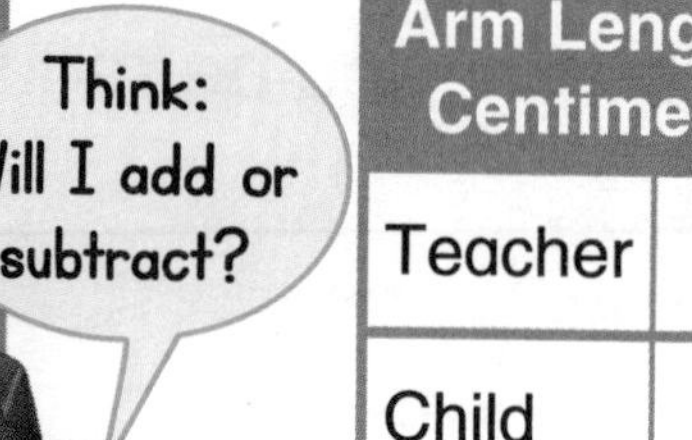

Arm Length in Centimeters	
Teacher	66
Child	47

Subtract to compare measurements.

$66 - 47 = ?$

47 → 40, 7; 7 → 6, 1

$66 - 40 = 26$

$26 - 6 = 20$

$20 - 1 = 19$

The teacher's arm is 19 centimeters longer than the child's arm.

Convince Me! Explain how to find the distance around a square park that is 2 miles long on each side.

Guided Practice

Decide if you need to add or subtract. Then write an equation to help solve each problem.

1. What is the distance around the baseball card?

$10 + 7 + 10 + 7 = 34$

Distance around: 34 cm

2. What is the distance around the puzzle?

____

Distance around: _____ in.

Name ____

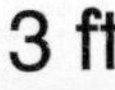

Independent Practice

Decide if you need to add or subtract.
Then write an equation to help solve each problem.

3. What is the distance around the door?

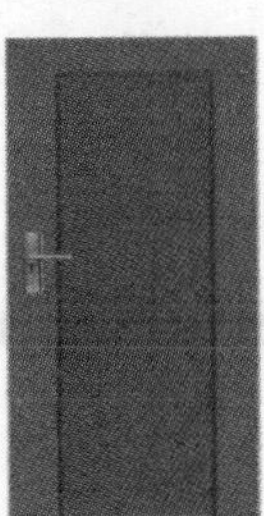

____

Distance around: _____ ft

4. What is the distance around the cell phone?

____

Distance around: _____ in.

5. How much longer is the red scarf than the blue scarf?

____

_____ in. longer

6. **Algebra** What is the length of the shorter side of the rectangle? Complete the equation to solve.

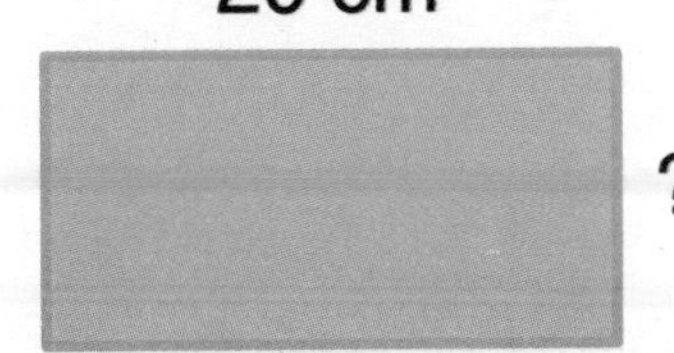

20 + _____ + 20 + _____ = 60

The shorter side is _____ centimeters.

Problem Solving

Decide if you need to add or subtract. Then write an equation to help solve each problem.

7. **Model** Ashley's sunflower is 70 inches tall. Kwame's sunflower is 60 inches tall. How much taller is Ashley's sunflower than Kwame's sunflower?

________________ ______ inches taller

8. **Model** Ben compares the length of a leaf and a plant. The leaf is 15 centimeters. The plant is 37 centimeters. How much shorter is the leaf than the plant?

________________ ______ centimeters shorter

9. **Higher Order Thinking** Tyler threw a ball 42 feet and then 44 feet. Sanjay threw a ball 38 feet and then 49 feet. Who threw the longer distance in all? Show your work.

10. **Assessment Practice** What is the distance around the placemat?

Ⓐ 28 in.

Ⓑ 39 in.

Ⓒ 56 in.

Ⓓ 66 in.

Name ______________________________

Lesson 14-2

Find Unknown Measurements

I can ...
add or subtract to solve problems about measurements.

I can also make sense of problems.

Solve & Share

Julie and Steve each cut a piece of yarn.
The total length of both pieces is 12 cm.

Measure each piece of yarn.
Circle Julie and Steve's pieces. Then explain your thinking.

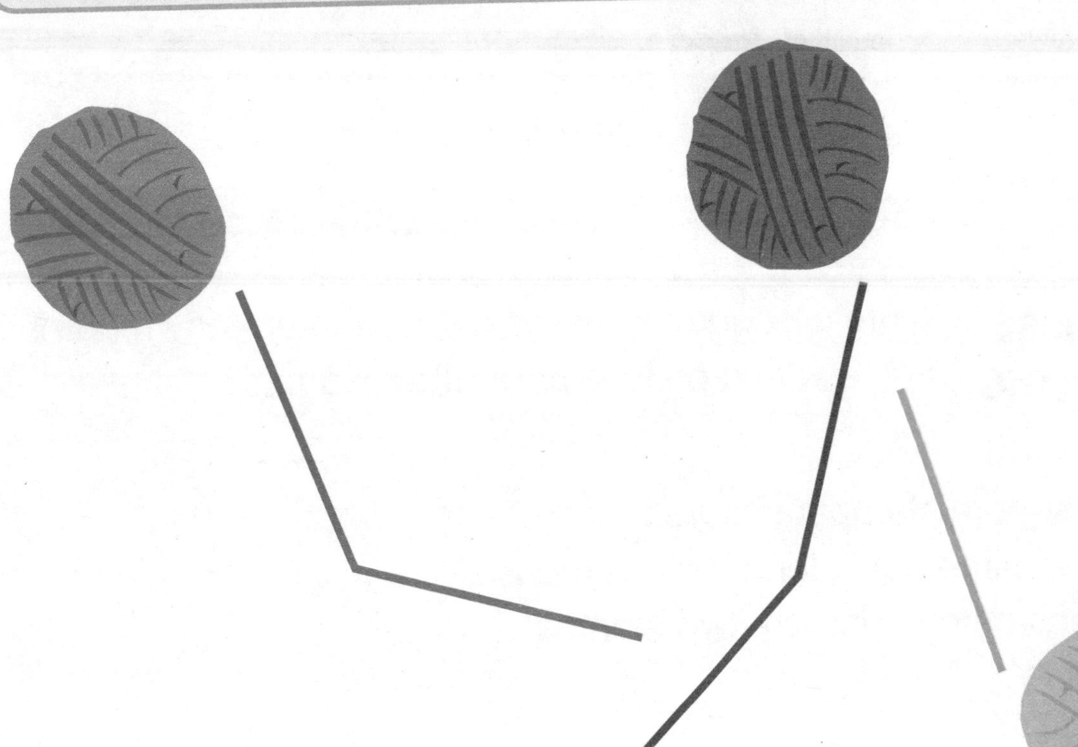

____

____

____

Michelle jumped 24 inches. Tim jumped 7 fewer inches than Michelle. How far did Tim jump?

What operation should I use?

You can write a subtraction equation to show the problem.

The length of Tim's jump is unknown.

24 − 7 = ?

24: length of Michelle's jump
7: fewer inches
?: length of Tim's jump

You can draw a picture, such as a yardstick. Then count back to solve the problem.

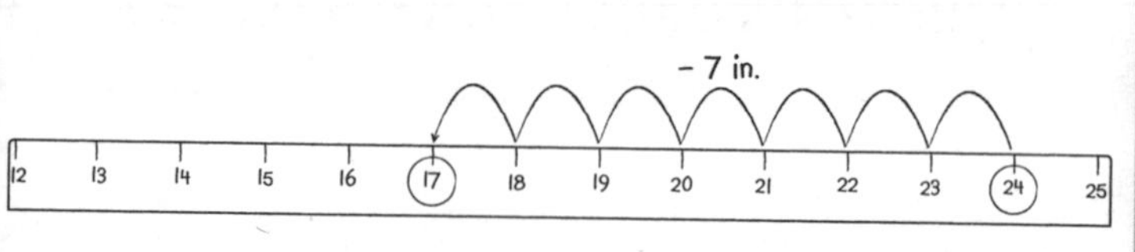

Tim jumped 17 inches.

Convince Me! How does drawing a yardstick help you solve the problem above?

Guided Practice Write an equation using a ? for the unknown number. Solve with a picture or another way.

1. A square stamp measures 2 centimeters in length. How many centimeters long are two stamps?

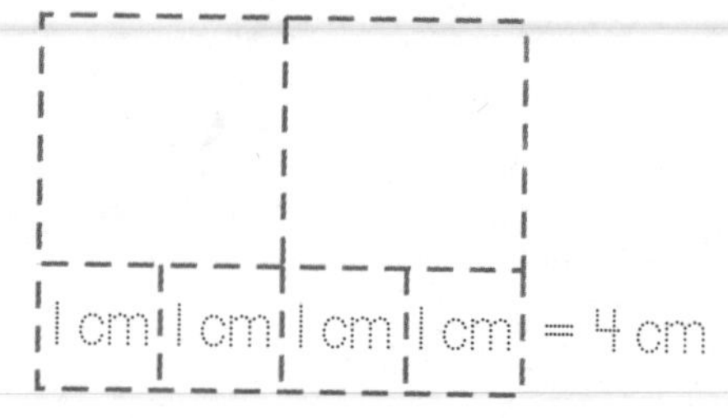

_____ cm

2. Stuart's desk is 64 centimeters long. His dresser is 7 centimeters longer than his desk. How long is Stuart's dresser?

_____________________ _____ cm

Name ______________________________

Tools Assessment

Independent Practice

Write an equation using a ? for the unknown number. Solve with a picture or another way.

3. Filipe's pencil box is 24 centimeters long. Joe's pencil box is 3 centimeters shorter than Filipe's. How long is Joe's pencil box?

______________________ ______ cm

---

4. Clark threw a red ball and a blue ball. He threw the red ball 17 feet. He threw the blue ball 7 feet farther. How far did Clark throw the blue ball?

______________________ ______ ft

---

5. **enVision**® STEM Ashlie's map shows where animals, land, and water are at a zoo.

The distance around her map is 38 inches. What is the length of the missing side?

____

______ inches

8 in.

11 in. 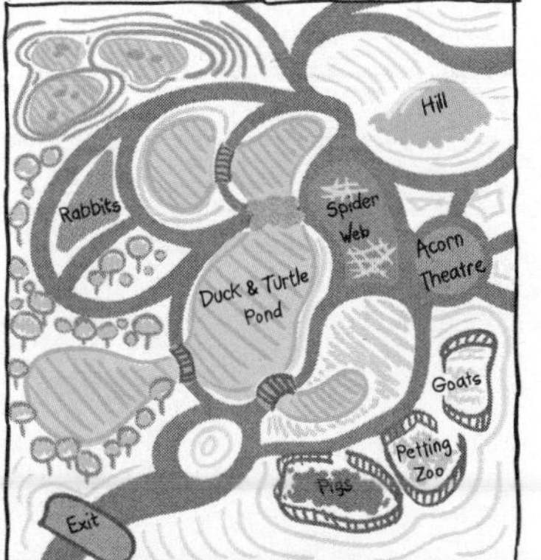 ? in.

8 in.

Problem Solving Solve each problem.

6. **Make Sense** A brown puppy is 43 centimeters tall. A spotted puppy is 7 centimeters shorter than the brown puppy. A white puppy is 14 centimeters taller than the brown puppy. How tall is the spotted puppy? Think about what you need to find.

_____ cm

7. **Vocabulary** Complete the sentences using the terms below.

foot **yard** **inch**

A paper clip is about 1 _______ long.

My math book is about 1 _______ long.

A baseball bat is about 1 _______ long.

8. **Higher Order Thinking** Jack jumped 15 inches. Tyler jumped 1 inch less than Jack and 2 inches more than Randy. Who jumped the farthest? How far did each person jump?

9. **Assessment Practice** Kim was 48 inches tall in January. She grew 9 inches during the year. How tall is Kim at the end of the year? Write an equation with an unknown and then draw a picture to solve.

____

_____ in.

Name ______________________________

Lesson 14-3

Continue to Find Unknown Measurements

Solve & Share

Alex has a piece of ribbon that is 45 feet long. He cuts the ribbon. Now he has 39 feet of ribbon. How many feet of ribbon did Alex cut off?

Draw a picture and write an equation to solve. Show your work.

I can ...
add and subtract to solve measurement problems by using drawings and equations.

I can also make sense of problems.

A string is 28 cm.
Alex cuts off a piece.
Now the string is 16 cm.
How long is the piece of string Alex cut off?

You can write an addition or subtraction equation.

28 − ? − 16

↑ length at first ↑ length cut ↑ length now

16 + ? = 28

↓ length now ↓ length cut ↓ length at first

You can draw a picture for 28 − ? = 16 or 16 + ? = 28.

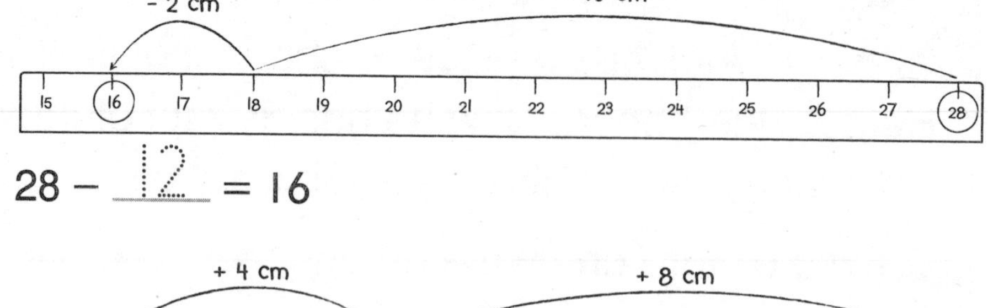

28 − <u>12</u> = 16

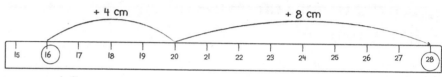

+ 4 cm   + 8 cm

15 16 17 18 19 20 21 22 23 24 25 26 27 28

16 + <u>12</u> = 28

Alex cut off 12 cm of string.

Convince Me! How does writing an equation help you solve the problem above?

Write an equation using a ? for the unknown number. Solve with a picture or another way.

1. A plant was 15 inches tall. It grew and is now 22 inches tall. How many inches did the plant grow?

+ 5 in.   + 2 in.

14 15 16 17 18 19 20 21 22 23

15 + ? = 22 ______

2. Each bus is 10 meters long. Each boat is 7 meters long. What is the total length of two buses and two boats?

______ ______

Name ________________________________

Independent Practice

Write an equation using a ? for the unknown number. Solve with a picture or another way.

3. Brent's rope is 49 inches long. He cuts off some of the rope and now it is 37 inches long. How much rope did Brent cut off?

_______________ _______________

4. Sue ran for some meters and stopped. Then she ran another 22 meters for a total of 61 meters in all. How many meters did she run at first?

_______________ _______________

5. **Algebra** Solve each equation. Use the chart.

○	=	12
☆	=	39
△	=	42
□	=	57

○ + ☆ = ____

□ − ☆ = ____

☆ + △ + ○ = ____

Problem Solving Solve each problem.

6. **Make Sense** The yellow boat is 15 feet shorter than the green boat. The green boat is 53 feet long. How long is the yellow boat? Think about what you are trying to find.

Write an equation to solve. Show your work.

_____ ft

7. **Vocabulary** Steve measured the length of his desk. It measured 2 units.

Circle the unit Steve used.

meter **foot** **centimeter** **inch**

Lori measured the length of her cat. It measured 45 units.

Circle the unit Lori used.

centimeter **yard** **inch** **foot**

8. **Higher Order Thinking** Lucy's ribbon is 1 foot long. Kathleen's ribbon is 15 inches long. Whose ribbon is longer and by how many inches? Explain your thinking.

____

____

____

____

____

9. **Assessment Practice** Mary's water bottle is 25 cm long. Joey's water bottle is 22 cm long. Ella's water bottle is 17 cm long.

Which statements are correct? Choose all that apply.

- ☐ Mary's bottle is 8 cm longer than Ella's.
- ☐ Joey's bottle is 6 cm longer than Ella's.
- ☐ Joey's bottle is 3 cm shorter than Mary's.
- ☐ Ella's bottle is 8 cm longer than Mary's.

Name ______________________________

Lesson 14-4

Add and Subtract on a Number Line

I can ...
add and subtract on a number line.

I can also model with math.

Solve & Share Amelia walks 18 blocks on Monday and 5 blocks on Tuesday. How many blocks does she walk in all?

Use the number line to show how many blocks Amelia walks. Then write an equation to show your work.

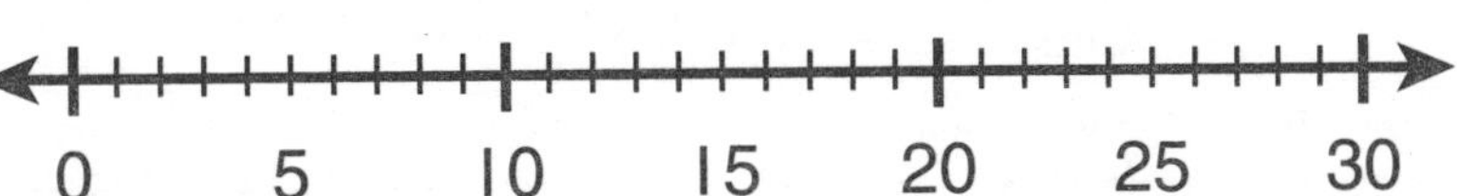

Amelia walks 17 blocks before dinner. She walks 8 blocks after dinner. How many blocks does she walk in all?

You can use a number line to add lengths.
First, show the 17 blocks Amelia walks before dinner.
Then, add the 8 blocks she walks after dinner.

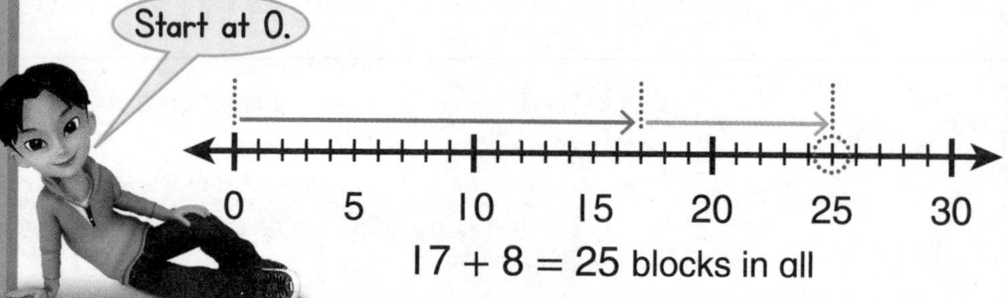

17 + 8 = 25 blocks in all

Amelia buys 17 feet of rope. She cuts off 8 feet of rope to make a jump rope. How many feet of rope does she have left?

You can also use a number line to subtract lengths.
First, show the 17 feet of rope.
Then, subtract the 8 feet of rope she cuts off.

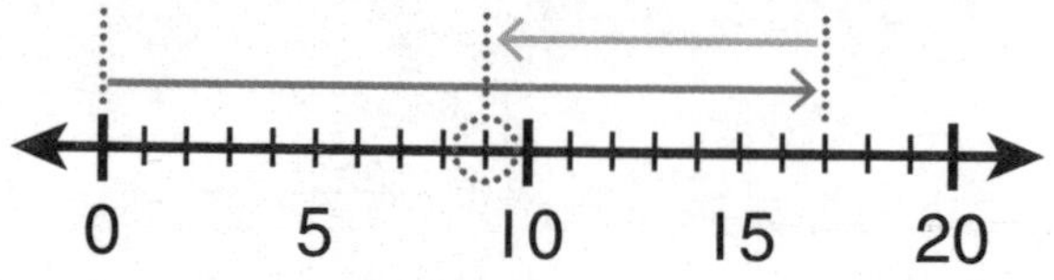

17 − 8 = 9 feet of rope left

Convince Me! Explain how to add 14 inches and 11 inches using a number line.

Guided Practice Use the number lines to add or subtract.

1. 21 + 7 = 28

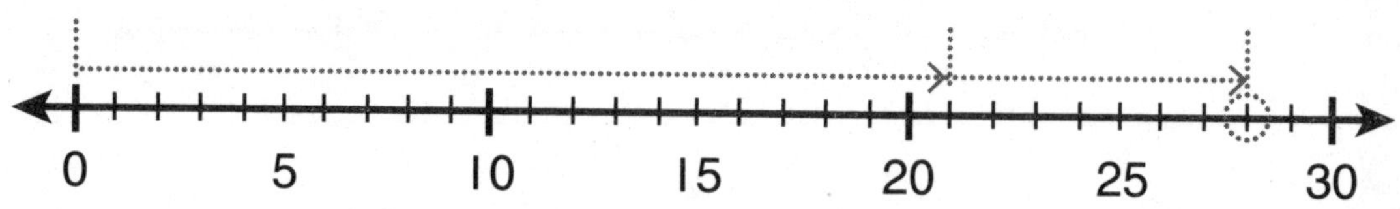

2. 28 − 14 = ____

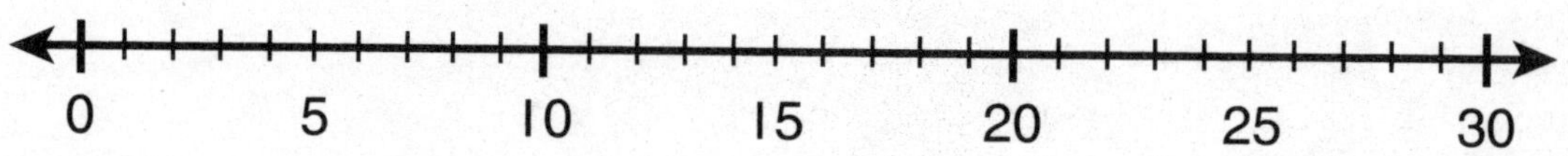

Name ______

Independent Practice

Use the number lines to add or subtract.

3. 80 − 35 = ______

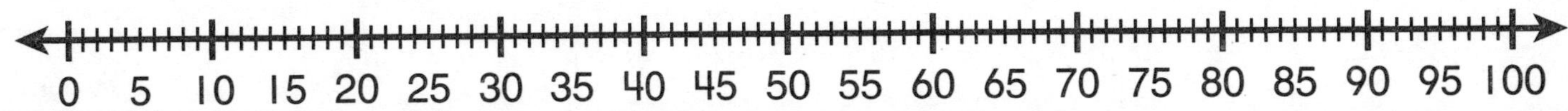

4. 19 + 63 = ______

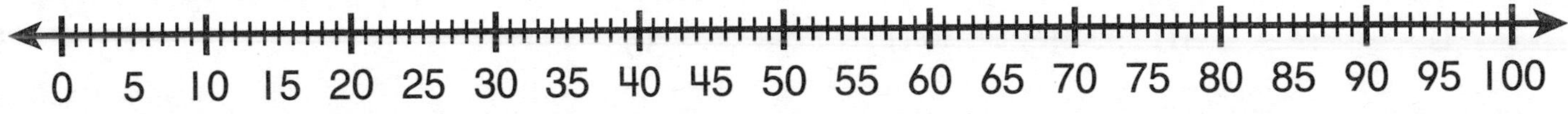

5. Higher Order Thinking Use the number line to show 15 inches plus 0 inches. Explain your thinking.

______

6. Number Sense Show each number below as a length from 0 on the number line. Draw four separate arrows.

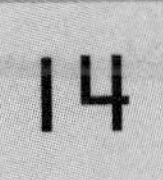

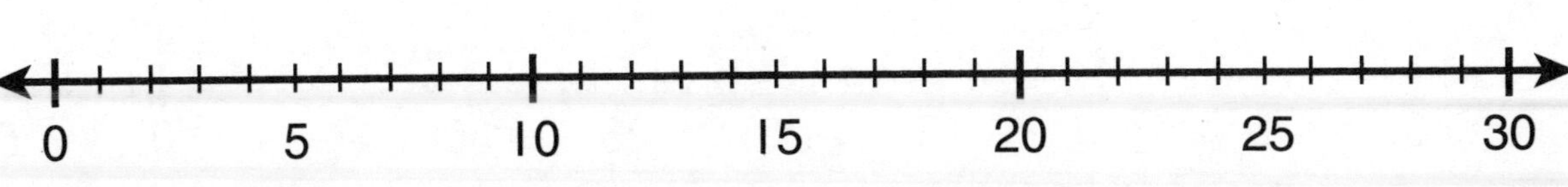

Problem Solving

Use the number line to solve each problem.

7. Use Tools A football team gains 15 yards on its first play. The team gains 12 yards on its second play. How many yards does the team gain in two plays?

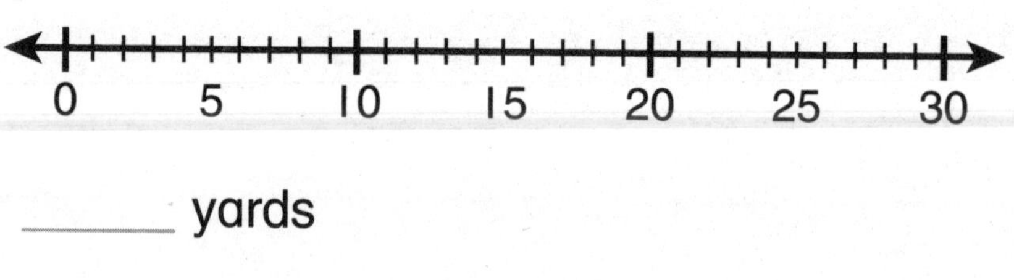

_____ yards

8. Use Tools Mia buys 25 feet of board. She uses 16 feet of board for a sandbox. How many feet of board does she have left?

A number line is a tool you can use to add and subtract.

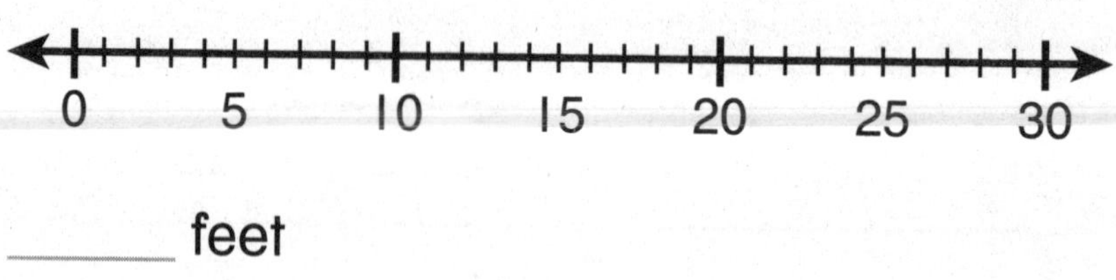

_____ feet

9. Higher Order Thinking The runners on the track team ran 12 miles on Monday. On Tuesday, they ran 6 more miles than they ran on Monday. How many miles did they run in all on both days?

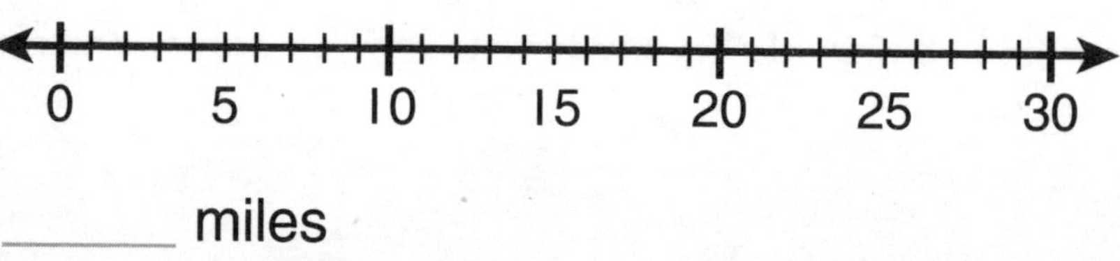

_____ miles

10. Assessment Practice Deb has two pencils. One pencil is 9 cm long and the other pencil is 13 cm long. What is the total length of both pencils?

Use the number line to show your work.

0 5 10 15 20 25 30

_____ centimeters

Name ______________________

Activity

Problem Solving

Lesson 14-5

Use Appropriate Tools

I can ...
choose the best tool to use to solve problems.

I can also measure and compare lengths.

Solve & Share

Choose a tool to solve each part of the problem. Be ready to explain which tools you used and why.

Which line is longer? How much longer? Draw a line that is that length.

Thinking Habits

Which of these tools can I use?

counters	paper and pencil
cubes	place-value blocks
measuring tools	string
number line	technology

Am I using the tool correctly?

Sara plays soccer. She is 56 feet away from the goal. Then she runs 24 feet straight toward the goal.

How many feet from the goal is Sara now?

How can I use a tool to help me solve the problem?

I can think of tools that could help me. Then I can choose the best tool to use.

Tools

counters	paper and pencil
cubes	place-value blocks
measuring tools	string
number line	technology

I don't need a measuring tool. The units are given in feet. I need to subtract. I will draw a number line.

56 − 24 = ?

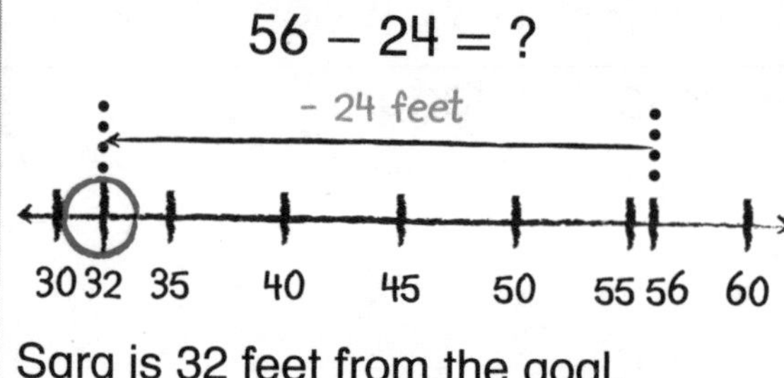

Sara is 32 feet from the goal.

I can use paper and pencil to check my work.

Convince Me! Explain why counters are **NOT** the best tool to use to solve the problem above.

Guided Practice Choose a tool to use to solve the problem. Show your work. Explain why you chose that tool and how you got your answer.

1. Sara cut 19 centimeters of ribbon into two pieces. One piece is 11 centimeters long. How long is the other piece?

Name ______________________________

Tools Assessment

Independent Practice

Solve each problem. Show your work.

2. Work with a partner. Measure each other's arm from the shoulder to the tip of the index finger. Measure to the nearest inch. Whose arm is longer and by how much?

Choose a tool to use to solve the problem. Explain why you chose that tool and how you got your answer.

3. Marcel jumped 39 centimeters high. Jamal jumped 48 centimeters high. How much higher did Jamal jump than Marcel?

Which tool would you **NOT** use to solve this problem? Explain.

Problem Solving

Performance Task

Sailboats

Zak is measuring sailboats at the dock.
Mr. Lee's sailboat is 64 feet long.
Ms. Flint's sailboat is 25 feet shorter than Mr. Lee's boat.

Help Zak find the length of Ms. Flint's boat.

4. **Use Tools** Which tool would you **NOT** use to solve this problem? Explain.

____

____

____

____

5. **Be Precise** Will you add or subtract to solve the problem?

____

Write an equation. Use ? for the unknown.

____

What unit of measure will you use?

____

6. **Explain** What is the length of Ms. Flint's boat? Did you use a tool to solve the problem? Explain.

____

____

____

Name ______________________________

Fluency Practice Activity

Color a path from **Start** to **Finish**. Follow the sums and differences that are odd numbers. You can only move up, down, right, or left.

I can ... add and subtract within 100.

I can also be precise in my work.

Start

80 − 23	94 − 73	21 + 22	45 + 36	19 + 24	86 − 53	14 + 15	25 − 17	35 + 49
65 − 21	97 − 35	35 + 23	12 + 20	98 − 12	74 − 48	27 + 48	54 + 46	53 − 31
51 + 21	35 + 52	28 + 43	18 + 31	51 − 38	79 − 24	95 − 30	61 − 29	30 + 24
55 − 27	60 − 17	27 + 39	29 + 49	62 − 28	36 + 56	59 − 31	42 − 26	87 − 45
36 + 16	38 + 25	88 − 53	33 + 18	34 + 49	45 − 32	62 − 23	97 − 38	19 + 74

Finish

Vocabulary Review

Word List

- centimeter (cm)
- foot (ft)
- height
- inch (in.)
- length
- mental math
- meter (m)
- yard (yd)

Understand Vocabulary

Choose a term from the Word List to complete each sentence.

1. The length of your finger can best be measured in centimeters or ________________.

2. 100 ________________ equals 1 meter.

3. ________________ is how tall an object is from bottom to top.

Write T for *true* or F for *false*.

4. ______ 1 yard is 5 feet long.

5. ______ 12 inches is 1 foot long.

6. ______ A centimeter is longer than a meter.

7. ______ You can do mental math in your head.

Use Vocabulary in Writing

8. Tell how to find the total length of two pieces of string. One piece of string is 12 inches long. The other piece is 9 inches long. Use terms from the Word List.

____

____

____

____

Name ____________________

Set A

Reteaching

What is the distance around the front of the bookcase?

Add the lengths. Write an equation.

4 + 3 + 4 + 3 = 14

Distance around: 14 feet

Write an equation to help solve.

1. What is the distance around the front of the crayon box?

____

Distance around: ______ cm

Set B

A kite string is 27 feet long.
Some of the string is cut off.
Now the kite string is 18 feet long.
How many feet of kite string were cut off?

Write an equation and draw a picture.

27 – ? = 18 or 18 + ? = 27

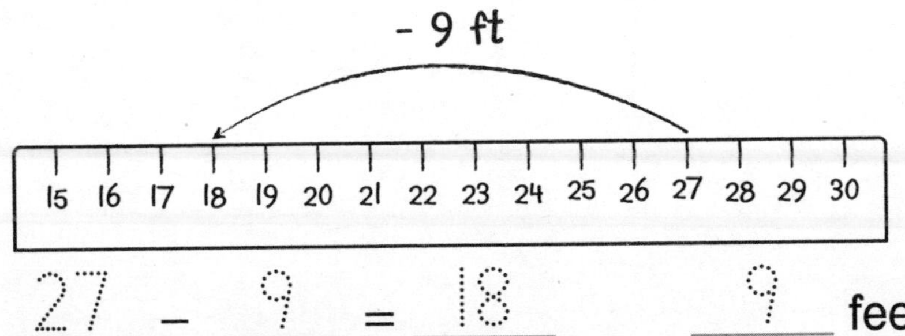

27 – 9 = 18   9 feet

Write an equation using a ? for the unknown number. Then draw a picture to solve.

2. A piece of yarn is 42 inches long. Mia cuts some of it off. It is now 26 inches long. How much yarn did Mia cut off?

____

Set C

A book measures 10 inches long. Another book measures 13 inches long. What is the total length of both books?

You can show 10 + 13 on a number line.

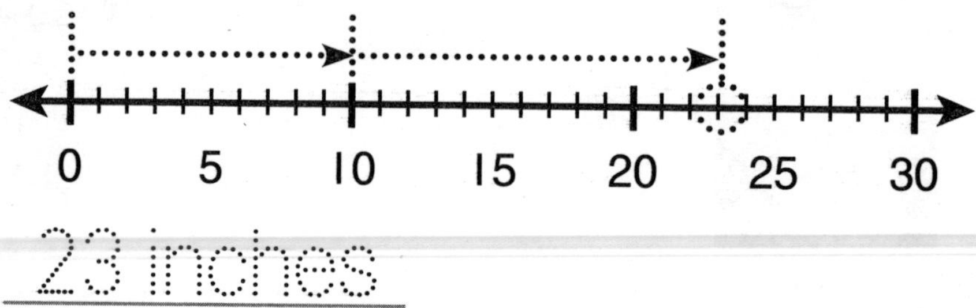

23 inches

Solve the problem using the number line.

3. One room in Jackie's house is 15 feet long. Another room is 9 feet long. What is the total length of both rooms?

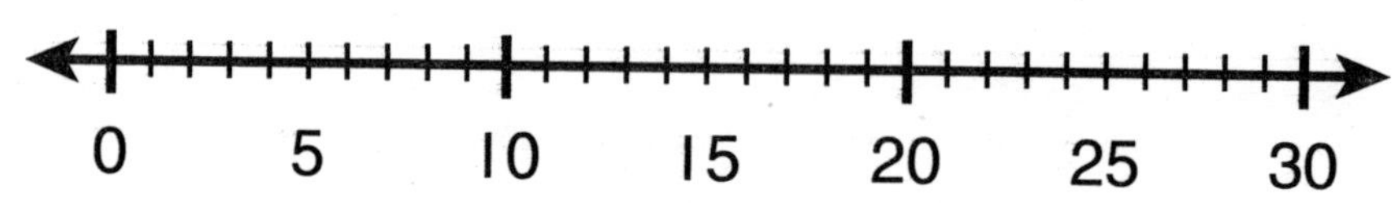

____

Set D

Thinking Habits

Use Tools

Which of these tools can I use?

counters	paper and pencil
cubes	place-value blocks
measuring tools	string
number line	technology

Am I using the tool correctly?

Choose a tool to solve the problem.

4. Damon's shoelace is 45 inches long. His shoelace breaks. One piece is 28 inches long. How long is the other piece?

Explain your solution and why you chose the tool you used.

Name ______________________________

Assessment Practice

1. A notebook has a length of 7 in. and a width of 5 in. What is the total distance around the notebook? Use the image below for help.

5 in.

7 in. 7 in.

5 in.

Distance around: ______ in.

2. Kate is 48 inches tall. Tom is 2 inches taller than Kate. James is 3 inches shorter than Tom.

How tall is James?

Ⓐ 45 inches
Ⓑ 47 inches
Ⓒ 50 inches
Ⓓ 53 inches

3. Alexis has a rope that is 7 feet long. Mariah's rope is 9 feet long. Sam's rope is 3 feet longer than Mariah's rope.

Use the measurements on the cards to complete each sentence.

2 feet	5 feet	12 feet

Sam's rope is ________ long.

Alexis's rope is ________ shorter than Mariah's rope.

Sam's rope is ________ longer than Alexis's rope.

4. Joe rides his bike 18 miles. Then he rides 7 more miles.

Use the number line to find how far Joe rides. Then explain your work.

5. Pat says that each unknown equals 25 cm. Do you agree? Choose Yes or No.

47 cm + ? = 72 cm	○ Yes	○ No
? + 39 cm = 54 cm	○ Yes	○ No
99 cm − 64 cm = ?	○ Yes	○ No
93 cm − ? = 68 cm	○ Yes	○ No

6. Grace got a plant that was 34 cm tall. The plant grew and now it is 42 cm tall. How many centimeters did the plant grow?

Ⓐ 8 cm
Ⓑ 12 cm
Ⓒ 42 cm
Ⓓ 76 cm

7. Claire rides her bike 26 miles on Saturday and Sunday. She rides 8 miles on Sunday. How many miles does she ride on Saturday?

Write an equation to show the unknown. Then use the number line to solve the problem.

_____ ○ _____ = _____

_____ miles

8. Chris had a string that is 18 cm long. He cut off 7 cm. How much string is left?

A. Which of these tools could you use to solve the problem? Choose all that apply.

☐ centimeter ruler
☐ paper and pencil
☐ measuring cup
☐ number line
☐ inch ruler

B. Write an equation to show the unknown. Then draw a number line to solve.

_____ ○ _____ = _____

_____ cm

Name ______________________________

Fishing Fun

Jim and his family go on a fishing trip. They use a boat and fishing gear to help them catch fish.

1. Jim takes this fishing box with him. What is the distance around the front of the fishing box? Write an equation to help solve the problem.

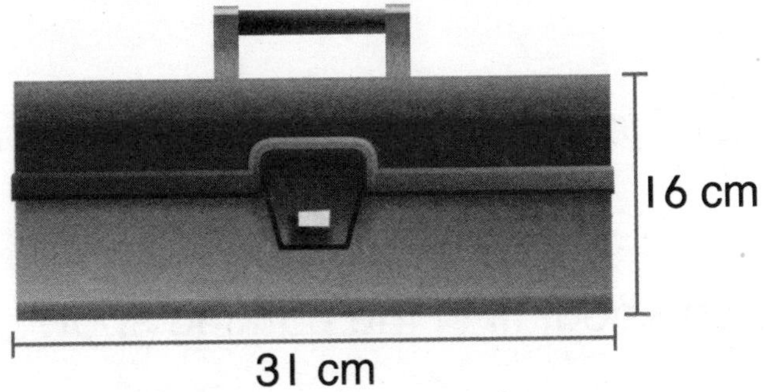

____

Distance around: ______ centimeters

2. Jim's fishing pole is 38 inches long. His dad's fishing pole is 96 inches long. How much shorter is Jim's pole than his dad's pole?

Part A Write a subtraction equation that shows the problem.

____

Part B Solve the problem.

______ inches shorter

3. Jim catches a fish 49 yards away from the shore. Later, he helps row the boat closer to the shore. Now he is 27 yards away from the shore. How many yards closer to shore is Jim now than when he caught the fish?

Part A Write an addition equation that shows the problem.

____

Part B Solve the problem.

______ yards

4. Jim catches a silver fish that is 12 inches long. His sister catches a green fish that is 27 inches long.

What is the total length of both fish? Use the number line to solve.

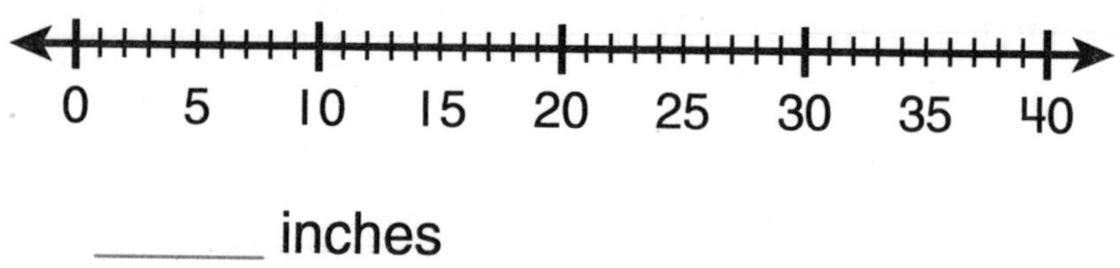

_____ inches

5. Jim has 27 yards of fishing line. He gives 12 yards of line to a friend. How many yards of line does Jim have left?

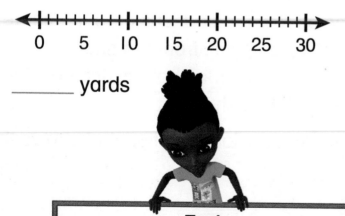

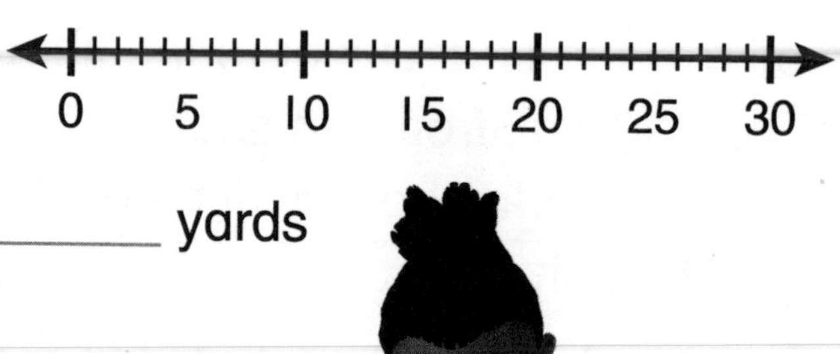

_____ yards

Tools

counters	paper and pencil
cubes	place-value blocks
measuring tools	string
number line	technology

6. Jim's family meets a man with a big boat. A parking spot at the dock is 32 feet long. Will the man's car and boat fit in the parking spot?

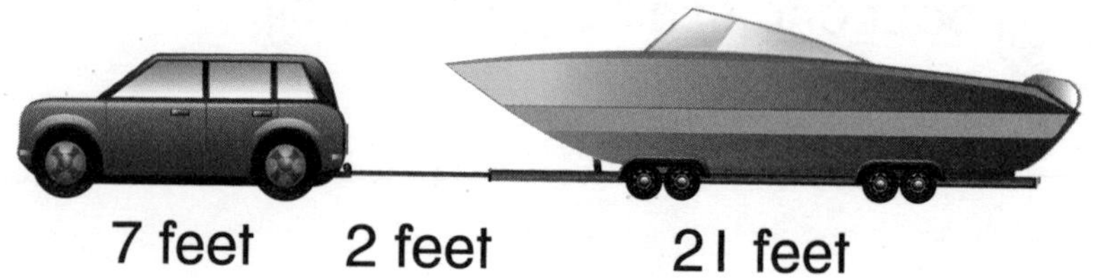

Part A

What do you need to find? _____

_____

_____

_____

Part B

What is the total length? Write an equation to solve.

_____ _____

Will the car and boat fit in the parking spot? Explain.

_____

_____

What tool did you use? _____

Graphs and Data

Essential Question: How can line plots, bar graphs, and picture graphs be used to show data and answer questions?

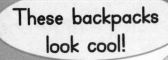

These backpacks look cool!
But which one would work better for you?
Wow! Let's do this project and learn more.

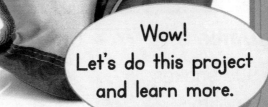

enVision® STEM Project: Comparing Objects and Data

Find Out Work with a partner. Compare two backpacks. Which one holds more? Which one has more parts? Which one is easier to put on? Think of other ways to compare.

Journal: Make a Book Show what you learn in a book. In your book, also:

- Tell one good thing and one bad thing about each backpack.
- Draw line plots, picture graphs, and bar graphs to show and compare data.

Name ______________________

Review What You Know

Vocabulary

1. Circle the number that has a 6 in the **tens** place.

406

651

160

2. Circle the **tally marks** that show 6.

Favorite Toy	
Car	𝍸 II
Blocks	IIII
Doll	𝍸 I

3. Circle the **difference**.

22 − 9 = 13

34 + 61 = 95

Comparing Numbers

4. A zoo has 405 snakes. It has 375 monkeys. Compare the number of snakes to the number of monkeys.

Write > or <.

405 ◯ 375

Interpret Data

5.

Picnic Tickets Sold	
Jean	16
Paulo	18
Fatima	12

Who sold the most picnic tickets?

____

Addition and Subtraction

6. Byron scores 24 points in a game.
Ava scores 16 points in the same game.
How many more points does Byron score than Ava?

_____ more points

Name ______________________

Pick a Project

PROJECT 15A

What types of flowers grow in your neighborhood?

Project: Graph Data About Flowers

PROJECT 15B

How many birds do you see every day?

Project: Create a Bird-Watching Poster

PROJECT 15C

Why should you plan a Florida vacation?

Project: Make a Florida Travel Brochure

Before watching the video, think:
How do you know what size clothing you should wear? Is there a way you can find out without trying the clothes on?

I can ...
model with math to solve a problem that involves making graphs to study data.

Name ______________________________

Lesson 15-1
Line Plots

I can ...
measure the lengths of objects, then make a line plot to organize the data.

I can also make math arguments.

Solve & Share

Find four objects that are each shorter than 9 inches. Measure the length of each object to the nearest inch. Record the measurements in the table.

Then plot the data on the number line.

Which object is longest? Which is shortest?

Object	Length in Inches

Lengths of Objects

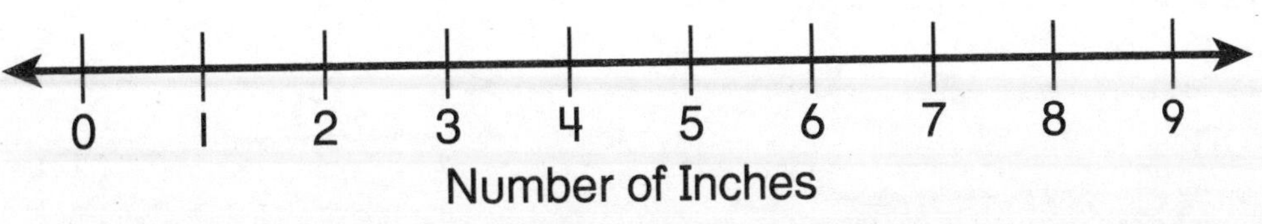

Visual Learning Bridge

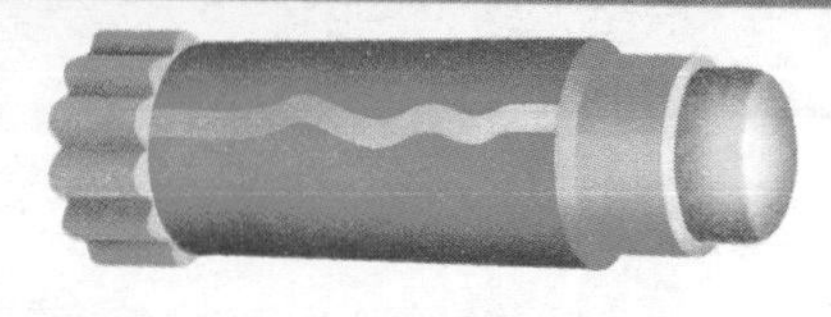

2 inches long

You can measure the length of objects. This glue stick is 2 inches long.

You can use a table to record the measurement **data**.

Object	Length in Inches
Glue Stick	2
String	4
Feather	6
Scissors	4

You can make a **line plot** to show the data. Place a dot over the number that shows each length.

The two dots above the 4 tell me that two objects are 4 inches long.

Lengths of Objects

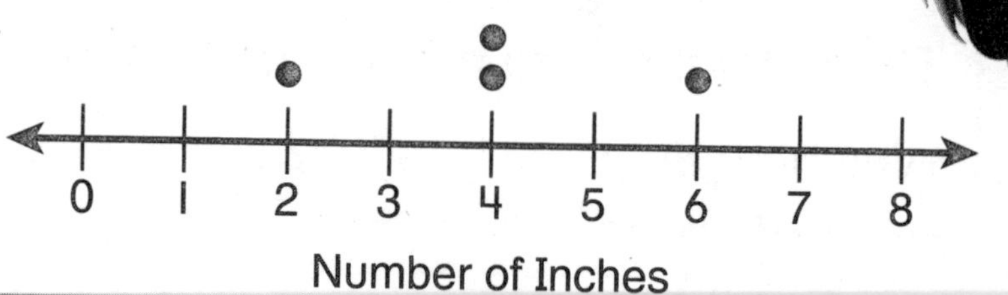

Number of Inches

Convince Me! Measure the length of your pencil to the nearest inch. Record your measurement on the line plot above. How does it change the data?

Guided Practice Use a ruler to measure each object in inches. Record each length in the table. Then make a line plot. Show each length on the line plot.

1. 4 inches long

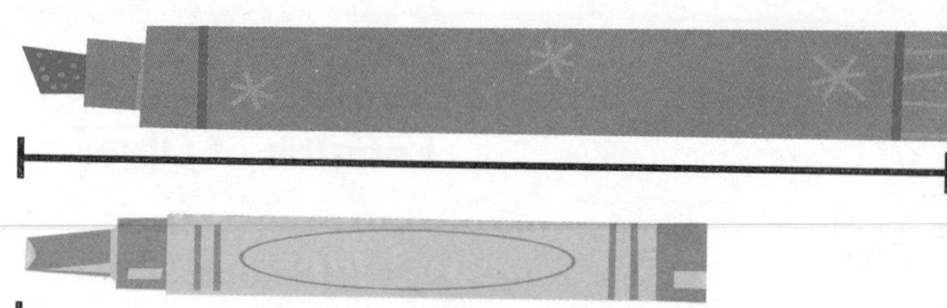

____ inches long

2.

Object	Length (in.)
Marker	4
Crayon	

Lengths of Objects

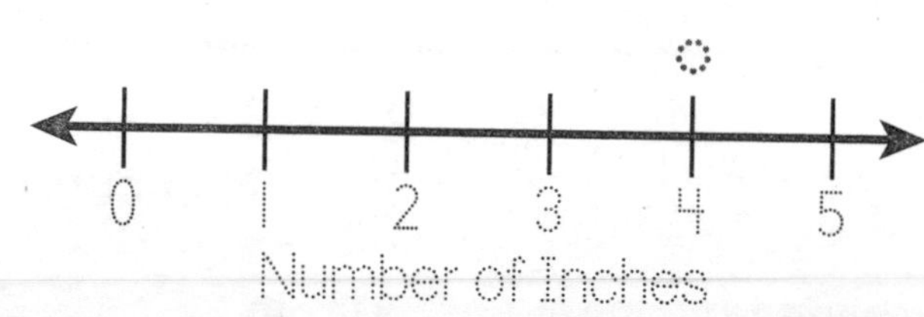

Name ____________________

Tools Assessment

Independent Practice Use a ruler to measure each object in inches. Record each length in the table. Show each length on the line plot.

3. The paintbrush is _____ inches long.

4. The chalk is _____ inches long.

5. The straw is _____ inches long.

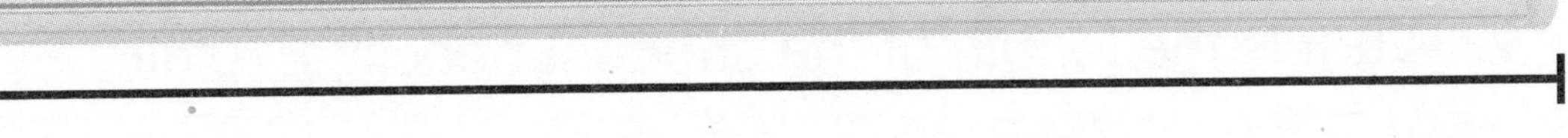

6. The feather is _____ inches long.

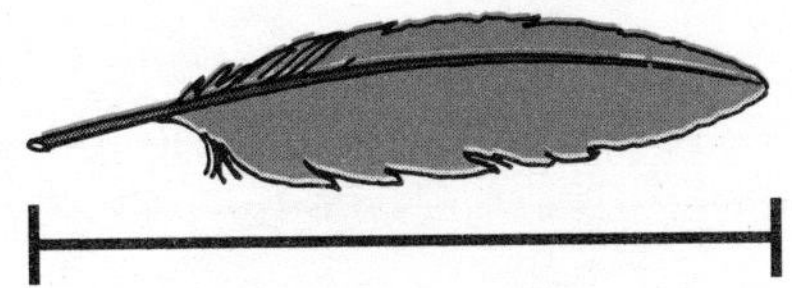

7.

Object	Length in Inches
Paintbrush	
Chalk	
Straw	
Feather	

Lengths of Objects

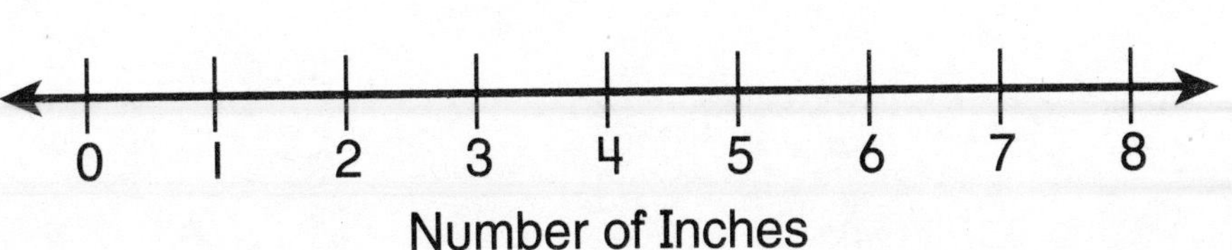

Problem Solving Solve each problem. Use the line plot.

8. Be Precise Sophia measured the lengths of her colored pencils and made a table. Use the data to make a line plot.

Pencil Color	Length in Inches
Red	4
Blue	3
Green	7
Yellow	9

You can use dots or Xs to record data in a line plot.

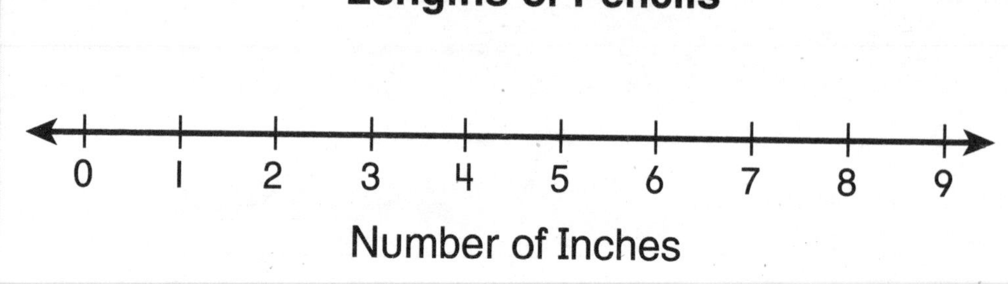

9. What is the length of the shortest pencil? Explain.

____

____

10. Higher Order Thinking What are the lengths of the two pencils have a total length of 16 inches? Explain.

____

____

____

11. Assessment Practice Measure the length of the purple pencil in inches. Write the length below. Record your measurement on the line plot above in Item 8.

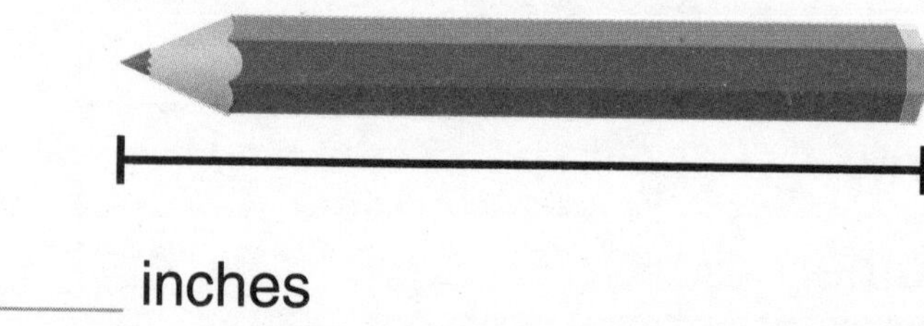

_____ inches

Name ____________________

Activity

Lesson 15-2
More Line Plots

I can ...
measure the lengths of objects, then make a line plot to organize the data.

I can also look for patterns.

Solve & Share

Measure the length of your shoe to the nearest inch. Then use your data and data from your class to make a line plot.

Tell one thing you learn from the data.

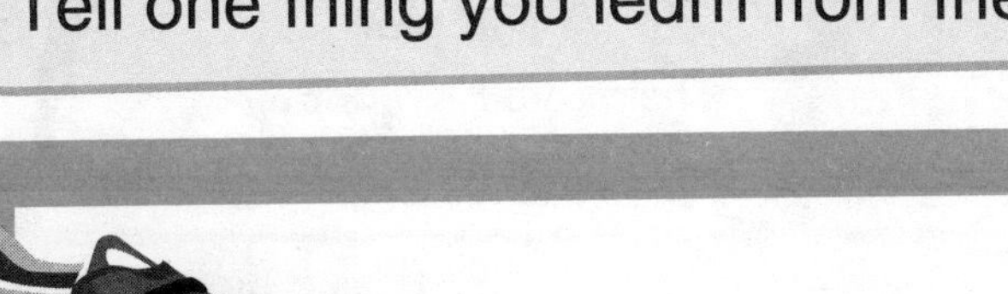

Shoe Lengths

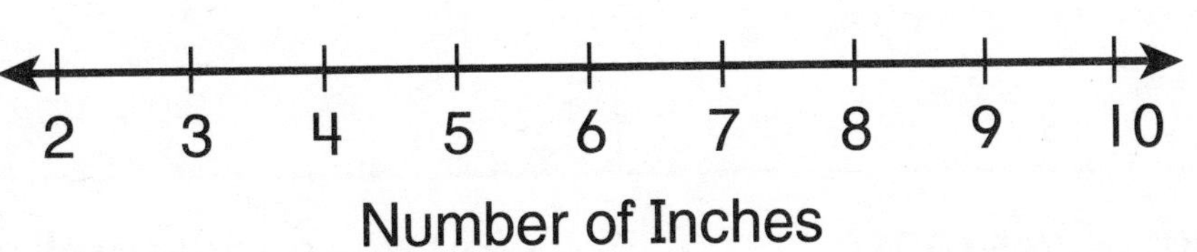

Some students measure their heights. They record the data in a table. Are there any patterns in the data?

Student Heights in Inches			
46	48	47	49
49	47	46	48
48	49	50	47
49	48	49	51

You can make a line plot to look for patterns.

To make a line plot, draw a number line, and write a title and labels to fit your data.

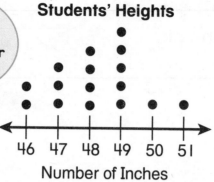

Students' Heights

46 47 48 49 50 51

Number of Inches

The most common height is 49 inches tall!

A line plot helps you organize data.

What else does the data show?

Convince Me! In the example above, how many students measured their height? Tell how you know.

Guided Practice Use the table to make a line plot. Then use the line plot to answer each question.

1.

Feather Lengths (cm)			
7	5	6	4
9	4	7	6
6	8	6	4
7	5	8	6

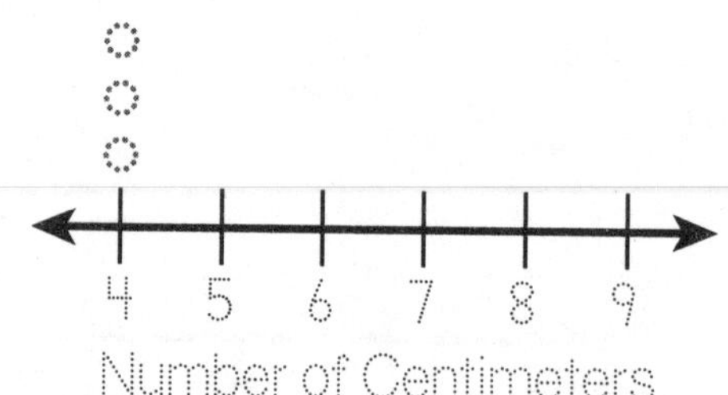

2. What is the most common feather length? 6 cm

3. Why does the number line use the numbers 4 through 9?

Name ______________________

Tools Assessment

Independent Practice Collect data and use the data to complete the line plot. Then use the line plot to solve the problems.

4. Measure the length of your pencil in centimeters. Collect pencil-length data from your classmates. Make a line plot with the data.

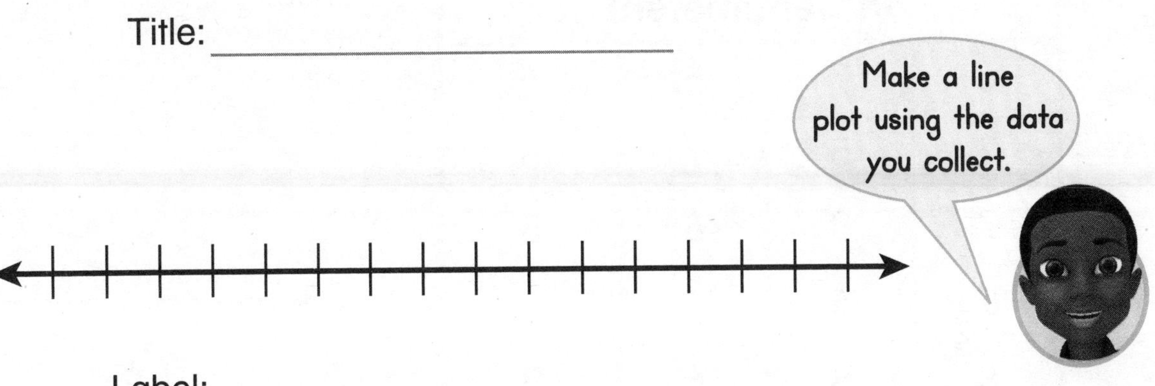
Title:
Make a line plot using the data you collect.
Label:

5. What is the length of the longest pencil?

______

6. What is the sum of the lengths of the shortest and longest pencils?

______

7. What is the difference in lengths between the shortest and longest pencils?

______

8. What is the most common pencil length?

______

9. **Vocabulary** Use these words to complete the sentences. **longest** **line plot** **order**

A ______ can help you see the data in ______.

A line plot can show the lengths of the shortest and ______ objects.

Problem Solving

Model Use the data in the table to complete the line plot. Then use the line plot to solve the problems.

10.

Crayon Lengths in Centimeters			
6	7	5	6
7	5	7	6
7	8	6	5
5	6	7	6
8	8	6	8

Title: ______________________

Label: ______________________

What numbers will you use to make your line plot?

11. Higher Order Thinking Measure the length of one of your crayons in centimeters, 5 different times. Make a line plot of the data on a separate sheet of paper. Did you get the same measurement each time? Explain.

____

____

____

____

12. Assessment Practice Measure the length of the blue crayon to the nearest centimeter. Write the length below.

____

Then record your measurement on the line plot above that you made in Item 10.

Name ______________________

Lesson 15-3
Bar Graphs

I can ...
draw bar graphs and use them to solve problems.

I can also be precise in my work.

Solve & Share

The graph shows the number of birthdays in each season for a class.

Use the graph to write the number of birthdays in the table. How many more birthdays are celebrated during spring, fall, and winter than during summer? Be ready to explain how you know.

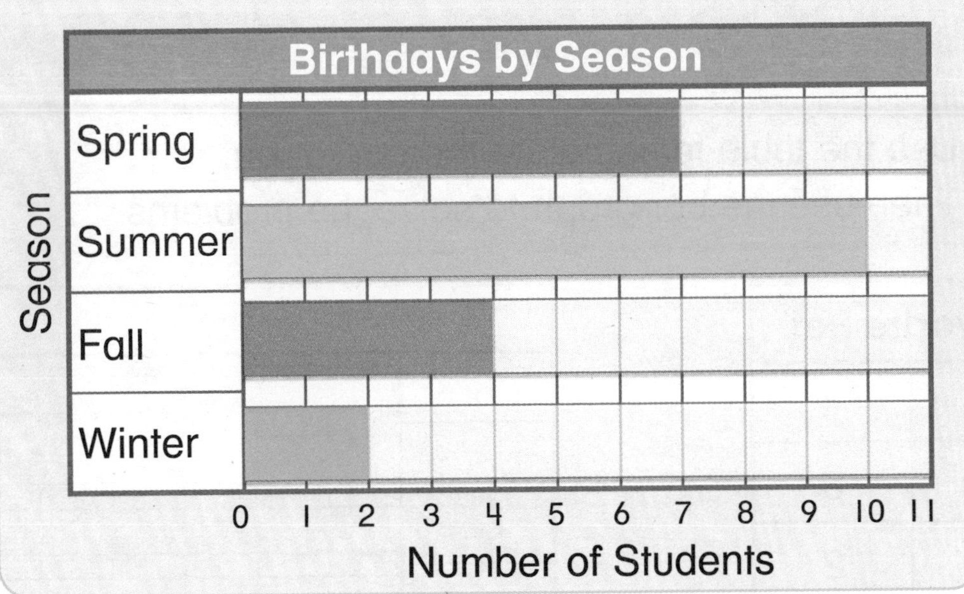

Birthdays by Season	
Spring	
Summer	
Fall	
Winter	

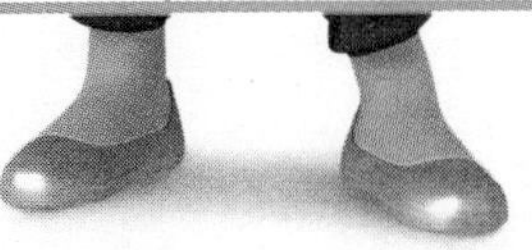

Visual Learning Bridge

Use the table to make a **bar graph**.
First, write a title and label the graph.

Favorite Activities	
Music	3
Dance	4
Art	1
Drama	6

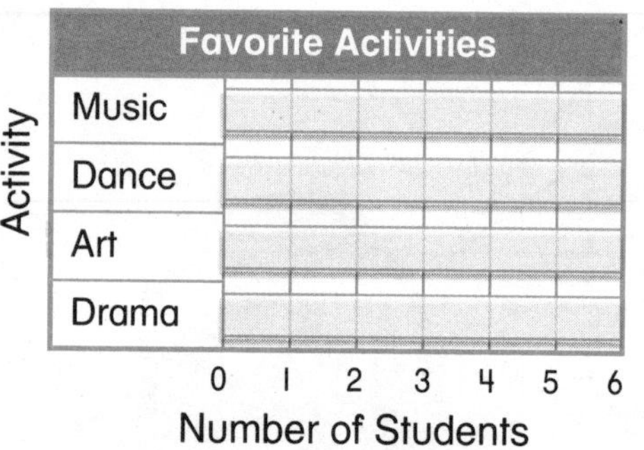

Then color boxes for each activity to match the data.

The length of the bars tell you how many students like each activity.

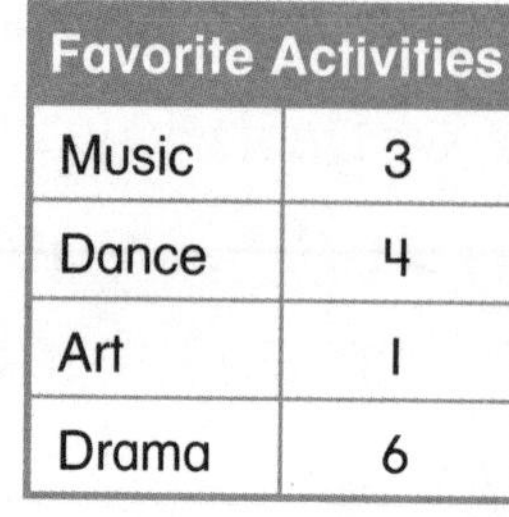

Favorite Activities	
Music	3
Dance	4
Art	1
Drama	6

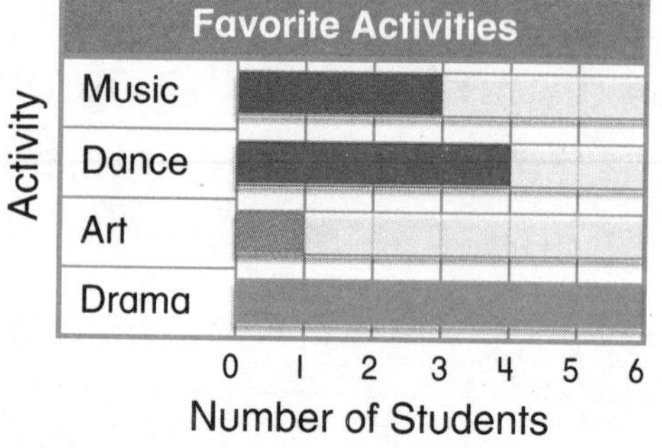

Convince Me! Which activity did the most students choose? Explain how you know.

Use the table to complete the bar graph. Then use the bar graph to solve the problems.

Favorite Pet	
Cat	4
Dog	6
Bird	2
Turtle	3

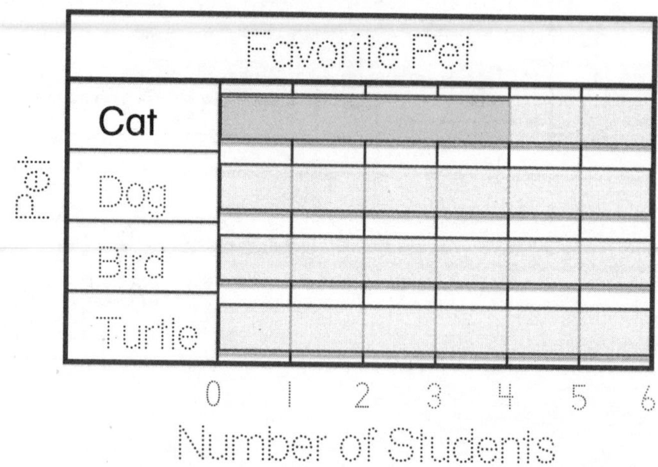

1. How many students chose cat?

   4

2. How many students chose bird or dog?

   ____

Tools Assessment

Name ______________________________

Independent Practice

Use the bar graph to solve the problems.

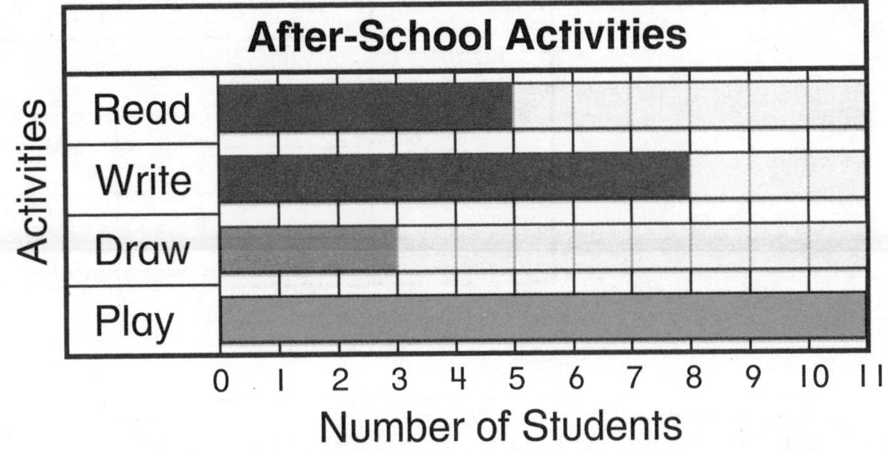

3. How many students write after school?

_____

4. How many fewer students draw than write after school? _____ fewer students

5. Which activity do the fewest students do after school? ______________

6. How many students read or draw after school? _____

7. Which activity do the most students do after school? ______________

8. How many more students play than read after school? _____ more students

9. **Higher Order Thinking** How would the graph be different if 2 students changed their after-school activity from play to read?

Problem Solving Solve the problems below.

10. Model Wanda goes to the farm. She buys 8 pears, 5 oranges, 2 apples, and 9 peaches.

Use this data to make a bar graph.

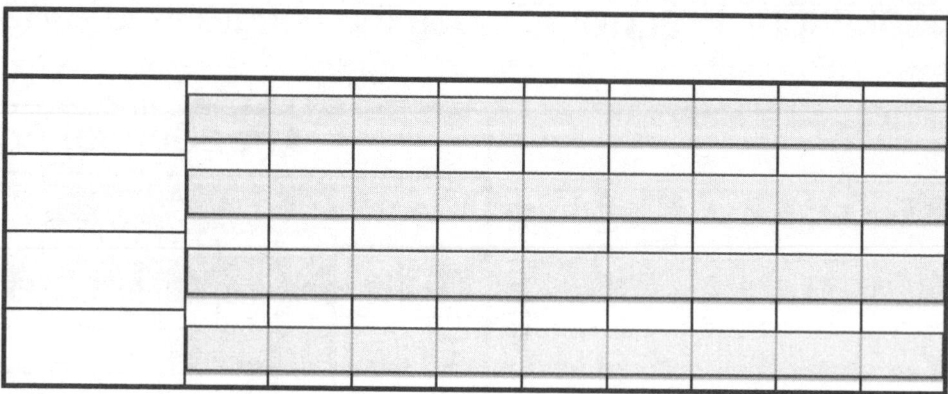

11. Higher Order Thinking Look at the graph you made in Item 10. How would the graph change if Wanda returns 3 of the pears that she buys?

____

____

12. Assessment Practice Look at the bar graph you made in Item 10. Which are correct? Choose all that apply.

- ☐ Wanda buys the same number of pears and peaches.
- ☐ Wanda buys 3 more oranges than apples.
- ☐ Wanda buys 24 pieces of fruit in all.
- ☐ Wanda buys 3 fewer oranges than pears.

Name ______________________________

Activity

Lesson 15-4
Picture Graphs

I can ...
draw picture graphs and use them to solve problems.

I can also look for patterns.

Solve & Share

The picture graph shows the favorite subjects of a class. Draw a smiley face on the graph to show your favorite subject. Then interview two classmates and add their data.

How many students responded to the survey?
Which subject do most students like best?
How many students like math or science best?

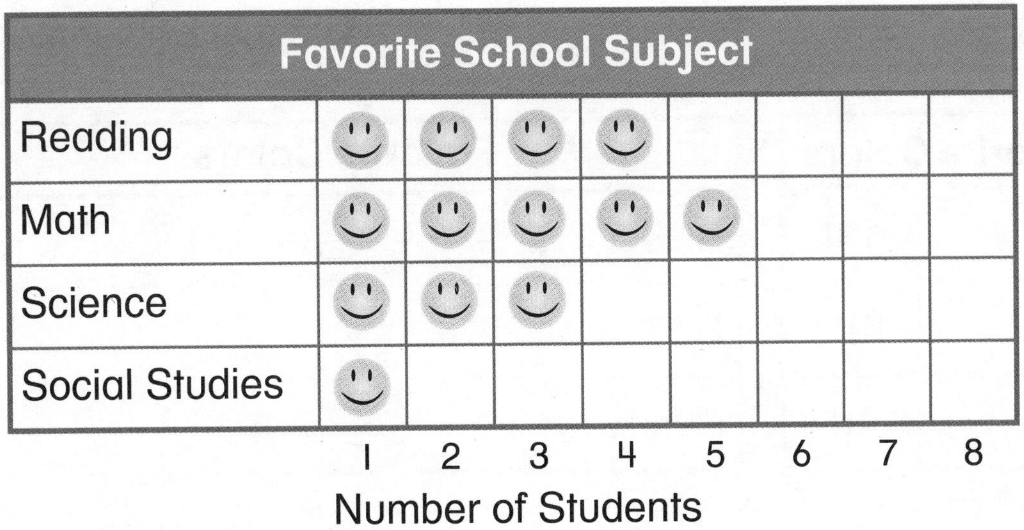

Favorite School Subject								
Reading	🙂	🙂	🙂	🙂				
Math	🙂	🙂	🙂	🙂	🙂			
Science	🙂	🙂	🙂					
Social Studies	🙂							
	1	2	3	4	5	6	7	8

Number of Students

 Visual Learning  Glossary

Visual Learning Bridge

The tally chart shows the favorite ball games of Ms. Green's class.

Favorite Ball Games	
Baseball	II
Soccer	~~IIII~~ III
Tennis	IIII

You can show the same data in another way.

Choose a **symbol** to represent the data.

The symbol will be 🯅. Each 🯅 represents 1 student.

A **picture graph** uses pictures to show data.

You can draw the symbols to show the data.

8 students chose soccer!

Favorite Ball Games	
Baseball	🯅🯅
Soccer	🯅🯅🯅🯅🯅🯅🯅🯅
Tennis	🯅🯅🯅🯅

Each 🯅 = 1 student

Convince Me! How are the tally chart and the picture graph for the favorite ball games of Ms. Green's class alike?

Guided Practice Use the tally chart to complete the picture graph. Then use the picture graph to solve the problems.

Favorite Colors	
Blue	~~IIII~~
Red	~~IIII~~ I
Purple	III

Favorite Colors	
Blue	✏✏✏✏✏
Red	
Purple	

Each ✏ = 1 vote

1. How many students like blue or red best?

   11

2. Which color is the favorite of most students?

   ______

Name ______

Tools Assessment

Independent Practice

Use the tally chart to complete the picture graph. Then use the picture graph to solve the problems.

3.

Favorite Season	
Spring	IIII
Summer	~~IIII~~ ~~IIII~~
Fall	~~IIII~~ I
Winter	II

Favorite Season	
Spring	
Summer	
Fall	
Winter	

Each 🯅 = 1 vote

4. How many students like fall best?

______

5. Which season do exactly 4 students like best? ______

6. Which season do the fewest students like?

______

7. How many fewer students voted for winter than for summer? ______

8. How many more students voted for summer than for spring and winter combined? ______ more students

9. How many students like the season with the most votes? ______

10. **Higher Order Thinking** Look at the picture graph above. How would the graph change if 2 students changed their votes from summer to fall?

______

______

Problem Solving

Use the tally chart to complete the picture graph.
Use the picture graph to solve the problems.

11. Model Bob made a tally chart to show the trees in a park.

Trees in the Park	
Birch	III
Oak	~~IIII~~ I
Maple	~~IIII~~
Pine	II

Trees in the Park	
Birch	
Oak	
Maple	
Pine	

Each [tree] = 1 tree

You can model data using a picture graph.

12. enVision® STEM Birch, oak, maple, and pine trees are common in North America. Which type of tree is most common in the park?

____

13. Higher Order Thinking How many birch and maple trees are there in all?

____

14. Assessment Practice Draw a picture graph to show the data in the table.

Favorite Drink	
Milk	III
Juice	IIII
Water	I

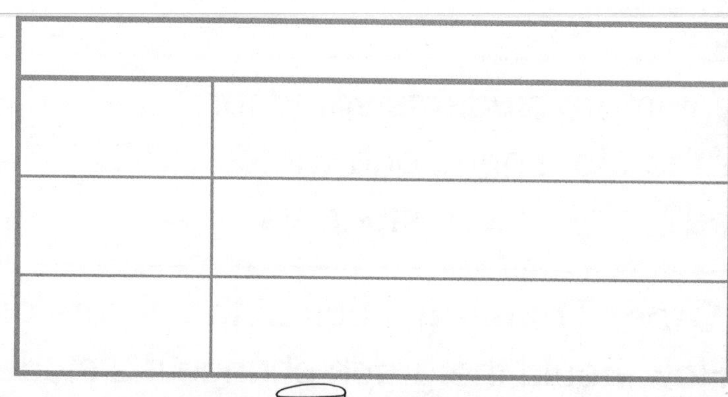

Each [cup] = 1 vote

Name ___

Activity

Lesson 15-5

Draw Conclusions from Graphs

I can ...
draw conclusions from graphs.

I can also model with math.

Solve & Share

7 students voted for Turtle as their favorite pond animal. 10 students voted for Frog. 4 students voted for Fish. Make a picture graph to show the data. Write two things you notice about the data.

Favorite Pond Animals

Turtle	
Frog	
Fish	

Each ★ = 1 vote

1. ___

2. ___

Look at the bar graph. What does it show?

You can also compare information and solve problems.

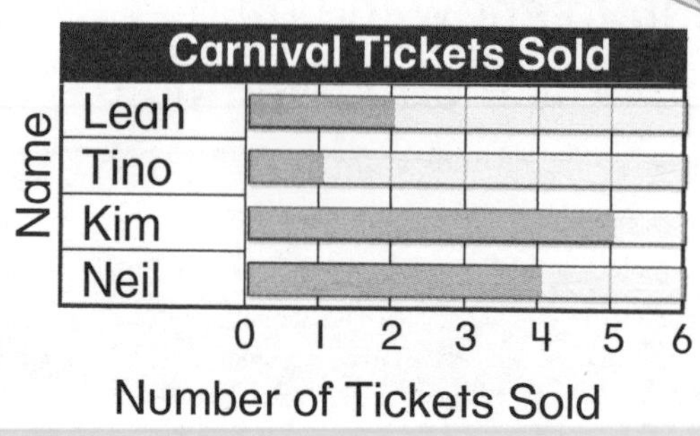

Convince Me! Look at the graph above. How many tickets did Kim and Neil sell in all? How do you know?

Guided Practice Use the bar graph to solve the problems.

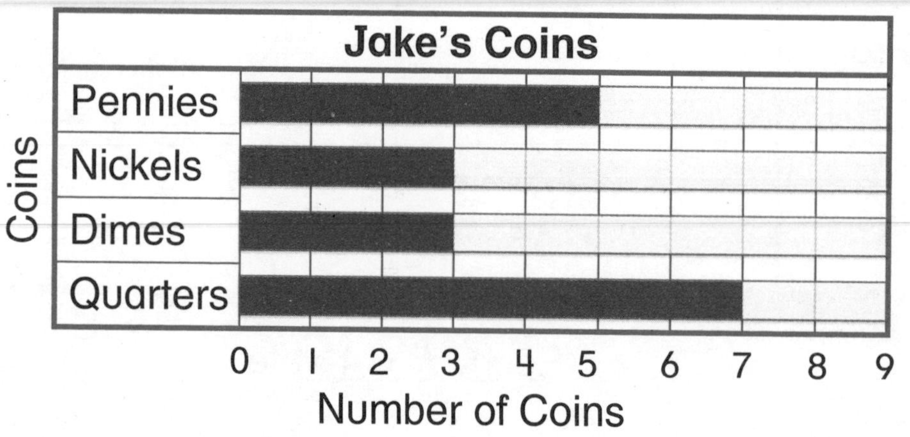

1. How many pennies does Jake have?
   5

2. Jake spends 3 of his quarters. How many does he have left?
   ____

Name ______________________

Tools Assessment

Independent Practice

Use the bar graph to solve the problems.

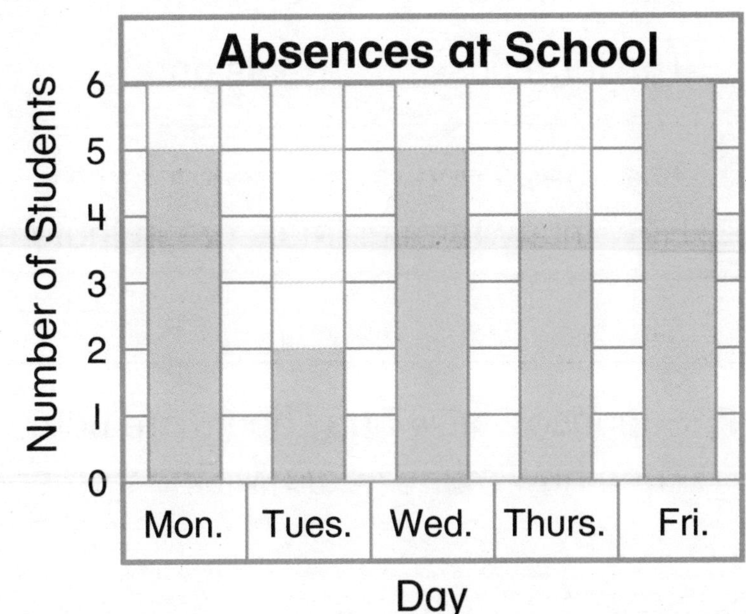

3. How many absences were there in all on Tuesday and Thursday?

____

4. Were fewer students absent on Monday or Friday? How many fewer?

____

5. Three of the students absent on Friday were boys. How many girls were absent on Friday?

____

6. On which two days were the same number of students absent?

____

7. Were more students absent on Wednesday or Thursday? How many more?

____

8. **Higher Order Thinking** The graph shows the number of absences last week. This week, there are 19 absences. Compare the number of absences this week to the number of absences last week.

____

____

____

Problem Solving Use the bar graph to solve each problem.

9. **Make Sense** Complete each sentence.

The farm has _____ cows and _____ horses.

The farm has _____ goats and _____ sheep.

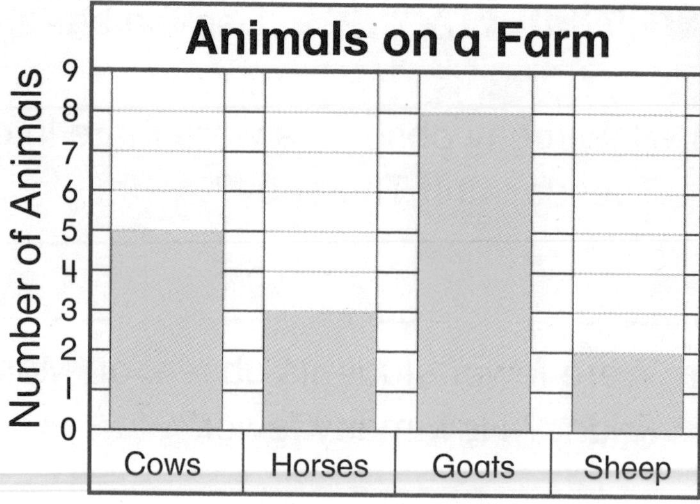

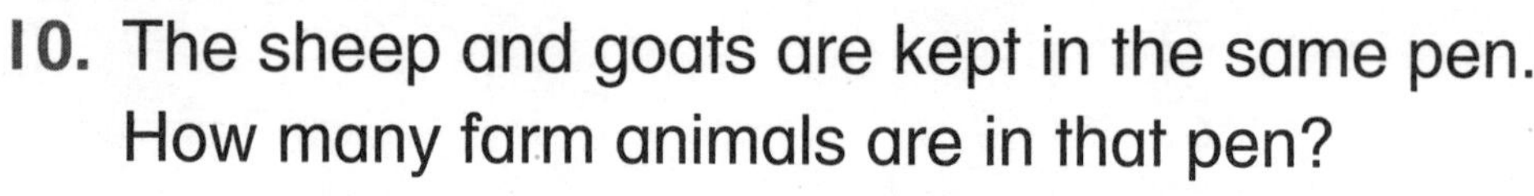

10. The sheep and goats are kept in the same pen. How many farm animals are in that pen?

_____

11. Suppose 3 new baby goats are born. Then how many goats will the farmer have?

_____

12. How many fewer horses than cows are on the farm?

_____ fewer horses

13. Write the order of animals on the farm from the greatest number to the least number.

____

14. **Higher Order Thinking** Do you think the bars on a bar graph should all be the same color? Explain.

____

____

15. **Assessment Practice** The farmer wants to buy some sheep. He wants to have as many sheep as cows. How many more sheep should the farmer buy?

_____ more sheep

Name ____________________

Activity

Problem Solving

Lesson 15-6
Reasoning

I can ...
reason about data in bar graphs and picture graphs to write and solve problems.

I can also show equal shares in shapes.

Solve & Share

Make a picture graph to show how many connecting cubes, counters, and ones cubes you have. Then write and solve a problem about your data.

Math Tools	
Connecting Cubes 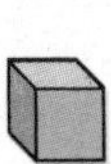	
Counters	
Ones Cubes	

Each ______ = 1 math tool

____

____

____

Thinking Habits
What do the symbols mean?
How are the numbers in the problem related?

The bar graph shows the number of stamps each student has collected.

Write and solve a problem about the data in the bar graph.

Stamp Collections

Student: Ben, Lara, David, Gail

0 1 2 3 4 5 6 7 8 9 10 11 12 13 14 15 16 17 18 19 20 21 22 23 24 25

Number of Stamps

How can I use reasoning to write and solve a problem?

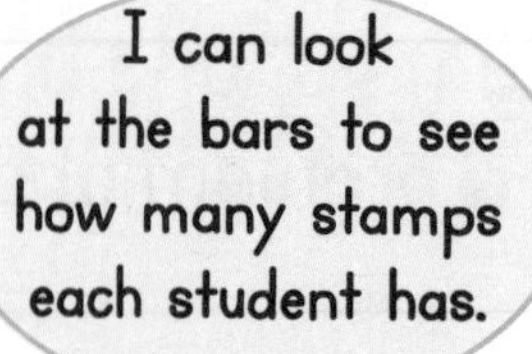

I can look at the bars to see how many stamps each student has.

I can write a problem to compare the number of stamps two students have.

My Problem

How many more stamps does Lara have than Gail?

25 - 15 = 10

10 more stamps

Convince Me! Use reasoning to write your own problem about the data in the graph. Then solve it.

☆ Guided Practice ☆ Use the bar graph to write and solve problems.

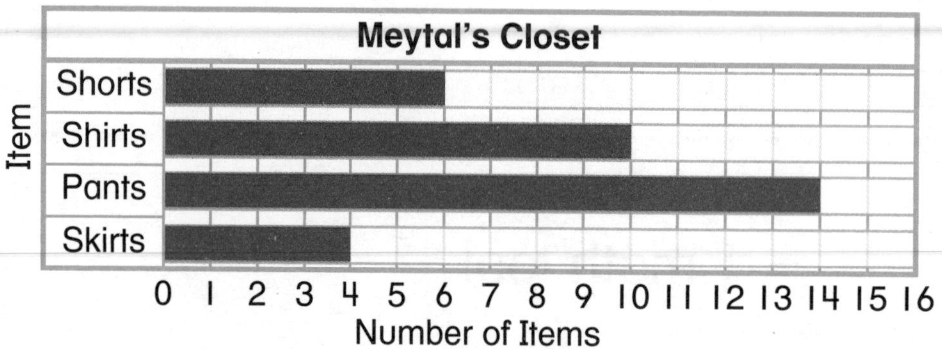

1. How many shirts and skirts are there in all?

____ ◯ ____ = ____

2. ____________

____ ◯ ____ = ____

Name ______________________

Independent Practice

Use the bar graph to write and solve problems.

3. ______________________

____

____

___ ◯ ___ = ___

____

____

4. ______________________

____

____

___ ◯ ___ = ___

____

____

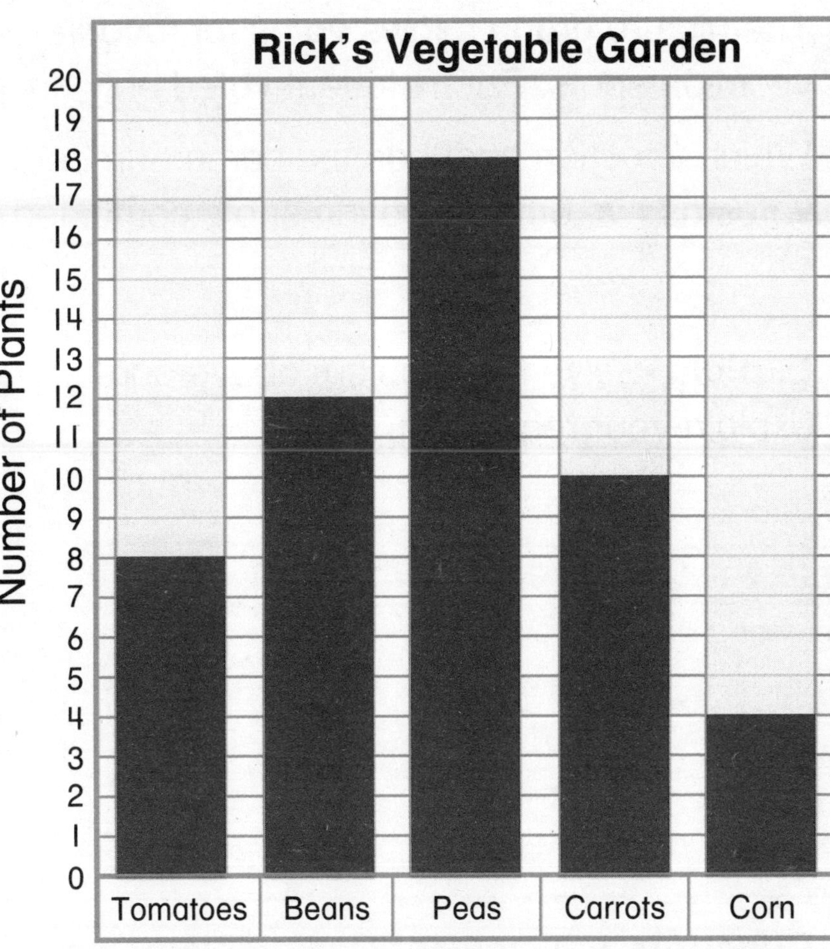

Use reasoning to think about how the numbers, bars, and plants are related.

Problem Solving

 **Performance Task**

Vacation Time!

The picture graph shows votes for favorite vacation spots. Each student voted only once.

Which vacation spot has the same number of votes as two other vacation spots combined?

Votes for Favorite Vacation Spot	
Beach	✔✔✔✔✔✔✔✔✔✔✔
Mountains	✔✔✔✔✔✔✔
City	✔✔✔✔
Theme Park	✔✔✔✔✔✔✔✔✔✔✔✔

Each ✔ = 1 vote

5. **Explain** Solve the problem above and explain your reasoning.

____

____

____

____

____

6. **Make Sense** How many students voted in all? Tell how you know.

____

____

____

____

____

7. **Reasoning** Write your own problem about the data in the graph. Then solve it.

____

____

____

___ ◯ ___ = ___

____

____

____

Name ______________________________

Fluency Practice Activity

I can ... add and subtract within 100.

I can also be precise in my work.

Find a partner. Point to a clue. Read the clue.

Look below the clues to find a match. Write the clue letter in the box next to the match.

Find a match for every clue.

Clues

A The difference is less than 16.

B The sum equals 43 + 25.

C The difference equals 75 − 46.

D The sum equals 53 + 20.

E The difference equals 96 − 19.

F The sum equals 75.

G The sum is between 60 and 65.

H The difference is between 25 and 28.

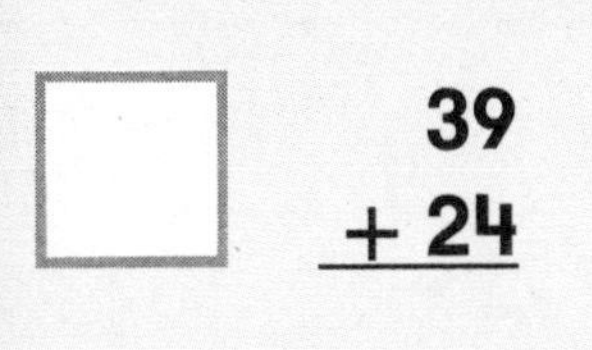

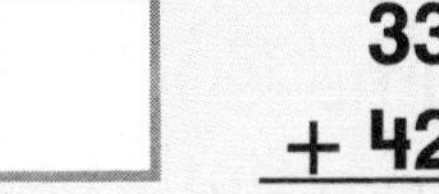

☐ 39 + 24	☐ 81 − 52	☐ 33 + 42	☐ 35 + 38
☐ 73 − 59	☐ 67 − 40	☐ 88 − 11	☐ 17 + 51

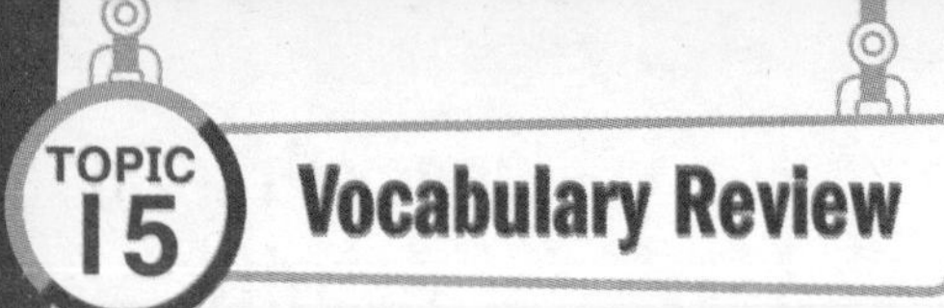

Word List
- bar graph
- data
- line plot
- picture graph
- symbol

Understand Vocabulary

Label each data display. Write *line plot, bar graph,* or *picture graph.*

1.

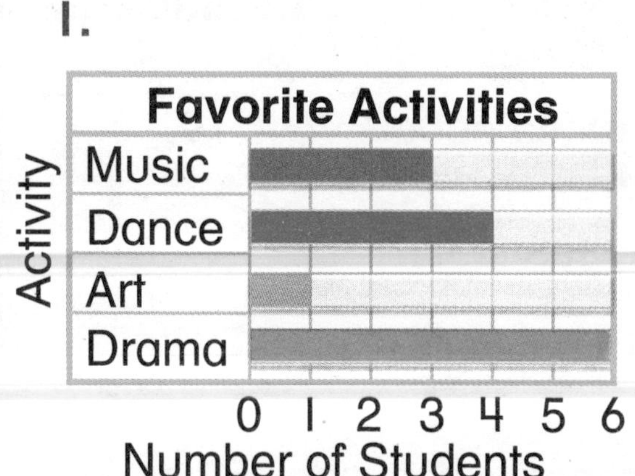

____

2.

Favorite Ball Games	
Baseball	🯅🯅
Soccer	🯅🯅🯅🯅🯅🯅🯅🯅
Tennis	🯅🯅🯅🯅

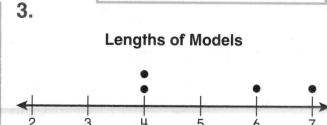

Each 🯅 = 1 student

____

3.

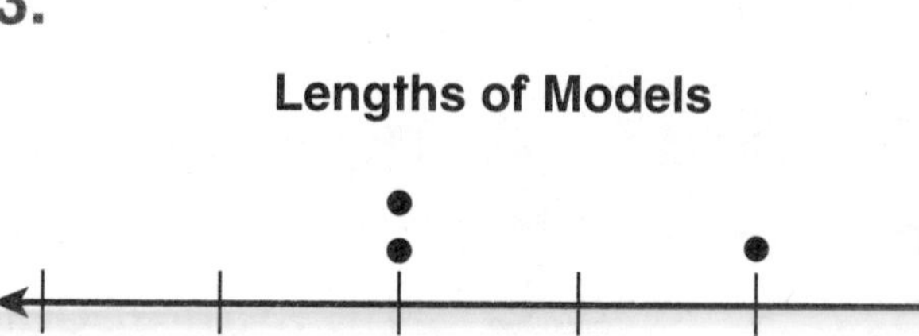

____

Use Vocabulary in Writing

4. Look at the graph in Item 2. Use words to tell how to find which ball game is the most popular. Use terms from the Word List.

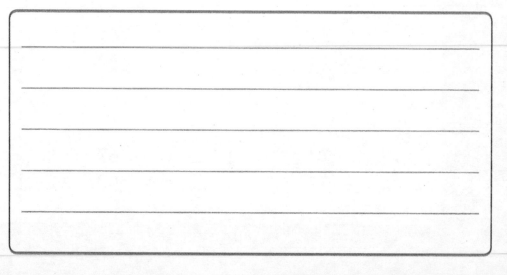

____

____

____

____

____

Name ______________________________

Set A

Reteaching

Line plots show and organize data.
Use an inch ruler. Measure the length of the toy car. Then record the measurement in the table.

Toy	Length in Inches
Car	3
Airplane	5
Doll	5
Block	1

Place a dot over the number that shows the length of each toy.

Length of Toys

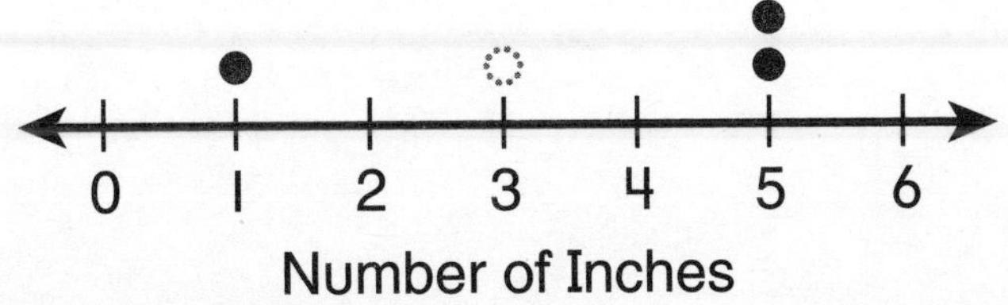

Complete the table and show the data on a line plot.

1. Use an inch ruler. Measure the length of the pencil. Then record the measurement in the table.

Object	Length in Inches
Pencil	
Stapler	6
Scissors	6
Eraser	3

2. Make a line plot to show each length in the table.

Length of Objects

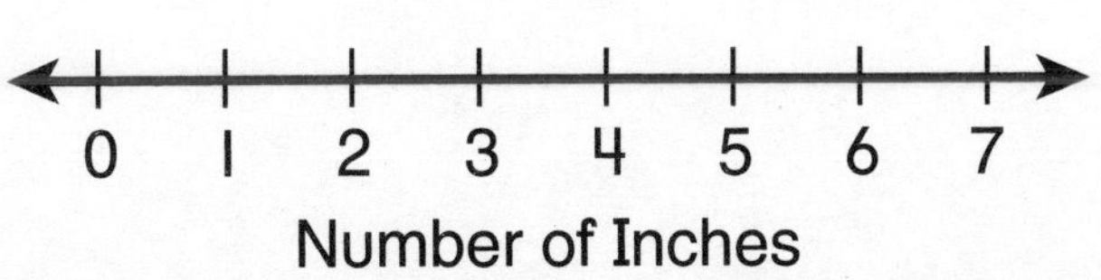

Set B

You can make a bar graph to show the data in a table.

Students voted for their favorite nut. The table shows the number of votes.

Favorite Nut	
Peanut	7
Almond	4
Cashew	5

Color one space for each vote in the bar graph.
Then use the graph to solve the problem.

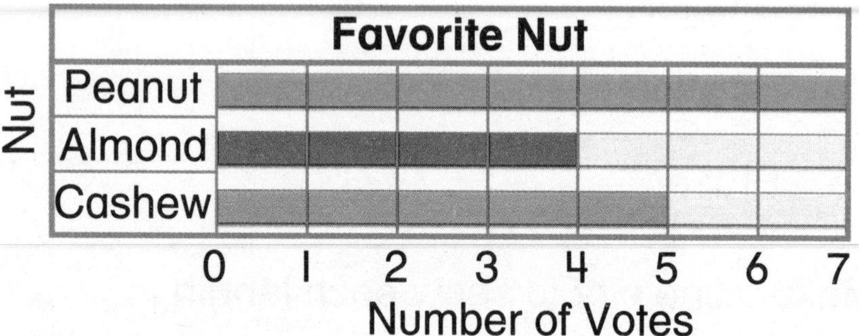

How many students voted? 16

Use the table to complete the bar graph. Then solve each problem.

3.

Favorite Yogurt	
Lemon	3
Vanilla	7
Banana	6

Favorite Yogurt

Flavor

Lemon

Vanilla

Banana

0 1 2 3 4 5 6 7

Number of Votes

4. How many more students voted for vanilla than banana? _____

5. How many fewer students voted for lemon than vanilla? _____

Name ________________________________

TOPIC 15

Set C ________________________________

Reteaching
Continued

A picture graph uses pictures or symbols to show data.

The tally chart shows votes for favorite sea animals.

Favorite Sea Animals	
Whale	卌 I
Dolphin	II
Seal	IIII

Use the data to make a picture graph. Each 웃 stands for 1 vote.

Favorite Sea Animals	
Whale	 웃웃웃웃웃웃
Dolphin	웃웃
Seal	 웃웃웃웃

Each 웃 = 1 vote

Which sea animal has the fewest votes?

dolphin

Use the tally chart to complete the picture graph.
Then solve each problem.

6.

Favorite Birds	
Blue Jay	卌
Robin	卌 III
Seagull	卌 卌

Favorite Birds	
Blue Jay	
Robin	
Seagull	

Each 🐦 = 1 vote

7. How many votes did seagull get?

_____

8. Which bird had the fewest votes?

____

Set D

Thinking Habits

Reasoning

What do the symbols mean?

How are the numbers in the problem related?

How can I write a word problem using the information that is given?

How do the numbers in my problem relate to each other?

How can I use a word problem to show what an equation means?

Use the picture graph to solve each problem. Each student voted once.

Favorite Winter Sport	
Skiing	❄❄❄❄❄❄❄
Snowboarding	❄❄❄❄❄❄❄❄❄❄
Skating	❄❄❄❄❄❄❄❄
Ice Fishing	❄❄❄❄

Each ❄ = 1 vote

9. How many fewer students chose ice fishing than snowboarding? ____

10. Write and solve your own problem about the data.

____

____

____ ◯ ____ = ____

____

Name ________________________________

TOPIC 15

Assessment Practice

1. Pam has 5 pennies, 2 nickels, 8 dimes, and 9 quarters. Show this data in the bar graph below. Draw the bars.

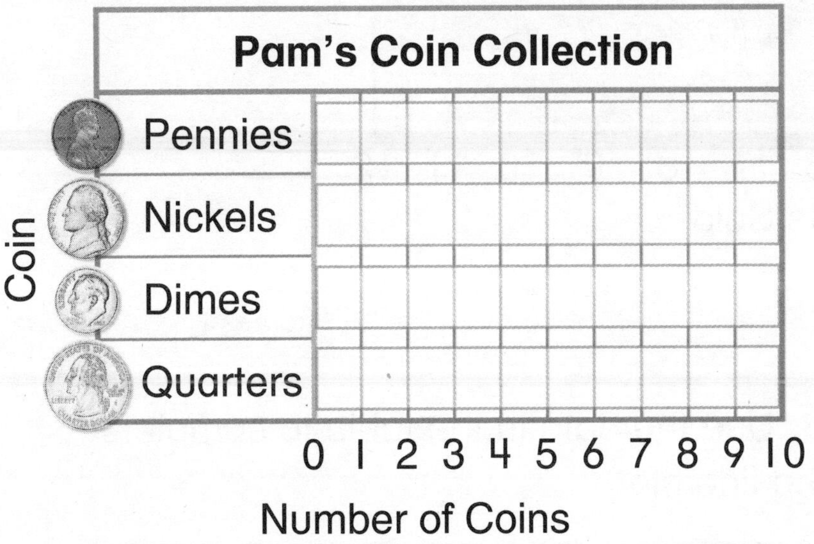

Pam's Coin Collection

Coin	0	1	2	3	4	5	6	7	8	9	10
Pennies											
Nickels											
Dimes											
Quarters											

Number of Coins

2. Use the bar graph you made above. Pam spends 5 of her dimes to buy an apple. Now how many dimes does Pam have left?

Ⓐ 13

Ⓑ 5

Ⓒ 3

Ⓓ 0

3. Is each sentence about the picture graph correct? Choose Yes or No.

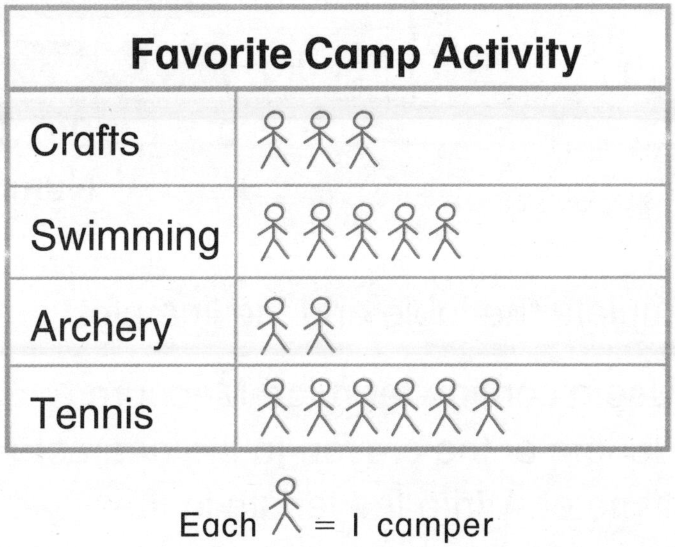

Favorite Camp Activity

Crafts	웃웃웃
Swimming	웃웃웃웃웃
Archery	웃웃
Tennis	웃웃웃웃웃웃

Each 웃 = 1 camper

7 students voted for tennis. ○ Yes ○ No

16 students voted in all. ○ Yes ○ No

2 more students voted for swimming than for crafts. ○ Yes ○ No

3 fewer students voted for tennis than for crafts. ○ Yes ○ No

4. How many more tickets did Kendra sell than Leon?

 5

 6

 11

Ⓓ 17

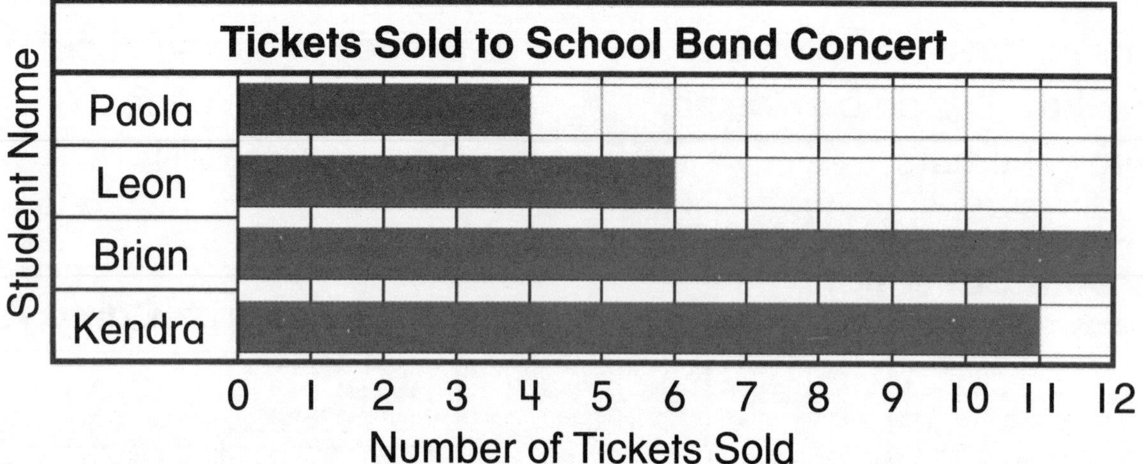

5. Complete the table and the line plot.

A. Use a centimeter ruler. Measure the length of the crayon to the nearest centimeter. Write the length in the table below.

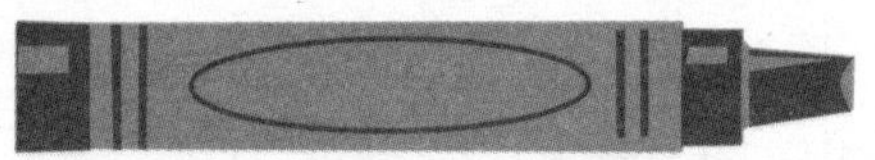

Crayon Lengths in Centimeters			
5	7	7	8
4	7	5	

B. Use the data in the table to complete the line plot.

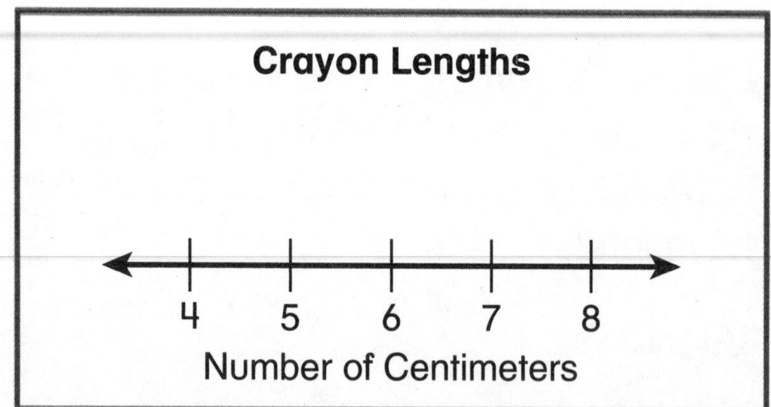

What is the difference in length between the shortest and longest crayon?

____

6. Scott is making a picture graph from the data in the tally chart. How many symbols should he draw in the bottom row?

Favorite Fruit	
Apple	IIII
Banana	卌I
Pear	I
Orange	卌

Favorite Fruit	
Apple	☺☺☺☺
Banana	☺☺☺☺☺☺
Pear	☺
Orange	

Each ☺ = 1 student

Ⓐ 3 Ⓑ 4 Ⓒ 5 Ⓓ 6

---

7. Mary gets new stamps every month. The bar graph shows the number of stamps she collects each month.

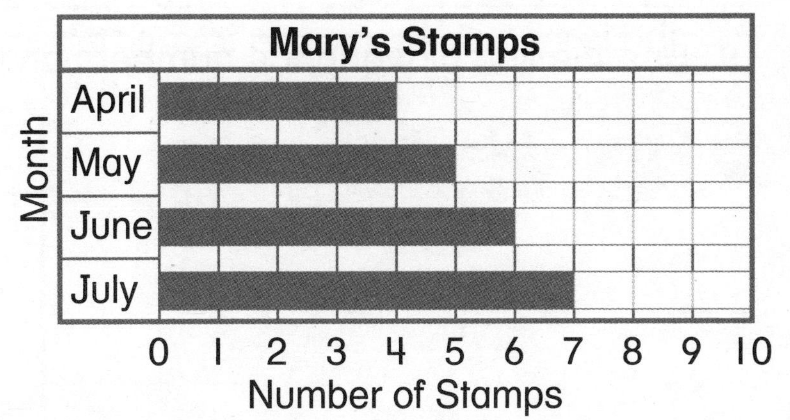

Which statements are true? Choose all that apply.

- ☐ Mary collects 1 more stamp in May than she does in April.
- ☐ Mary collects 2 fewer stamps in June than she does in July.
- ☐ Mary collects a total of 11 stamps in May and June.
- ☐ Mary collects one additional stamp each month from May to July.
- ☐ Mary collects the most stamps in June.

8. Use the tally chart to complete the picture graph.
Then use the picture graph to solve the problems.

Favorite Flower	
Rose	卌 I
Daisy	III
Tulip	卌
Lily	卌 III

Favorite Flower	
Rose	
Daisy	
Tulip	
Lily	

Each (flower) = 1 vote

How many students voted for Lily? _____

Which flower is the least favorite? __________

9. Use the line plot and the numbers on the cards to complete each sentence.

5

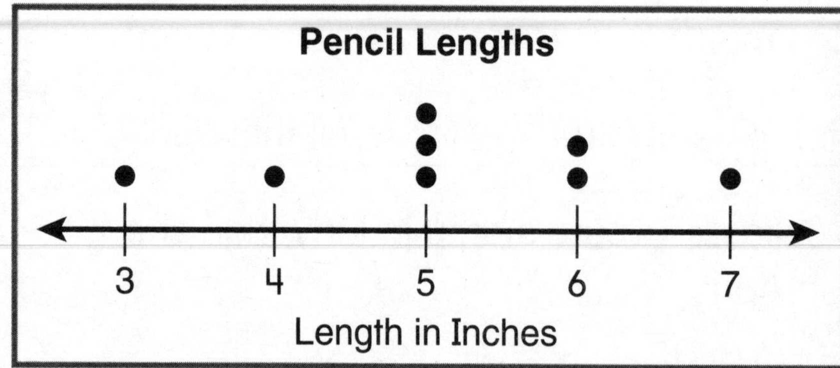

3 pencils are _____ inches long.

The longest pencil is _____ inches long.

The shortest pencil is _____ inches long.

The difference between the shortest and longest pencil is _____ inches.

Name ______________________________

TOPIC 15

Performance Task

School Surveys

Some students asked their classmates different questions.

George asked his classmates to vote for their favorite lunch. This table shows the results.

Favorite Lunch	
Taco	5
Pizza	8
Hamburger	9
Salad	6

1. Use the table to complete the bar graph.

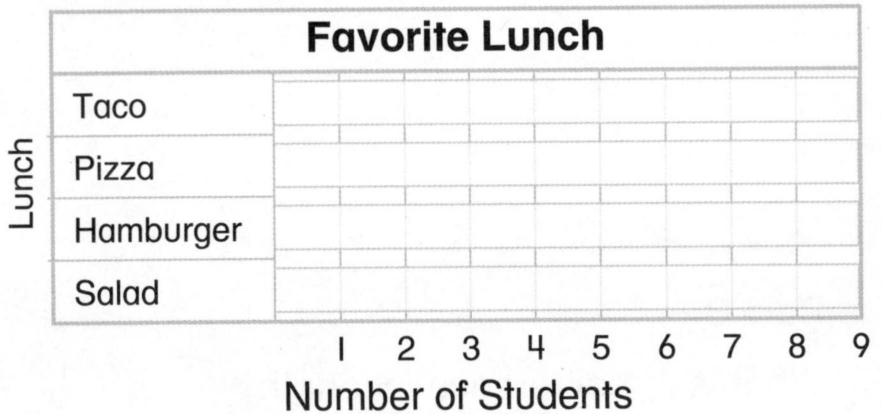

2. Use the Favorite Lunch table to complete the picture graph.

Favorite Lunch	
Taco	
Pizza	
Hamburger	
Salad	

Each ✔ = 1 student

3. Use the graphs you made to answer these questions.

How many students chose salad as their favorite lunch? _____

How many fewer students chose taco than hamburger? _____ fewer students

How would the bar graph change if two more students chose taco?

____

____

4. Write and solve a math story about the Favorite Lunch graphs you made.

Part A

Use the bar graph or the picture graph about favorite lunches to write a math story problem. The problem should include addition or subtraction.

____

____

____

____

Part B

Solve your math story problem. Explain how you solved the problem.

____

____

____

____

____

____

5. Gina asked her classmates to measure the length of their favorite storybook in inches. She recorded their measurements in this table.

Lengths of Books in Inches			
12	9	8	10
6	10	11	9
10	9	9	12
12	10	7	7

Part A

Use the table to make a line plot.

Part B

What is the difference in length between the longest and shortest books?

_____ inches

Photographs

Every effort has been made to secure permission and provide appropriate credit for photographic material. The publisher deeply regrets any omission and pledges to correct errors called to its attention in subsequent editions.

Unless otherwise acknowledged, all photographs are the property of Savvas Learning Company LLC.

Photo locators denoted as follows: Top (T), Center (C), Bottom (B), Left (L), Right (R), Background (Bkgd)

1 (TL) Africa Studio/Fotolia, (TC) Africa Studio/Fotolia, (TR) karandaev/Fotolia, (BL) Lori Martin/Shutterstock; (BR) An Nguyen/Shutterstock, **3** (T) 123RF, (C) Sean Pavone/Shutterstock, (B) Trinet Uzun/Shutterstock; **4** (Bkgd) Russo Photography/Shutterstock, (T) Sergey Sarychev/Shutterstock, (C) Lesinka372/Shutterstock, (B) Corinna Huter/Shutterstock, 123RF; **57** (TL) Shadowmac/Shutterstock, (TR) Rose Thompson/Shutterstock, (BL) Tory Kallman/Shutterstock, (BR) Jo Crebbin/Shutterstock; **59** (T) Steve Byland/Shutterstock, (B) Islavicek/Shutterstock; **60** (T) Smileus/Shutterstock, (B) 123RF; **89** (L) FiCo74/Fotolia; (R) Antonio Scarpi/Fotolia, **91** (T) Pisaphotography/Shutterstock, (C) Aviation Images/Alamy Stock Photo, (B) Lazyllama/Shutterstock; **92** (Bkgrd) 123RF, S_Rouse/Shutterstock; **133** Beboy/Shutterstock; **135** (T) Echo/Juice Images/Getty Images, (B) Peter Leahy/Shutterstock; **136** (T) Universal Images Group North America LLC/Alamy Stock Photo, (B) Charles O. Cecil/Alamy Stock Photo; **185** Deborah Benbrook/Fotolia; **187** (T) Cturtletrax/iStock/Getty Images, (C) Inxti/Shutterstock, (B) Horizon International Images Limited/Alamy Stock Photo; **188** (Bkgrd) Evgeny Atamanenko/Shutterstock, (T) Nisakorn Neera/Shutterstock, (B) Thomas M Perkins/Shutterstock; **233** GlebStock/Shutterstock; **235** (T) Joe McDonald/Corbis Documentary/Getty Images, (B) Hero Images Inc./Alamy Stock Photo; **236** (T) Charles Wollertz/123RF, (B) Vchal/Shutterstock; **277** Paylessimages/Fotolia; **279** (T) Kiselev Andrey Valerevich/Shutterstock, (C) Mr. Ned Klezmer/Shutterstock, (B) IrinaK/Shutterstock; **280** (Bkgrd) Mikhail Zahranichny/Shutterstock; Good Shop Background/Shutterstock; **325** Ambient Ideas/Shutterstock; **327** (T) Chuck Pefley/Alamy Stock Photo, (B) Masterchief_Productions; **328** (B) (T) Will Hart/PhotoEdit, Christopher Villano/Image Source/Alamy Stock Photo; **331** B Brown/Shutterstock; **363** B Brown/Shutterstock; **367** B Brown/Shutterstock; **373** Es0lex/Fotolia; **375** (T) Christos Georghiou/Shutterstock, (C) Gilles Barbier/imageBROKER/Alamy Stock Photo, (B) Brian J. Skerry/National Geographic/Getty Images; **376** (Bkgrd) People Image Studio/Shutterstock, (T) Fashion iconography/Shutterstock; (B) Brandon Alms/Shutterstock; **429** Tonyz20/Shutterstock; **431** (T) Karin Hildebrand Lau/Alamy Stock Photo, (B) Richard Paul Kane/Shutterstock; **432** (T) CharlieTong/Getty Images, (B) Corey Rich/Aurora Photos/Alamy Stock Photo; **469** Klagyivik Viktor/Shutterstock; **471** (T) Felix Lipov/Shutterstock, (C) Skynesher/Vetta/Getty Images, (B) Stephen Vincent/Alamy Stock Photo; **472** (Bkgrd) Sergiy Bykhunenko/Shutterstock, Gino Santa Maria/Shutterstock; **505** Ant Clausen/Fotolia; **507** (T) Peter Bernik/Shutterstock, (B) Westlee Jay Appleton/Shutterstock; **508** (T) Samuel Borges Photography/Shutterstock, (B) Steven Hogg/Shutterstock; **557** Yurakr/Shutterstock; **559** (T) EFesenko/Shutterstock, (C) Franck Boston/Shutterstock, (B) Creeed/Shutterstock; **560** (Bkgrd) SuriyaPhoto/Shutterstock; Studio Kiwi/Shutterstock, **568** StudioSmart/Shutterstock; **605** Bonita R. Cheshier/Shutterstock; **607** (T) Angelo Ferraris/Shutterstock, (B) Tanawat Palee/Shutterstock; **608** (B) Naramit/Shutterstock; (T) Business stock/Shutterstock, **628** Lledó/Fotolia; **637** (R) Ivonne Wierink/Fotolia, (L) Karichs/Fotolia; **639** (T) Karamysh/Shutterstock, (C) Noxnorthys/Shutterstock, (B) Gabriele Maltinti/Shutterstock; **640** (Bkgrd) Bowie15/123RF, Koya979/Shutterstock